Erving Goffman

Exploring the Interaction Order

Edited by

PAUL DREW and ANTHONY WOOTTON

Polity Press

This collection copyright © Polity Press 1988

Chapter 1, 'Introduction', copyright © Paul Drew and Anthony Wootton 1988. Chapter 2, 'Goffman's Approach to Face-to-Face Interaction', copyright © Adam Kendon 1988. Chapter 3, 'Theoretical Continuities in Goffman's Work', copyright © Randall Collins 1988. Chapter 4, 'Understanding Goffman's Methods', copyright © Robin Williams 1988. Chapter 5, 'Goffman and the Analysis of Conversation', copyright © Emanuel A. Schegloff 1988. Chapter 6, 'Embarrassment and Interactional Organization', copyright © Christian Heath 1988. Chapter 7, 'Putting Linguistics on a Proper Footing: Explorations in Goffman's Concepts of Participation', copyright © Stephen C. Levinson 1988. Chapter 8, 'Minor Courtesies and Macro Structures', copyright © P. M. Strong 1988. Chapter 9, 'Goffman as a Systematic Social Theorist', copyright © Anthony Giddens 1988.

First published 1988 by Polity Press
in association with Blackwell Publishers Ltd

Reprinted 1996

Transferred to digital print 2003

Editorial office:
Polity Press, 65 Bridge Street,
Cambridge CB2 1UR, UK

Marketing and production:
Blackwell Publishers Ltd
108 Cowley Road, Oxford OX4 1JF, UK

ISBN 0-7456-0392-0
ISBN 0-7456-0393-9 (pbk)

A CIP catalogue record for this book is available from the British Library

Typeset in 11 on 12pt Baskerville
by DMB (Typesetting) Abingdon

Printed and bound in Great Britain by
Marston Lindsay Ross International Ltd,
Oxfordshire

Contents

Contents

List of Contributors

Randall Collins, Department of Sociology, University of California at Riverside, USA.

Paul Drew, Department of Sociology, University of York, England.

Anthony Giddens, Professor of Sociology, University of Cambridge, England.

Christian Heath, Department of Sociology, University of Nottingham, England.

Adam Kendon, Philadelphia, Pennsylvania, USA.

Stephen C. Levinson, Max Planck Institute for Psycholinguistics, Nijmegen, The Netherlands.

Emanuel A. Schegloff, Department of Sociology, University of California at Los Angeles, USA.

P. M. Strong, formerly Department of Public Health and Policy, London School of Hygiene and Tropical Medicine, University of London, England. Phil Strong died in the summer of 1995, aged 49.

Robin Williams, Department of Sociology and Social Policy, University of Durham, England.

Anthony Wootton, Department of Sociology, University of York, England.

1

Introduction

PAUL DREW and ANTHONY WOOTTON

A trademark of much intellectual work which Erving Goffman publicly deprecated was scholasticism. By this he was referring to the preoccupation that some scholars have with charting memberships, influences and lineages within the academic community, one facet of this often being the tendency to pigeonhole a writer's work 'as if (it) . . . is a unitary thing' (1981a: 61), as though that work had been generated throughout in a seamless fashion by a single and coherent quest. If these are considered traps then a volume such as this risks falling into them, for several of the contributors take as their topic the nature of Goffman's contribution to the study of forms of human association. So we will begin by explaining why we think it necessary to venture down avenues in which Goffman himself, by all accounts, would never have been seen.

Although opposed to scholasticism Goffman's work was, of course, immensely scholarly; and his singular, and frequently exquisite, literary style is renowned. But these merits should not obscure the fact that for him scholarship and style were only resources to be used in the service of his primary objective, which was that of unravelling the procedures employed by people in their face-to-face dealings with each other. In the last analysis he saw himself as an empirical investigator, and his eclectic use of both scholarly and not-so-scholarly texts, drawn from his astonishingly wide reading, together with his own observations of human behaviour were intended to form part of a cumulative body of enquiry into this domain. So we are entitled to ask, without meaning to be unsympathetic, how he set about investigating this domain; whether and in what ways this domain is separable from other realms of human life; what were the main discoveries that he made;

what kinds of research can take his discoveries and insights further; and so on. In their various ways the papers in this collection set out to address just such questions. However the obstacles to the twin tasks of considering the nature of his work and the lines of research that can now further it are well known. Goffman offered few explicit guides as to his research strategies, usually just the briefest of indications in his prefaces and footnotes. He employed apparently shifting conceptual distinctions across his various texts. Furthermore his work is not presented in any conventionalized form: there are, for example, no clear hypotheses, no standard research designs, nor even a theory that could be tested or used to make sense of a variety of research findings. Nevertheless in order to deliver news of our own we need to be clear about what, after all, the news was that Goffman delivered.

There are further reasons which make it pertinent to explore these questions. On the face of it there is a paucity of empirical research which actually picks up Goffman's 'golden shovel' (Hymes 1984: 625) either to dig in his own patch or on untilled land. Attention was drawn to this paucity at the conference for which the papers in this volume were originally written.[1] Reviewing research in the fields of communication studies and medical sociology respectively, Leeds-Hurwitz (1986) and Strong (1986)[2] found (with a few notable exceptions)[3] a general absence of research connected closely to Goffman's insights into these areas – surprising conclusions in view of the interest that Goffman showed in them. In one sense the absence of a Goffmanian tradition is consistent with, and perhaps partly an outcome of, the position he took up *vis-à-vis* other academic groupings. He was reluctant, for example, to affiliate with the intellectual clubs and traditions of his time. Hymes quotes him as saying about a paper he had been sent to review for *Language in Society* '. . . I'm getting very tired of slogans and flags and kinship acknowledgements and membership badges . . .', though adding with characteristic ambivalence '. . . no doubt because I have employed so many myself' (quoted in Hymes 1984: 626). But whilst he may have done so in the politics of his citations, he pointedly stood apart from his neighbours in symbolic interactionism, ethology, structuralism – and conversation analysis. About the latter he could be especially acerbic, even though several of the main figures in this movement were his own pupils, and committed to lines of investigation in some ways similar to his own.

However the absence of a Goffmanian tradition must also partly be explained by tensions existing between his work and parallel work in the two disciplines into which he might have become domiciled, namely sociology and psychology. For sociologists, his writings excluded systematic analysis of social structure, of class, types of organizations, political formations and so on. And it was difficult to cast within conventional ways of relating the individual to social structure: for example, sociologists, as well as anthropologists, have regarded as one of their major achievements the demonstration of links between personality and group structures, but Goffman's endeavour cut across this kind of connection insofar as he was identifying a separate form of order existing at the interpersonal level, one which had its own forms of systematicity, the investigation of which would require a distinctive kind of conceptual apparatus. A tension also existed between Goffman's treatment of individuals in interaction, and their treatment in various branches of psychology. Although his concepts sometimes suggest connections with psychology, the mechanisms of defence and protection introduced in *The Presentation of Self in Everyday Life* being obvious examples, these are usually recast in interactional terms, that being his purpose in appropriating them. And even in the domain of interactional process, where there might have seemed to be a close connection with social psychology, Goffman demurred, later describing himself as having tried '. . . to treat face-to-face interaction as a domain in its own right in my dissertation . . . to rescue the term "interaction" from the place where the great social psychologists and their avowed followers seemed prepared to leave it' (Goffman 1981a: 62). Kendon's chapter in this volume brings out clearly how this concern with the properties of interaction *per se* represented a radical departure from existing social psychological work.

Members of adjacent disciplines therefore found, and continue to find, Goffman's work puzzling; and in his lifetime it does not appear that Goffman ever became identified with any particular investigative tradition of research, though, in his later years, perhaps he came to have closest working links with certain linguists and anthropologists at the University of Pennsylvania. Nevertheless by the end of his career it becomes clear that Goffman certainly saw his work as identifying a new domain of behaviour, and that he saw this as a thread running through his writing. In his own summary statement of his life's work, which he wrote as an address to be given on his inauguration as president of the American Sociological Association in 1982 (published a year later), Goffman plainly states that:

My concern over the years has been to promote acceptance of this face-to-face domain as an analytically viable one – a domain which might be titled, for want of any happy name, the *interaction order* – a domain whose preferred method of study is microanalysis.

(Goffman 1983b: 2)

Although his primary concern in his address is to examine connections between the interaction order and other forms of social organization, he takes time to re-acquaint us with familiar themes from his past work. The territories of the self, normal appearances, the dangers of hallways, contact rituals and many other icons are mentioned to remind us of what he has investigated. If then there is to be a unifying theme in his work it must centre around the notion of an 'interaction order', and this is our warrant for claiming, through the title of this volume, this unity to Goffman's writing.

The details of this legacy however, for reasons already mentioned, are by no means clear-cut. The absence of a clear tradition around Goffman's work, his avoidance of programmatic statements and so on mean that anyone inclined to follow in his footsteps will have an uncertain path ahead of them. So one of our aims in collecting this volume together is to get clear how far along which path Goffman has taken us, and for this reason several chapters, notably those of Kendon, Collins and Giddens, contain lengthy exegetical sections to this end. We hope that they will be taken as attempts at scholarly understanding of what Goffman was about when he investigated social interaction, rather than as merely scholastic enterprises. And with the same intention we now sketch out, in a preliminary way, some of what we see as the key themes of his work.

In his presidential address Goffman is at pains to justify his treatment of 'the social situation as the basic working unit in the study of the interaction order', a position which, on the face of it, might seem unpromising as a sociological perspective. Since we bring some knowledge of one another to encounters, a store of memories and cultural assumptions, all of which are in obvious ways both particularized and trans-situational, then these background 'givens' might be thought the proper province of the sociologist, not the workings and forms of situations themselves. Goffman's line of enquiry into situations in various ways runs contrary to such a position. His analysis respects, of course, the unique sense of any occasion that participants have: all his work claims to be ingrained in such particulars. So he does not at all deny, or relegate, the significance of knowledge that people bring to interaction, or, in his words, their knowledge of 'the biography of the occasion and its participants'. But to bring an occasion to life requires us to select, mobilize and arrange, *in fine detail*, ways of presenting ourselves to others, ways which will 'render our behaviour understandably relevant to what the other can come to perceive is going on' (Goffman 1983a: 51). Our behaviour can then be designed so as to enable our fellows to see in it evidence of our broader cultural knowledge, memberships and identities. Furthermore:

> It is not only that our appearance and manner provide evidence of our statuses and relationships. It is also that the line of our visual regard, the intensity of our involvement, and the shape of our initial actions, allows others to glean our immediate intent and purpose, and all this whether or not we are engaged in talk with them at the time. Correspondingly, we are constantly in a position to facilitate this revealment, or block it, or even misdirect our viewers.
>
> (Goffman 1983b: 3)

Of necessity, therefore, there is a sense in which people fashion the situations in which they participate through the ways in which they conduct themselves and read the conduct of others.

Instead of focusing on the trans-situational givens that people bring with them to occasions, what was for Goffman interestingly trans-situational was the set of procedures that informed the ways in which people managed the face-to-face domain. In the last analysis, as is evident from all his writing, it was these trans-situational practices that interested him: he rarely dwells for long on any particular encounter or interactional event. To identify such practices involved finding resemblances across quite different occasions of interaction 'so that what they share can be extracted and analysed, and so that the forms of social life they derive from can be pieced out and catalogued sociologically, allowing what is intrinsic to (such instances of) interactional life to be exposed thereby. In this way one can move from the merely situated to the situational' (Goffman 1983b: 3). Elsewhere Goffman gives us a succinct account of what such a strategy might involve in analysing handshakes:

> By this practice we 'express' our pleasure in renewing contact with a friend not seen for a time. That's what someone shaking hands during a greeting might feel and report about his feeling. But surely for the student *some* of the significance of the act is to be found in the fact that in American society only male to male cannot employ a 'social' kiss as a functional equivalent; that we mark departures with

a handshake too, and therefore students may have need for a concept
such as 'access ritual' which brings together what those who use
handshakes during hello's and goodbye's don't bother to assemble;
that handshaking as a behavioral ingredient is also found in introduction routines, congratulatory practices, dispute settlements, and
contract finalizations, these several sequences – as sequences – being
otherwise appreciably different, raising the issue of how our ritual
idiom is organized; and that whenever handshaking occurs, brackets
are being provided with respect to some episode of face-to-face
activity or/and state of social relationship.

(Goffman 1981a: 61–2)

Goffman's concern then was to investigate the procedures and
practices through which people organized, and brought into life,
their face-to-face dealings with each other. To investigate this
domain required finding means of access to these procedures and,
initially, ways of conceptualizing the resemblances between different
occasions. To this end a host of concepts are introduced in his
writing for different types of interactional occurrence, some given
brief mention in his presidential address – ambulatory units,
contacts, conversational encounters, etc. Their merit is that they
draw our attention to the orderly ways that people have for
distinguishing, for each other, the varied nature of the occasions in
which they are engaged. Such concepts are not themselves the end-
points of analysis. Whether people share the interactional concerns
identified by Goffman, and whether they orient to such concerns in
the manner he suggests, are frequently questions which await
further enquiry. Goffman himself rarely went far down that road.
He was often content simply to indicate the potential relevance and
significance of the interactional parameters in question; as a result,
the maps he provides of this new terrain are often akin to those one
buys on holiday in certain countries – suggestive sketches rather
than definitive.

The interaction order was, for Goffman, not merely a technical
one. For him it consisted of more than rules, such as turn-taking
rules, which permit people to interact with each other in coordinated
ways. The technical mechanisms of interaction, the traffic rules,
were only of sociological significance insofar as they were the
vehicles for participants' *moral* enterprises (a point also given
emphasis in the chapter by Williams). For Goffman the world of
interaction was a moral one which could generate in people a sense
of effectiveness or ineffectiveness, success, disenchantment, fraud
and so on. One in which, for example, we continually draw

inferences about levels of engrossment shown by others in what we are saying or doing; in which offence can be given to, and concealed from, others; in which others can be relied on to display or to conceal various sentiments in their manner; in which there are patterns and sequences containing slots as to what *should* occur next. There were attempts to codify some of these matters in such places as etiquette books, and Goffman certainly did not ignore these. But he recognized that such manuals were at best codified forms of folk etiquette which did scant justice to the manners and practices he was trying to document. His working view was that people acted better than they knew how, and that more ingenious observations were needed to unravel this moral world. And Goffman's explorations of this world, of the nature of the offences that we can give to each other for example, and the remedies available for avoiding such eventualities, unfold for us in people's daily lives a range of everyday moral sensibilities and duties which speaks to the distinctively human condition.

At the centre of this essentially moral world of interaction is the individual, a revered object as revealed by Goffman's analysis of the ways in which the individual is treated both by self and others. Perhaps even a sacred object in anthropological parlance – a possibility dwelt on at length in the chapter by Collins. But by the same token an object that can be made vulnerable, and desecrated, through manipulation of the normal means through which such reverence is displayed. In this sense the abnormal, for Goffman, could always tell one something about the normal, about the props whereby a sense of our integrity as individuals is maintained, and in his earliest writings these sites of individual desecration were to receive detailed attention. Especially in the papers 'On face work' and 'Embarrassment and social organization', and in his books *Asylums* and *Stigma*. But the emphasis on the moral character of the face-to-face domain persisted throughout his writing, perhaps becoming most explicit in his distinction between system and ritual requirements in *Forms of Talk*, and his use of that distinction to criticize certain forms of discourse analysis for paying insufficient attention to the ritual/moral domain. That distinction, and issues pertaining to it, are discussed by several authors in this book (e.g. Kendon, Collins and Schegloff).

If Goffman saw the purpose of his enquiries as being to make discoveries about the properties of the interaction order, his methods for accomplishing this were, to say the least, singular. He selected strategies which were consistent both with his general enterprise and with the results of his early investigations, one such strategy being the investigation of the normal through the abnormal, to which reference has already been made. More broadly, and most obviously, his methods had to be inductive and comparative. Inductive because he wished to identify features of interaction to which people actually attend in their conduct, such features being discoverable in and through the ways in which they are oriented to. Comparative because his concern all along, as we have stressed, was to explore the possibility of there being definable parameters of interaction that were common to a great variety of settings. In his presidential address he writes that '. . . pedestrian traffic rules can be studied in crowded kitchens as well as in crowded streets, interruption rights at breakfast as well as in courtrooms, endearment vocatives in supermarkets as well as in the bedroom' (1983b: 2). Though this comparative emphasis was out of kilter with part of the symbolic interactionist tradition that helped to nurture him at the University of Chicago, it is clear that it was not peculiar to Goffman in his early days, as is evidenced by the following observation of Garfinkel published in 1956:[4]

> A useful form of the method of free variation is found in a technique that is known around the Department of Sociology at the University of Chicago where it was developed as the use of 'natural metaphors'. By this is meant that there are formal similarities in the situations of persons located at different places in the social order. These structurally repeated situations, though they may be known to the participants by different names, are organizationally identical. The participant's ways of describing their own situations may be used as the metaphor or model for appreciating the formally identical features in the situations of others.
>
> (Garfinkel 1956: 190)

This method of the 'natural metaphor', used as a technique of comparative analysis, was however one that Goffman came almost to make his own; the transparent symmetry between this method and the fondness of metaphor displayed in his literary style being striking. Such a strategy of comparative analysis can be clearly seen, for example, in Goffman's early essay 'On cooling the mark out' (1952), where he draws parallels between the techniques used by con men to assist their victims in adjusting to misfortune, and those used by others in society who exercise skills in managing the failure of others.

Another feature of Goffman's methodology can be illustrated by this same article. One of the problems which we have mentioned he had to overcome was that of finding ways to uncover the skills and practices people employ in interaction, but about which they are generally unaware. Among the strategies with which he tried to come to terms with that problem was to focus in on occasions when it was in people's interests to exercise, consciously, some control over these skills. This is hinted at in something already quoted, when he said that precisely because we are gleaning one another's intentions and purposes from appearances in interaction, '. . . we are constantly in a position to facilitate this revealment, to block it, or even to misdirect our viewers' (1983b: 3). Recurrently he emphasizes how the rules of the interaction order can be manipulated to achieve specific interactional effects. Thus, methodologically, the categories of persons and events from whom we can initially learn much about the ground rules for 'normal' interaction are those who, by deliberately exploiting them to manipulate situations to their advantage, make these rules more visible. Con men are one such category, and in their organization of cooling out the mark they have occasion to spell out the rationale and incentives attached to this form of behaviour, published versions of this then constituting a useful methodological resource. But other deviants and non-deviants have an interest in making interactional rules explicit, and Goffman makes copious use of their confessions in his writing. So much so, perhaps, that some have been misled into believing that for Goffman we are all manipulative con men, indeed that interaction itself is a con. Here, as elsewhere, serious exegesis of Goffman's work is needed as a corrective: for once one looks beneath the surface, behind his disdain for methodological comment, it is possible to see Goffman exercising a sharp and shrewd methodological imagination.

There are many aspects of the interaction order and of Goffman's methods for uncovering its laminations that we have not touched on. The authors of the various papers in this collection take up and develop these, and many issues besides. We have tried to sketch something of the programme which Goffman set himself, especially his aim to uncover the trans-situational, standardized practices through which people manage their face-to-face dealings with one another, whilst locating these practices and explicating them via analysis of the details of their local appearance in particular settings. It is to be hoped that the reader will find in these papers some further illumination of Goffman's domain, and of ways in which this domain might now be explored. For the authors by no means adhere to an uncritical acceptance of the procedures whereby Goffman pursued his programme: there are other methods through which discoveries can be made about interaction which can also satisfy the rather stringent requirements involved in meeting his objectives.

Nevertheless through the last quarter of a century or more of sociological schisms, self-doubts and other denunciations, Goffman sustained his view of a domain of social life to which he sought to cut a path, despite the fact that, as he put it, 'My colleagues have not been overwhelmed by the merits of the case'. We owe to him that through the integrity of his purpose and the standards which he expected of his own and others' work, he is largely responsible for making the meticulous, naturalistic and unsponsored study of ordinary social interaction a respectable enterprise, 'respectable' not at all in that distorted meaning of conventionally, almost stolidly well mannered, but in that it is deserving of our respect, indeed an enterprise in which we would ourselves wish to engage.

We have said that the purpose of the papers in this volume is not to engage in a scholastic exercise, but to throw some light on what Goffman's enterprise was, and on what it might become. To this end some are exegetical, some are critical, and some try to take up and develop some theme(s) in his work. Kendon's chapter is positioned first because it clearly articulates the main parameters of the interaction order as they evolved in the course of Goffman's work. This he does partly through an examination of the prefaces Goffman wrote to his books, in which he was usually most explicit about the nature of his work, and partly by bringing together, from various textual sources, Goffman's observations about certain key interactional processes. He draws particular attention to the means whereby people in interaction display differing states of involvement with one another, and he shows how Goffman's observations on these matters make it possible to discriminate different kinds of social gathering. The chapter by Collins is also primarily exegetical, but his focus is on the Durkheimian influences on Goffman, transmitted partly through such teachers as W. Lloyd Warner and C. W. M. Hart. Collins outlines what he sees as the central tenets of the Durkheimian approach to ritual, and then attempts to trace these features, and their transformations, in Goffman's work, especially in relation to *Frame Analysis* (1974) and *Forms of Talk* (1981b). In the course of this he argues for the existence of important continuities in these respects throughout Goffman's writings.

The next two chapters, by Williams and Schegloff respectively, take up more explicit alignments in relation to Goffman's work. Williams identifies three methodological criticisms frequently made of Goffman, namely the arbitrary selection of topic, imprecision in the use of concepts and apparent lack of care in handling data.

Drawing on a description of the development of sociological knowledge put forward by Baldamus, Williams argues that the tendencies identified in such criticisms in fact represent strengths of Goffman's work in that they are outcomes of a way of working which respects the trial and error way in which knowledge is accumulated. So, for example, Williams argues that Goffman's use of hypothetical/ non-empirically observed sequences played an important part in refining the conceptual frameworks that he was developing. Schegloff's line of argument, however, adopts a more critical stance. For him Goffman's avoidance of sustained and detailed attention to carefully described occasions in social life made it possible for him to avoid also the challenge of devising ways of handling the orderly properties of actual interactional events. Goffman was often pointedly critical of other research workers who did take up this challenge, and Schegloff, as a leading figure in one such group (conversation analysis), addresses these criticisms and evaluates them in the light of their relevance to understanding actual stretches of conversation.

The chapters by Heath, Levinson and Strong represent three rather different lines of enquiry which nevertheless display an intellectual debt to Goffman, and which exemplify ways in which future research may further the investigation of the interaction order. Heath examines the phenomenon of embarrassment by exploring in detail some video-recorded instances of doctor–patient consultations. He makes a case for the view that rather than being irrational and disorganized, a view which Goffman and many others have taken, it is possible to see the behaviour of the embarrassed as designed to manage highly specific matters associated with the event in question. Heath's argument is that to understand the details of such conduct, in such moments, requires us to consider the nature of the sequences in which they occur, and the socially organized properties of those sequences. Levinson's chapter develops a theme that recurred frequently in Goffman's writings, but which received its final and most explicit treatment in his short essay called 'Footing' (1979). Goffman was concerned to identify the limitations of dyadic, speaker–hearer ways of thinking about encounters. The fact that talk can be designed for other parties present who are not the official recipients of the message, for example, suggests that there may be a variety of ways in which people can 'participate' in encounters. Levinson further develops the set of participation categories suggested by Goffman, and demonstrates both how these distinctions are built into the grammatical structures of different languages, and how these distinctions are actually attended to in the way language is used in a number of different societies. In all this Levinson's aim is to develop a universal set of categories consonant with the various types of participant role encoded through people's linguistic practices. Strong reports on his extensive research into interaction practices in paediatric clinics, both in Britain and the USA. Drawing especially on Goffman's 'Fun in Games' (1961c) paper he highlights the way that rules of relevance and irrelevance are the means by which participants document the nature of these ceremonial orders. His analysis also suggests, however, that in considering particular types of relationship, such as the service relationship, Goffman wrote in terms of there being one form of ritual order which shaped the relationship's various manifestations. Strong takes issue with this, arguing that in the encounters he has examined various types of ritual order are evident, and he argues for a more thorough-going attempt to locate such ritual orders within the social structural arrangements that generate them.

The final chapter, by Giddens, begins by defending Goffman against various arguments which betray misunderstandings of his work. Giddens goes on to delineate what he sees as the central parameters of this work, and he suggests that it constitutes an important social theory in spite of the fact that Goffman himself may have been uneasy with it being identified in such terms. Giddens' exegesis dwells especially on Goffman's presidential address to the ASA, and the shortcomings he identifies in Goffman's work centre principally around Goffman's views on the nature of the micro-macro link as revealed in that address, and in his other writings. Broadly, Giddens argues that the analysis of what takes place when people are co-present is central to the ways in which social structures are reproduced, and that Goffman, in attempting to separate out a distinctive interaction order, placed himself in a position where the potential contained in his sort of work for establishing such connections lay dormant.

NOTES

1 This conference was called *Erving Goffman: an interdisciplinary appreciation*, and was held at the University of York, in July 1986. It was organized by the editors of this book on behalf of the British Sociological Association's Sociology of Language group, and was financed by the British Economic and Social Research Council.
2 All the chapters but one in this book represent versions of papers given at the conference mentioned in note 1 (above): the only exception is the

chapter by Strong, which radically departs from his conference presentation.

3 As some of these references are not mentioned elsewhere in the book it may be useful to mention two of the more important ones here, namely King, Raynes and Tizard (1971) and Heilman (1979).

4 We are grateful to Phil Strong for drawing these remarks of Garfinkel to our attention.

2

Goffman's Approach to Face-to-Face Interaction

ADAM KENDON

FACE-TO-FACE INTERACTION AS AN AUTONOMOUS FIELD OF STUDY

In this paper I shall review some of the concepts Goffman developed for the study of face-to-face interaction. I hope to show that these concepts provide for a framework of great generality in terms of which a thoroughly integrated study of interaction becomes possible. As I shall argue at the end of this paper, a major theoretical challenge that students of interaction face is that of showing how the seemingly different components of human conduct that play a part in it are articulated in relation to one another. In his late writings, especially, Goffman was at pains to remind us that face-to-face interaction in general, and conversation in particular, is far from a matter of spoken words alone. In doing so he pointed the way towards a truly integrative view of human communicative conduct. I believe that further development of the framework that is implicit in Goffman's work on this topic provides the best way forward toward a theory of human face-to-face interaction that will permit an integrated view of it.

I will begin with a discussion of Goffman's claim that the study of face-to-face interaction should be regarded as a separate branch of sociology. He suggested that there is what he called an 'interaction order' (Goffman 1983b) that can be regarded as a field of study in its own right. This is a view that is expressed in some of his earliest writings. It may be found in his doctoral dissertation (Goffman 1953, referred to in Williams 1980: 210–11) and it is a main premise of such early papers as 'On face work' (1955) and 'Alienation from interaction' (1957). It is made explicit in the preface to *Encounters*

(1961a). He returns to defend the idea repeatedly in subsequent works, as in the introductory pages of *Behavior in Public Places* (1963), the preface to *Interaction Ritual* (1967), and in the prefaces to *Strategic Interaction* (1969) and *Relations in Public* (1971). The way in which he presents and defends this idea differs somewhat from one work to another. A comparison between them is instructive, for it suggests how the theoretical context within which Goffman expected his work to be placed, changed from one occasion of publication to the next.

In *Encounters*, written in 1961, when the study of 'small groups' was very popular in sociology and social psychology, Goffman is concerned to show that the study of interaction, as he conceived of it, is not the same thing as the study of 'small groups'. He there argues that such a unit of organization as the focused gathering or the encounter is not the same as the 'small group' such as the street-corner gang, the family, the army platoon or the psychotherapy group. Although there are certain similarities – for instance groups, like gatherings, have rules of recruitment and norms of conduct that members must adhere to if they are to continue as participants – in the study of interaction as such we must be concerned with many matters that seem quite unimportant for the study of groups. These include issues of activity management such as the problem of regulating the giving up or taking over of the speaker role or the allocation of positions of participants in space.

In *Behavior in Public Places* we find a different emphasis, one in which an attempt is apparently being made to justify the study of interaction as a separate branch of sociology. Goffman here proposes a notion of a 'public order' by which he means the order that governs the conduct of persons when they are in each other's immediate presence. 'Public order' is proposed as a species of 'social order'. A 'social order' is defined as 'the consequence of any set of moral norms that regulates the way in which persons pursue their objectives' (Goffman 1963: 8). He goes on: 'The set of norms does not specify the objectives the participants are to seek, nor the pattern formed by and through the coordination or integration of these ends, but merely the modes of seeking them.' The rules of traffic and the orderliness of traffic that results is an obvious example. The domain of face-to-face interaction, thus, is to be concerned with the 'traffic rules' of interaction, not with why people interact or what they achieve when they do so. The 'public order', as a species of 'social order' is comparable to the 'legal order' or to the 'economic order' of a society. As such it has as much a claim to a separate study as do these. In proposing the domain to be studied in these terms, I think we may detect Goffman's first more or less explicit attempt to propose, in public, the study of the interaction order as a separate branch of sociology and an attempt, accordingly, to justify to sociological colleagues the importance of the area (Goffman had already argued along these lines in his dissertation, as has been pointed out by Leeds-Hurwitz, 1986).

In the preface to *Interaction Ritual*, written in 1967, he is concerned to show that what he is advocating is not to be confused with psychology. In this preface he draws attention to the then recent emergence of interest in what is sometimes known as 'non-verbal behaviour' or 'non-verbal communication' (although Goffman does not use these terms). This interest developed largely at the hands of psychologists and here we find that Goffman maintains that in the field of interaction study, as he conceived of it, it is not the psychology of individuals that is of primary interest. In this study we must be concerned, to be sure, with 'the glances, gestures, positionings and verbal statements' (Goffman 1967: 1) that participants in interaction continuously provide, for these are the 'external signs of orientation and involvement'. However, what is of interest is not the psychology of orientation and involvement, but their social organization. He then goes on to say: 'I assume that the proper study of interaction is not the individual and his psychology, but rather the syntactical relations among the acts of different persons mutually present to one another' (Goffman 1967: 2).

In *Strategic Interaction* (1969) Goffman makes his concern to establish the study of interaction even more explicit. In the preface to that book he says that his 'ultimate aim' is to 'develop the study of face-to-face interaction as a naturally bounded, analytically coherent field – a sub-area of sociology' (p. ix). He then goes on to raise the issue of 'communication' and whether, as had become commonplace by that time, it was appropriate to say that all interaction was communication. Goffman's argument in *Strategic Interaction* is that there are limits to what we may call 'communication' but that these limits are not the same as the limits to what we may call 'interaction'.

By the time we reach *Relations in Public* (1971) we find that Goffman now recognizes that something like what he is calling for has begun to emerge. He notes that some workers, in particular certain linguists and ethologists, are engaging in efforts quite parallel to his own. He suggests the area be called 'interaction ethology' although he is at pains to urge that we 'politely disattend' the Darwinian outlook of the ethologists, while recognizing that their methods answer well for the sorts of questions he wished to raise and pursue. In particular, he upholds the methods of these kinds of workers, while severely criticizing the methods of experimental psychologists and sociologists, from whom he appears to be consciously distancing himself.

Ten years later, in *Forms of Talk* (1981b), there is no longer any need to outline and justify the field as such. The papers in this collection are now addressed to others who, like himself, have been undertaking the study of interaction practices. The issues raised, concerned as they are with the place of language in interaction, are presented as important questions for discussion within what is taken to be an already well-established field.

At the very end of his career, in his presidential address to the American Sociological Association – entitled 'The interaction order' (1983b) – he again discusses the place within sociology of the study of the interaction order. In this address he attempts to spell out at some length the ways in which the study of the interaction order is both distinct from the study of other aspects of the social order but is also articulated with them. A central issue in that paper is the question of how the subject matter of 'macro-sociology' – status, power, social structure and the like – relates to the microstudy of particular bits or strips of interaction. Here he seems concerned to show that, not only is the study of the interaction order a legitimate concern in itself (there is really no longer any need to argue this, for the field is by now established, at least in an informal way), but that it can contribute helpfully to the concerns of the other sub-fields of sociology.

We see then, how, in the earlier prefaces and introductions, Goffman makes explicit his aim of establishing a sub-field of sociology that is to be concerned with interaction. He makes the object of such a study very clear, but in the course of doing so he is at some pains to establish that what he was advocating was not part of the study of 'small groups', was not part of the study of psychology, and was not the same thing as the study of communication. In writing in this way, Goffman gives the impression of attempting to establish something altogether new. He states repeatedly that the study of interaction had received very little attention, despite the work on small groups, social psychology and communication that might have suggested otherwise.

GOFFMAN AND THE STUDY OF INTERACTION
IN AMERICAN SOCIOLOGY

At first sight this emphasis on the newness of the field seems somewhat curious. The study of 'interaction' had appeared as a well-
established tradition in American social science well before Goffman
matured as a scholar. For example, in the 1920s, the work of Georg
Simmel became available to American readers (see Park and
Burgess 1924, Spykman 1925). His concept of a 'formal sociology'
and his attempts to describe the structures of 'pure sociation' which
he saw exemplified in the details of interpersonal behaviour, is
perhaps the first explicit introduction into American sociology of the
idea that interaction can be studied in its own right. Such an interest
fitted well with the line of thought that begins with William James
(1890: vol. 2) and continues through the work of George Herbert
Mead (1934), in which the 'self' is seen not as actor but as a product
of interaction. Such a view encouraged an interest in the details of
interaction and it was an important part of the background that led
to the emergence of its empirical study. This began in the late 1930s,
when pioneering investigations were carried out by workers such as
Eliot Chapple (1939, 1940), George Homans (1950), Robert Bales
(1950; see also Hare, Borgatta and Bales 1955), and Kurt Lewin and
his associates in 'small-group dynamics' – Cartwright and Zander
(1953) is a typical product of this tradition. An enormous amount of
observational and experimental laboratory work followed. Although
Goffman shows indebtedness to the earlier workers, such as Simmel
and Mead, with the exception of the naturalistic observational work
in 'psychological ecology' (e.g. Barker and Wright 1955), he rarely
mentions any of this later empirical work in interaction. Reading
between his lines we gain the strong impression that he owed this
tradition very few debts.

A closer consideration shows that Goffman was justified in
disregarding this work, and in claiming that the study of interaction
that he was advocating was new. It will be seen that in Goffman's
approach quite new questions were being raised. In the tradition just
referred to, interaction was studied because it seemed that to do so
was the best way to get at other questions. Thus Chapple developed
his ingenious method of 'interaction chronography' as a way of
'measuring human relations'. As a disciple of Percy Bridgman's
'operationalism' (Bridgman 1936) he was impatient with the literary
style of social anthropologists (he had been a student of Lloyd

Warner and had worked on the 'Yankee City' studies). He sought to
find a way of directly observing the stuff out of which social relations
are made. He hit upon the idea of measuring the amount of time
people spend interacting with one another and, more specifically, of
measuring how their actions are patterned in time in relation to one
another. As a result, he was able to report findings of great interest;
but since he was using the study of interaction as a means to an end,
he sought as narrow an aspect of it as he could as a suitable object of
measurement. Likewise, Robert Bales, whose method of 'interaction process analysis' set off a veritable flood of papers, developed
his system of categorizing 'acts' in interaction, not so much because
he was interested in interaction itself but because he was interested
in understanding such matters as the dynamics of leadership in small
groups and how groups of people could arrive at solutions to
problems.

Such approaches took the view that the phenomena of usual
concern to sociology and social psychology – leadership, social
stratification, organization of authority, and the like – must be
grounded in the patterning of specific acts of interaction between
society's members. Such acts were to form the basic data upon
which the investigation of such phenomena was to be based.
However, the acts of interaction were not themselves studied. Only
an aspect of them was seized upon as a means toward studying
something else. Goffman recognized this and made it clear that what
he was concerned with was different: it was to raise the question as
to how interaction is possible in the first place. Goffman was,
therefore, quite correct to observe, as he did several times in his
prefaces, that so far as he was concerned interaction as such had
really received very little attention. As he puts it in the preface to
Relations in Public: 'interaction practices have been used to illuminate
other things, but themselves are treated as though they did not need
to be defined or were not worth defining' (Goffman 1971: ix). And
for Goffman, of course, it is precisely the 'interaction practices' that
are at issue. Workers such as Chapple and Bales simply took for
granted that the people they observed could practice interaction.
They did not investigate how people succeeded in doing so or what
these practices were. Their focus was entirely upon the outcomes of
interaction. Goffman's was upon how it was done; upon how,
indeed, it was possible at all.

Goffman's attempt to set up the study of the practices of interaction
as a separate field was not an isolated one, although he recognized
perhaps more clearly than most that what was being attempted was

distinctive from what was generally understood as a concern with interaction.

The recognition of the importance of the question of how interaction could be accomplished, the issue of what it takes for people to 'do' interacting, had already begun to emerge in the work of a number of other authors. Gregory Bateson, had, by 1951, come to formulate an approach to the study of interaction as a communication system, and it was the organization of this system that was the focus of his interest (Ruesch and Bateson 1951). In this he had been much influenced by his contacts with the development of information theory and cybernetics (he was influenced by Norbert Weiner and von Neumann, especially – see Heims 1977) and with his collaboration with the interpersonal psychiatrist Jurgen Ruesch (see Ruesch 1972). For Ruesch, the issue in psychotherapy was not so much the internal psychological dynamics of the patient as it was the process of interaction between patient and psychiatrist. Likewise, there had been certain developments in structural linguistics that led workers such as Norman McQuown (1971) and Ray Birdwhistell (1952, 1970) to begin to examine the 'behavioural materials' of interaction in a spirit that was completely consonant with the approach that Goffman himself was to advocate later.

Several workers of this persuasion, under the inspiration of the interpersonal psychiatrist Frieda Fromm-Reichmann, gathered at the Institute for Advanced Study in Stanford in 1956 to undertake a detailed study of a film of an interaction in which every aspect of what could be observed was to be minutely charted and examined for its place in the communicative process. This project, known under the name of "the Natural History of an Interview", involved Gregory Bateson, Norman McQuown, and Ray Birdwhistell, among others, all of whom were to be closely associated with the subsequent development of an approach which did indeed attempt to explicate, in a microscopic way, the details of interaction practice (McQuown 1971, Zabor 1978, Leeds-Hurwitz 1987).

Goffman maintained a close interest in this development and was undoubtedly influenced by it. He has acknowledged the influence of Gregory Bateson and he was taught by Ray Birdwhistell when he was an undergraduate at Toronto University. He participated, with Gregory Bateson, in the second Josiah Macy Jr Foundation Group Processes Conference held in 1956; and he played a prominent role in the discussion at the Conference on Paralinguistics and Kinesics held at Indiana University in 1962 (Sebeok, Hayes and Bateson 1964). In later years he was himself to organize conferences at which the structuralist, natural history or 'context analysis' approach to interaction was the principal concern.

The main early exponents of the approach to the study of interaction, which attempts to examine the process itself and the manner in which it is accomplished, included Gregory Bateson, Ray L. Birdwhistell and Albert Scheflen. Each in their own way attempted to develop a theoretical framework in terms of which the process or practice of interaction as a system of behaviour could be understood. A particularly notable feature of this approach is its integrativist view of the interaction process. As much attention is paid to the management of bodily activity and the part this plays in the interactive process as is paid to verbal utterance. Furthermore, these authors consistently struggled toward formulating a view in which the system of relationships between the acts of the participants is the focus, rather than the participants themselves. It could very well have been this work that Goffman had in mind when he wrote, in the passage already quoted from the preface to *Interaction Ritual*, that the proper study of interaction entailed the study of the "syntactical relations among the acts of different persons mutually present to one another". Goffman's use of the word 'syntactical' is significant here, for it shows that he had already begun to employ linguistic analogies in respect to the analysis of interaction. In the development of the approach to interaction by such people as Birdwhistell and Scheflen, concepts from linguistics played an important role (Birdwhistell 1952, 1970; Scheflen 1963, 1964, 1974; McQuown 1971. For discussions of this approach see Kendon 1972, 1979, 1982, McDermott and Wertz 1976 and McDermott and Roth 1978).

GOFFMAN'S FRAMEWORK FOR THE STUDY OF FACE-TO-FACE INTERACTION

Co-presence and Modes of Information Provision

At its broadest, Goffman takes the domain for the study of face-to-face interaction to be the gathering. This he defines as any occasion when two or more persons are, as he puts it, co-present with one another. He defines co-presence in the following way: 'Persons must sense that they are close enough to be perceived in whatever they are doing, including their experiencing of others, and close enough to be perceived in this sensing of being perceived' (Goffman 1963: 17).

He goes on to say that the conditions of co-presence are ordinarily expected to prevail within the bounds of a room, but in spaces that are not walled in, the boundaries of co-presence cannot always be sharply drawn. In a park, for example, if it is relatively crowded, persons 50 yards apart may not sense each other in the way that they may do if they are the only two in sight.

When people are co-present they are, as a rule, able to sense each other with their unaided senses. In such circumstances each can apprise himself of what the other is doing, but each can also see that the other can see that this is so. So a special mutuality arises. P can guage the actions of Q and adjust his own actions accordingly, but in co-presence Q can do likewise, and both P and Q can, therefore, adjust his actions to the fact that the other is adjusting to his own adjustings. In such circumstances a kind of agreement arises in which each takes the other's line of action on trust. This means that people do not have to continually monitor each other, because each person's current doings are construed by the other as a line of action. The other is seen as if he is engaged in some project or other, and can be relied upon in this; accordingly the perceiver can build his own line of action in the light of this. In addition, of course, he can do this in the light of his own assumption that the other will also take it that he is engaged in some project or other.

In establishing this notion of co-presence, Goffman makes us realize that in any situation where people are in a position to mutually perceive one another, some sort of interdependency of action is bound to arise. In this way the concept of 'interaction' is immediately broadened in a radical way. Hitherto, students of inter-action had been concerned only with instances where two or more people (but usually two) were actually talking with one another. Goffman showed that this was far too narrow a view.

In his discussion of co-presence, in addition, Goffman emphasized a further very important principle. This is that whenever people are co-present they are, all the time and inevitably, sources of infor-mation for one another. This was a point that Gregory Bateson had emphasized some years before (see Watzlawick, Beavin and Jackson 1967: 51), but Goffman gave it new life for he was able to show in what different ways people provide one another with information and what sorts of information it is.

He pointed out that in any gathering the participants take it that they provide information for one another in two ways: they *give* it, and they *give it off*. When people *give* information they provide it through actions that are taken to be voluntary, for the provider of given information is held responsible for what he provides. This means that, as a rule, given information is provided through the use of symbolic actions – that is, actions that are mutually acknowledged to refer to something other than themselves. When we talk, the information provided by the content of what we say is given, in this sense – although there are many other ways that information may be given besides by talk. Information that is *given off*, on the other hand, is taken to be provided whether the provider chooses to do so or not. It is an inevitable and unavoidable product of his presence and of his action. I may tell you the way to the Cathedral, but in doing so I provide, through my choice of words, through my accent, and so on, all sorts of additional information. This additional information is what I give off rather than give.

It is important to remember that the issue here is not whether the information provided is *in fact* provided voluntarily or involuntarily. It is, rather, whether the co-participants in the gathering *take it* that it is provided voluntarily or not. In any situation of interaction, it seems, participants treat only some aspects of each other's behaviour as if it is deliberately intended to convey something. In conversations it is usually the something called 'content of talk' that is treated in this way, not the manner of talk, and certainly not the bodily stagings and ecological arrangements within which the talk is carried on. However, it is not as if these other aspects of the situation play no role in the structuring of the interaction. Far from it. Their role is crucial to the whole way in which the event is organized. We owe Goffman a major debt for getting us to see this.

Goffman approaches this fundamental distinction between 'given' and 'given-off' information in a number of different ways. One of his more elaborate treatments of it is in *Frame Analysis* (1974). There he develops the notion of 'attentional tracks'. He suggests that in any social encounter there is always an aspect of the activity going forward that is treated as being within a 'main-line' or 'story-line track'. A domain of action is delineated as being relevant to the main business of the encounter, and it is oriented to as such and dealt with accordingly. The action that is treated in this way is taken to be voluntary, and the information that it provides is given. Other aspects of the activity that is going on are not treated in this way, but this does not mean that they play no part in the interactive process. Thus Goffman proposes that we distinguish a 'directional track' in which, in his words, there is 'a stream of signs which is itself excluded from the content of the activity but which serves as a means of regulating it, bounding, articulating and qualifying its various components and phases' (Goffman, 1974: 210). We may speak, too, of a 'disattend track', to which are assigned a whole variety of actions that are not counted as playing a part in the interaction at all. Goffman mentions here, in particular, various creature-comfort releases – scratching, certain kinds of postural adjustments, and so forth – that are, so to speak, allowable deviations from the behavioural discipline which all participants in co-presence follow as the price for passing as unnoticeable, normal, predictable human beings.

Now as Goffman himself makes clear, and as a moment's reflection will remind us, it is, of course, not that the actions treated as being in the 'disattend track' are not cognized and are not responded to by participants. On the contrary, they may be shown in many situations to play a major role in the interactive process. It is by way of actions that are mutually treated as being in the 'disattend track', for example, that participants in a conversational encounter may negotiate an agreement about when to end it. I may forewarn you of my need to move on somewhere else by a certain change in the pattern of my glances, by a certain postural restlessness, perhaps by a change in the pace with which I am managing a side involvement such as drinking or smoking. Such changes are not officially attended to, they are not even considered part of my expression, yet they may be treated, nonetheless, as conveying certain definite information about my current intentions, and they permit you to adjust your line of behaviour accordingly.

Types of Interactional Occasion: Focused and Unfocused Interaction

The *gathering*, as we have seen, is Goffman's term for any collection of individuals who are co-present. Gatherings themselves can be organized in many different ways. One important general distinction that Goffman proposed here was the distinction between what he called a *focused gathering* and an *unfocused gathering*. In a focused gathering the participants are organized so that they are maintaining among themselves a jointly sustained focus of attention. In an unfocused gathering no such focus can be discerned and the various participants are pursuing separate lines of concern. Unfocused gatherings include, for instance, pedestrians on a city street, users of a reading room, people waiting in a waiting room. Focused gatherings are exemplified by occasions of conversation of all sorts, games of tennis, dancing couples, pairs of workers co-operating to see through a task which requires their jointly sustained attention, interviews, psychotherapy sessions, and the like.

By drawing this distinction, and by showing that a wide variety of occasions of interaction could apparently be accommodated by it, Goffman suggested that seemingly very diverse kinds of occasions in fact had organizational features in common. By drawing our attention to these features he made us aware of aspects of inter-actional situations that had never been systematically considered before. Furthermore, through his characterization of the features of focused gatherings, especially, he was able to suggest ways in which various aspects of behaviour, hitherto disregarded in interaction studies, had a crucial role to play.

If we begin to work in terms of this dichotomy and, in thinking about different kinds of gatherings, try to decide whether they are focused or unfocused, we very quickly come to discover that this distinction can be considered to be no more than a first approximation. However, it is a fruitful exercise to compare various situations in terms of whether they meet the criteria for focusedness or unfocused-ness, for thereby we come to appreciate aspects of these situations that otherwise would be overlooked.

People walking along a city street comprise a collection of individuals who, though co-present, are each pursuing a separate line of action – as pure an example of unfocused interaction as one can get, it would seem. However, as Goffman showed, in his elegant discussions of this situation (in *Behavior in Public Places*, 1963: 83–8 and then, more elaborately, in *Relations in Public*, 1971: 5–18), there is nevertheless a good deal of mutual co-ordination between them. He identified a minimal interactive ritual which he termed 'civil inattention' in which passers-by each behaved to the other in such a way that they conveyed, at once, recognition of the passing of another human being and, at the same time, recognition of the other's right to his own, separate, line of action. Already, in this minimal kind of interchange in which, for example, the passers-by glance at one another but mutually agree not to let their eyes meet, and do so in a way that lets each know that the other is not scared, hostile or that he regards the other as an automaton, we see that there is more to the pedestrian situation than the mere steering of bodily vehicles past one another. In this seemingly most unfocused of situations, thus, we can nevertheless detect a series of momentary agreements not to sustain a joint focus of attention and in this, it seems, we have instances of interaction that have some of the properties of the focused interchange. For in these moments of 'civil inattention' we may observe two people co-ordinating their actions about a common objective, albeit in this case one that joins them in an agreement not to join.

Consider now another kind of gathering, the queue. Is this an example of an unfocused gathering or a focused one? A queue forms when there is something that a number of people want to do which can only be done by one person (or rather, to use another useful concept from Goffman, one 'participation unit')[1] at a time. Buying tickets to go into the cinema, for instance. For a moment you might think a queue is a focused gathering because every participant in it is wanting to do the same thing. They are all focusing their attention on the business of buying the ticket. But this would be wrong because, of course, each ticket-buying is a separate transaction which involves the members of the queue as separate participants. The ticket-buying transaction itself is a focused interaction, of course, but the members of the queue are not all participants in a gathering which sustains ticket-buying. In a queue, what you have is a collection of participation units, each one separately and independently focused upon the same thing. In focused interaction the common focus must be the joint responsibility of the participants.

Nevertheless a queue does have some features that are not unlike those that we can also observe in fully fledged focused gatherings such as conversations. For instance, a queue has a particular and characteristic spatial organization, it has boundaries, and would-be queue members must observe these boundaries, otherwise they may not be regarded as qualifying as members of the queue, and so may not hold a 'place' in it. If you stand too far to the side or too far back from the next person, questions may arise as to whether you are really in the queue or not. To engage in queueing, thus, participants must join in sustaining a spatial arrangement (or 'formation' as I have termed it elsewhere – Kendon 1977) and this must be done through a kind of interaction that can in fact be said to be governed by a jointly sustained attentional focus. Such a focus is rarely formulated as such, it does not become treated as the 'story-line' of the interaction. Nevertheless it is something to which all members of the queue are attentive, for it is easy to observe how they co-operate with one another to keep it going. It would not be right to say that a queue is a focused gathering, yet we cannot deny that, at least in terms of spatial and orientational manoeuverings, there is a kind of focused interaction going on.

Another example to consider from this point of view is the army platoon on the parade ground or, perhaps, pupils and teacher on a nature walk or in the classroom. Here you have a collection of individuals all attending to a single focus, the officer in charge, or the teacher. Once again, these occasions have a spatial organization which the participants co-operate to maintain and which must be participated in if one is to be counted as a participant. Here, too, there is a range of matters to which it is proper to attend, another range of matters which are improper – a pattern of glance and bodily posture is appropriate, and there are arrangements which govern the organization of moves and responses as in spoken-utterance exchanges between teacher and pupils or spoken-utterance–bodily movement exchanges between officer-in-charge and men. There are, thus, several ways in which all participants must co-operate together to sustain the occasion as a parade-ground occasion or a nature-walk occasion. Yet the focus that is 'official', the matters that are treated as 'story-line' or 'main-track', does not arise through the joint actions of the participants in the way it does in a conversation or a game of tennis. In the classroom or on the parade ground there is a single focus to which a collection of individuals are separately attending, and this focus does not change through co-operative action of the participants. In a conversation, however, the topic at hand is jointly created and jointly sustained; and if one of the participants, upon having a turn to talk, is unable to speak for some reason (perhaps because of a coughing fit, or perhaps because he can think of nothing to say) the conversation may have to be suspended. Or if, in a tennis game – another instance of a focused interaction – one of the parties suddenly strains a muscle and can't serve or respond to a serve, the play must be suspended. A soldier collapsing on the parade ground or a pupil on the nature walk who lags behind, on the other hand, does not bring about the suspension of the whole affair unless the officer-in-charge or the teacher decides that it should. Of course, pupils or soldiers can revolt, they can refuse to maintain the organization in which they each separately give their attention to the common focus, in which case the situation becomes transformed. However, my point is that the focus itself is not something that is jointly sustained, as a topic of conversation or play in tennis is. One is tempted thus to distinguish between a *common focused* gathering on the one hand, of which the platoon on the parade ground or the nature walk are examples, and the *jointly focused* gathering, such as the conversation or the tennis game, on the other.

Goffman himself suggested that we distinguish a *multi-focused* gathering from a singly focused one. The standard example of the multi-focused gathering is the cocktail party. Here you have a lot of participants, all within the boundaries of a well-defined space, where there are many separate jointly focused gatherings – a multiplicity of conversational 'knots' or 'huddles'. Such occasions are of particular interest because they bring out very clearly some important features of jointly focused gatherings. These include their boundedness, the way in which the participants co-operate to maintain the integrity of the occasion as a unit of jointly sustained activity. What is of interest in a multi-focused gathering is that one has a number of such bounded occasions of jointly sustained activity within the same physical space. Observation in such a setting provides one with good opportunities to see how the integrity of such occasions is maintained.

We observe, for instance, that each focused encounter maintains itself as a spatially distinct group. People manoeuvre in relation to one another so that the little world of talk that they establish is maintained as a separate world. The goings-on around are carefully treated as if they are irrelevant. We can observe, too, the procedures that people go through as they enter into such bounded units, and as they leave them. Goffman, in *Behavior in Public Places* (1963) provided a succinct introduction to these procedures, referring in particular to the way in which face-engagements must be opened up by a series of moves by which, prior to the beginning of the encounter, the prospective parties must each let the other know that they are open and available for engagement. This is often done through a subtle exchange of glances which may be followed by joint spatial manoeuvres which bring the participants into a suitable 'range' of one another. Typically, an exchange of talk and gesture then occurs – a 'greeting', that is – which serves to establish that the parties to the interaction have openly entered into it. These utterances and gestures of greeting serve as public announcements of the agreement to engage in a focused encounter. They make public the agreement both to the participants themselves but also to anyone else who may be around. And this is important because from this point others within the setting will behave very differently in respect to the two or more who are now engaged together in a focused encounter than they would to the same people not so engaged. The integrity of a jointly focused interaction, thus, is both a product of the sustained co-operation of the participants, and of the co-operation of others who are within the same setting, but not participants. Thus we may observe, in a setting such as a cocktail party, how the separate instances of focused interaction co-operate to keep themselves spatially distinct. Around each occasion of talk there is a sort of 'no-man's land', a reserve of buffer space. People may pass through such spaces, but when they do so, as a rule, they disattend the gatherings within them. If they stay, on the other hand, provided they establish themselves in a particular kind of orientation in relation to the on-going focused encounter, they are likely to be let in to it, or invited to join. On such occasions, thus, we may note how mere movement and orientation in space can constitute a move in an interactional exchange.

Goffman provides a detailed outline of the organization of what I have been referring to as jointly focused gatherings – he also calls them 'face-engagements', 'encounters' or 'situated-activity systems'. He says 'Face-engagements comprise all those instances of two or more participants in a situation joining each other openly in maintaining a single focus of cognitive and visual attention – what is sensed as a single mutual activity, entailing preferential communication rights' (Goffman 1963: 89). He points out how this organization can come to prevail not only in respect to occasions in which talk is the featured activity and the vehicle by which the mutual activity is carried forward, but in any instance where two or more individuals join to sustain a focus of common concern. He points out how people who have entered into a focused interaction tend to maintain a distinct spatial organization – 'an eye-to-eye ecological huddle . . . maximizing the opportunity for participants to monitor one another's mutual perceivings' (1963: 95). He goes on:

> A shared definition of the situation comes to prevail. This includes agreement concerning perceptual relevances and irrelevancies, and a 'working consensus' involving a degree of mutual considerateness, sympathy, and a muting of opinion differences. Often a group atmosphere develops – what Bateson has called ethos. At the same time a heightened sense of moral responsibility for one's acts also seems to develop. A 'we-rationale' develops, being a sense of a single thing that we the participants are avowedly doing together at the same time.
>
> (1963: 96–8)

Goffman's characterization of the properties of the focused encounter – developed slightly differently in several of his works – served to raise new issues for students of interaction and drew attention to the importance of analysing all sorts of aspects of behaviour that hitherto had been quite overlooked.

Thus by emphasizing the separateness of the interactional world that is established by such occasions, he drew attention to the importance of studying the means by which this is accomplished. That is, he pointed out that a consideration of those aspects of behaviour in interaction which serve in boundary maintenance is just as crucial to our understanding of how interaction is accomplished as the study of the actual interchanges that occur within such boundaries. He gave some indications as to what to look for – particularly to look to the spatial arrangements adopted by people engaged in interaction, and to look also to the way in which focused gatherings are organized in relation to the physical settings in which they take place. The study of formation systems (Scheflen and Ashcraft 1976, Kendon 1977, Ciolek and Kendon 1980) – that is, the study of how interactants enter into and maintain spatial-orientational arrangements – is a direct outcome of Goffman's account of focused interaction. Goffman insisted, too, that the physical settings in which gatherings take place is also extremely important from the point of view of how they maintain their integrity. Thus he directed attention to the wide variety of ways in which the environment is structured for interaction; and to the ways in which, in gatherings, participants make use of the various features of the physical environment in different ways according to how the interaction is being organized.

Goffman also drew attention to the problem that faces people who are potential participants in focused interaction. How do they get from the state of being 'unengaged' to the stage of being 'engaged'; from being separate participants engaging only in unfocused interaction, to being 'lodged in a state of talk' with one another? Thus the little rituals by which focused encounters are set up become a matter of interest. He showed that before people could exchange words or gestures of any sort there has to be a kind of prior agreement to do so. And to understand how this prior agreement is reached requires that one look beyond the actual utterances or gestures that are exchanged to the conditions that are organized beforehand: hence we must look at the glances, manoeuverings, posturings and orientations that lead up to the establishment of an exchange of explicit moves and responses. In the study of this we have a nice illustration of the way in which aspects of behaviour that are not explicitly organized as moves giving information to others – 'explicit acts', as I shall call them in a moment – are nevertheless scrutinized for the information they give off about the other's future intentions; and of how people can deliberately manipulate behaviour that is typically treated as belonging to the disattend track to provide information about their intentions so that others can organize their own intentions and behaviour accordingly (see also Kendon and Ferber 1973, Kendon 1985).

Analysis of Explicit Interchanges

In focused interaction participants engage in what Goffman has distinguished as 'interchanges'. In an 'interchange' it is common that first one person does something and then another does something, but these successive doings are treated by the participants as being somehow linked together, often in such a way that B's doing is regarded as some sort of a response to A's previous doing. It has been the preoccupation of many investigators to arrive at a characterization of the principles that govern the way in which the succession of 'doings' in an interchange are linked together and how, as a result, they are organized into a coherent unit of some sort – such as 'a conversation', 'a talk', a 'bout' of fighting, a 'turn' of dancing or a 'round' of cards.

Implied in the action of an interchange is a recognition that participants in interaction attend to each other's behaviour in a highly differentiated way. Earlier in this paper I discussed this in connection with the general point about 'given' and 'given-off' information, and in connection with the observations that Goffman makes about 'attentional tracks' in interaction. It seems that people deal with some aspects of another's behaviour always as if they were explicit acts of some sort, and other aspects of behaviour as if they were either 'background' activities or as if they were irrelevant. In interaction participants treat some aspects of what others' do as 'meant' acts, acts which are mounted as requiring an explicit response while, at the same time, other aspects are not treated in this way at all.

Fundamental to the occurrence of 'interchanges' as these are understood here, then, is the ability of participants to enter into a 'working consensus' as to what is and what is not relevant as an 'explicit act'. *Frame attunement*, thus, must be seen as a prior and fundamental process in the organization of any instance of an interchange (Kendon 1985).

Given frame attunement, we may then look at how the explicit acts that occur in the interaction are patterned. Goffman proposes two frameworks within which this may be done: the framework of *system requirements* and the framework of *ritual requirements*. System requirements are the requirements that an interaction system must have, given that the participants have certain anatomical, physiological and information-processing capacities. Ritual requirements refer to the rules that govern interaction, given that the participants are moral beings who are governed by reciprocally held norms of good or proper conduct. Most of Goffman's work on interchanges has been concerned with the explication of the ritual requirements that govern them. However, in *Forms of Talk* (Goffman 1981b) he outlines the system requirements first and then suggests how the ritual requirements and the system requirements of interaction reinforce one another. The outline of the system requirements that he provides draws together many of the findings of the detailed work that has been done on the organization of face-to-face interaction in recent decades. It is a useful summary of much that is now understood about this organization. He is also able to show very clearly why we also must have the concept of ritual requirements for a complete understanding of interaction.

In Goffman's outline there are eight system requirements. These are given below, with some commentary. I have also added some references to a selection of the work in interaction that lies behind the summary statements presented here.

First, there must be a two-way capability for sending and receiving adequate and clear messages. In his list Goffman specifies 'acoustically adequate' messages, but we may suppose that Goffman would accept the more general statement given here, insofar as messages may just as well be visual – a point to which he gives much emphasis, as a matter of fact, as shall be discussed below. This capability for message production and reception obviously depends upon suitable environmental conditions and upon circumstances which allow participants both to direct their sending apparatuses appropriately and to orient their receiving apparatuses. From this we may see that much of the ecology of conversational gatherings may be understood: people must be close enough to hear and see one another, they must be oriented appropriately, and so on (see Kendon 1977, Ciolek and Kendon 1980).

Second, there are requirements for signals that inform senders that reception is taking place. There are many aspects of the behaviour of listeners that can be interpreted as having this function. For example, there are certain postural and orientational patterns that are commonly adopted by listeners which serve to convey information about the sort of attention that is being given to a speaker – Scheflen (1964, 1972) provided some pioneering observations on this. There are patterns of gaze direction, and head and face gestures and short vocal utterances that serve to give speakers moment-to-moment feedback on how their utterances are being attended to and received (Yngve 1970, Duncan and Fiske 1977, Goodwin 1981).

Third, there must be signals which serve to announce that a channel is sought for and that a channel is open; and also signals that serve to close off communication channels. Such 'opening' and 'closing' functions provide part of the explanation for the occurrence of greeting and parting exchanges (Kendon and Ferber 1973, Schegloff and Sacks 1973).

Fourth, given that P cannot formulate a response to Q until he knows what Q's own relevant action is going to be, we find that participants in explicit interchanges tend to alternate, or take turns, in engaging in explicit actions. This implies that a set of signals or markers will be needed by which turns are marked as beginning and ending, and by which the expectations of the participants as to who is to take up the next turn is indicated.

It should be added that the issue of turn-taking in interaction and the explanation for it is much more complex than this paragraph suggests. For example, P may at times embark upon his next turn before Q's current turn is finished. This comes about not only in situations where P is trying to cut Q off. It also comes about because P is often able to anticipate the nature of Q's current relevant action. Such anticipations may be based upon such things as P's knowledge of what Q is talking about, P's grasp of the intonation structure of Q's utterance, or his grasp of the patterns of redundancy in the structure of Q's talk. This sometimes gives rise to P completing the utterance Q was in the midst of, and then going on to add something of his own. In some circumstances, furthermore, it appears that people can talk and listen at the same time. Nonetheless, alternation of explicit communicative acts is a striking feature of much interaction and is probably to be accounted for in large part by the limitations of the information-processing capacities of participants. To the extent that this is so, we may expect aspects of behaviour to serve as turn-regulation signals and probably all human interactions include these.

Fifth, there must be devices which permit messages to be re-run, to be held up, or for interruptions to occur.

Sixth, there must be ways in which messages may be framed as being messages of a certain type: that is, there must be metacommunication signals, to use Gregory Bateson's term (see Bateson 1956), which serve to instruct how a given message is to be read.

Seventh, there are norms that govern the deployment of content of messages in terms of its relevance to what has gone before.

Finally, there must be rules governing the relationship between people actively engaged in an interchange and those who, though within receiving range of what is going on, are not participants. That is, there must be ways in which a distinction between actual sender–receivers and potential sender–receivers may be maintained. Here again we find a principle in terms of which the spatial and orientational conduct of co-present persons may be accounted for, where some of whom are engaged in interchanges together and others are not, or not in the same interchanges (Kendon 1977, Ciolek and Kendon 1980).

Such system requirements can go a long way towards accounting for much of what we may observe about the organization of conduct in explicit interchanges. However, they do so on the assumption that participants have, in Goffman's words, already 'jointly agreed to operate (in effect) solely as communication nodes, as transceivers, and to make themselves fully available for that purpose' (Goffman 1981b: 15).

If a person is to undertake to operate as a 'communication node', however, he can do so only in respect to one system at a time (another 'system requirement'): and this has the consequence that he must relinquish, for a period, some other pursuit. To receive a request to open a channel with another, in other words, is to receive a request to put other demands aside. Such a request is an invasion of one's autonomy, therefore, and could be resented. By the same token, to transmit a request for an opening of channels to another is to risk being resented and refused, and this is to risk having one's worth as an individual person denied. And of course the other, in refusing, is thereby likely to be seen as a person who denies the worth of others – good grounds, this, for not sending requests for channel-openings to such a person in the future. Requests for channel-openings are risky for one's self-worth, therefore, but to refuse such requests is equally to put at risk the worthiness that others will accord one. Thus an addressee is under some obligation to respond, but an addressor is under an obligation to hedge his address around with devices that could allow the other to refuse him if he must, with a minimum of offence.

Hence we find that explicit interchanges have features that cannot simply be explained in terms of system requirements. In seeking to open conversations, for instance, people address various kinds of gestures and utterances to one another which, although serving as channel openings, also serve as means whereby the worthiness of the participants is given recognition. To close a conversation, one party does not simply turn off his receivers, rather an elaborate process of forewarning of closure is gone through. Prior agreement to close is sought and entered into; and the closing ceremony itself is hedged about with expressions that mutually assure the participants that the severing of the communication channels that is about to take place does not imply that neither will be willing to re-open them in the future, should circumstances permit. Hence we find that the processes of channel-opening and channel-closing become elaborated into rituals of greeting and departure. We can seek to account for their organization in terms of system requirements, but an understanding of their structure also requires an understanding of the ritual requirements of interaction. The pre-explicit-greeting manoeuvres that have been alluded to earlier, often composed of behaviour in the 'disattend' track, require the ritual framework of interaction for their understanding. Indeed, the very way in which persons choose to differentiate 'explicit' from 'inexplicit' action, is a function of the ritual structure of the interaction. To be sure, the selectiveness of our responses to each other's behaviour is a consequence of limitations in our attentional capacities. Differential response, thus, has its origin in a system characteristic. But what parties to an interaction agree to attend to and what not to attend to is part of the general agreement they have to entertain as to each other's worthiness as persons. The agreement that is arrived at is also, therefore, governed by ritual requirements.

Explicit Acts

A final issue raised in Goffman's analyses of explicit interchanges must now be discussed. This is the issue of the nature of the explicit acts out of which they are organized. I have tried, as far as possible, to leave it open as to what 'explicit acts' are. Most of the time, naturally, it seems, we assume that what counts as an 'explicit act' is an act of speech, or at least a vocalization, and virtually all work that has attempted to undertake a close analysis of interaction has been confined to occasions when exchanges of spoken utterance constitute the main involvement of the participants. This is true even where the main interest of the investigation has been on the non-verbal aspects of the communication. The number of investigations of interactions where speech is not involved or where it plays only a minor role are very few indeed, as far as I know.

Goffman, however, has always recognized that explicit interchanges need be neither verbal nor gestural to yet have all of the organizational features he has shown such interchanges to have. He has been at considerable pains to emphasize that the explicit acts out of which explicit interchanges are composed need be neither acts of speech nor of gesture, but can be anything that the participants agree to treat as explicit. A verbal act can be properly responded to by a physical action, as when I say 'Pass the salt' and the salt is passed; a physical action can properly be responded to with a verbal act, as when the waiter moves the spout of his coffee pot over my cup and I say 'just half a cup, please'; and a physical action can properly be responded to with another physical action – as when A takes out his cigarettes, offers one to B, who takes one and then B produces his lighter and holds out its flame to A so he can light up.

Or consider the transaction that takes place when a customer buys a chocolate bar in a cafeteria. The customer can approach the cashier at the cash register to say 'how much is this chocolate bar?' and the cashier may reply '50 cents'. A verbal question is provided with a verbal reply. However, the customer may just as well approach the cashier holding the chocolate bar upwards or forwards in a conspicuous fashion. This, too, will be taken as a move, and to it the cashier may again say, simply, '50 cents'. Here a physical manoeuvre combined with a marked act of object-holding gets a verbal response. Finally, knowing the price of the chocolate bar in advance, the customer may approach the cashier holding up both chocolate bar and money. To this the cashier may simply extend his hand, palm upwards, whereupon the customer may deposit his money therein, and go on his way. Here the entire transaction was conducted without a word being spoken. Yet in all three cases we have an example of an explicit interchange and one which, in each case, has the same fundamental structure.

For transactions of this sort we may identify an opening move, by which the customer establishes his wish to be a purchaser, moves by which the needed goods are identified and the price established, and a final set of moves by which money is proffered and received. Whether these moves and responses are accomplished by spatial manoeuvre and orientation, by facial or manual gesture, by object manipulation and transfer, by talk, or by any combination of these, the organizational pattern of the transaction remains the same.

A common structure for such purchasing transactions could thus be recognized. It could be shown how, in different circumstances, the moves themselves are expounded in different ways: now as spatial manoeuvres and object manipulations only, at other times as acts of speech and gesture. Such an analysis would show how, as Goffman has put it, 'interaction sequences establish slots, and slots can be effectively filled with whatever is available: if you haven't got a sentence, a grunt will serve nicely; and if you can't grunt, a twitch will do.' (Goffman 1971: 149, n. 38).

With examples of this sort, Goffman is able to conclude, as he does in his paper 'Replies and responses' (Goffman 1981b) that talk is but an 'example of that arrangement by which individuals come together and sustain matters having a ratified, joint, current and running claim upon attention, a claim which lodges them together in some sort of intersubjective, mental world' (Goffman 1981b: 70–1). He agrees that 'words are the great device for fetching speaker and hearer' into his intersubjective, mental world, but points out that though they may be the 'best means' for doing this, this does not imply that 'they are the only one or that the resulting social organization is intrinsically verbal in character'.

The resulting social organization is, as we have seen, a product of frame-attunement processes, system constraints and ritual requirements.

Frame-attunement processes allow the participants to arrive at the 'working consensus' of the encounter, by which it is agreed as to what aspects of behaviour are to count as 'moves' and what is relevant for the content of the encounter.

System constraints contribute to the ecological organization of the encounter and they also determine the kind of basic organization the move sequences will have, depending upon the nature of the behaviour that is serving as 'explicit action'. For instance, if talk is involved we may expect a turn-taking structure; if dance movements or caresses or wrestling actions are involved, a different sort of structure is likely.

Ritual requirements account for the ways in which the participants display their willingness to participate in the encounter, how they show appropriate levels of attention and response, and how they negotiate and arrive at an agreement to bring the encounter to a close.

The processes of frame attunement, the management of system constraints and the fulfillment of ritual requirements, involve a variety of actions which may include talk, but need not always do so – but which always involve modes of behaviour other than talk. Talk is thus not fundamental to the production of explicit interchanges; it may not even be required. Nevertheless, it retains a centrality in our experience which no one would wish to deny. The problem remains of stating what its place is within interaction. Goffman's discussion serves to raise this problem. Its solution is a matter for future work.

CONCLUSION

How may Goffman's contribution to the study of face-to-face interaction be summarized and what tasks has he left us with for the
future?

First, I think, he provided a powerful demonstration of the
validity of seeing occasions of interaction as systems that deserve
study in their own right. He gave a particularly clear expression of
the point that participants may engage in actions in interaction for the
sake of the system to which they become committed, and not necessarily because of something they have to express. Thus he showed the
importance of an approach that takes as its starting-point for analysis
not the individual, but the interplay of acts. This provided, for many
of us at least, a quite new framework, in terms of which the small
details of interactional behaviour could be interpreted which,
hitherto, had always been regarded in purely psychological terms.

Second, I think he opened our eyes and made us see that the
whole range of things that people do in each other's presence is
worthy of close study, that all of the orderliness of people's conduct
in co-presence deserves attention, not just those events that we are
normally expected to report. He showed us both the possibility for,
and the importance of, a natural history of social interaction and
greatly broadened the domain of observation.

Finally, he provided us with a terminology with which the complexities of interaction could be talked about. In particular, he
proposed a number of terms which serve to show how the various
commonplace features of everyday interaction are representatives of
whole classes of phenomena which, until Goffman, had never been
treated in this way before. To give just one example, by calling a
conversation a 'focused interaction' he thereby referred a 'conversation' to a wider class of interactional occasion, of which a conversation is but a species. In this way he provided the basis for a general
theory of face-to-face interaction.

For the future, there are many issues, but here are three that seem
to me of particular importance.

First, there is the question of the cultural generality of Goffman's
outline. To what extent is Goffman's analysis of interaction
practices appropriate only for the culture within which he lived and
wrote, or to what extent can it be applied more broadly? It is my
view that Goffman's analysis of interaction may be seen as an
attempt at a formulation that applies to human interaction in
general. The main concepts he developed, including those of

'gathering', 'participation unit', the contrast between 'focused' and 'unfocused' interaction, the analysis of the framing work that inter-actants must do to establish occasions of focused interaction, the ritual interchanges he identified, especially the 'bracketing' or 'access rituals' (Goffman 1971: 73–80) by which interactional frames become established and altered – these can be taken up as proposals for features of face-to-face interaction of an entirely general sort. However, comparative analyses of interaction practices still seem to be too far and few between for this statement to be much elaborated.

In order that more sophisticated comparative studies be under-taken, I think it would be especially valuable if there were further attempts at a systematics of social interaction. There is a whole range of terms that we use in everyday life to refer to different types of social occasion, different kinds of encounters; and Goffman himself makes use of many of these terms in a quasi-technical fashion, hinting at the possibility of a systematics of interactional occasions, although not really offering one himself. Thus he distinguishes 'focused' and 'unfocused' interaction, as we have seen, but he also points out how occasions differ in their participation frameworks – as in the differences between 'podium' events, and occasions where participation rights are more evenly distributed. Goffman provides a starting-point for such a classifi-cation of different kinds of interactional occasion. It remains for others to develop this aspect of his work further.

Finally, there is the question of the nature of the units from which explicit interchanges are composed. I have already alluded to this, pointing out how Goffman, especially in 'Replies and responses' and 'On footing', argues at considerable length that, as he puts it 'anything can be burnt in the fire of conversation'. Goffman is clearly correct here; yet to be left with the very general point that conversation – by which presumably he means any kind of focused interaction – 'is a sustained strip or tract of referencings, each referencing tending to bear, but often deviously, some retrospectively perceivable connection to the immediately prior one' (Goffman 1981b: 72), is to be left with a challenge, not an answer. The challenge is to work out the ways in which the different kinds of actions that can be used as referencings are articulated. What are the contexts, what are the situations, in which people follow the right constraints of conversational patterning, and when do they not do so? Just how are we to formulate the place of talk in human interaction, after all?

NOTES

I would like to thank Mathew Ciolek, Charles Goodwin, Allen Grimshaw, Wendy Leeds-Hurwitz, Stephen Mugford and Emanuel Schegloff for useful comments and suggestions on this paper. I am very grateful to Anthony Wootton and Paul Drew for providing the stimulus for this paper. Financial, institutional and technical support while this paper was being written came from the Australian Institute for Aboriginal Studies, the Department of Anthropology in the Research School of Pacific Studies at the Australian National University, Canberra and the National Science Foundation of Washington, DC.

1 The concept of 'participation unit' is introduced in *Relations in Public* (1971: pp. 19–27). Goffman points out how individuals may participate in occasions of interaction as 'solos' or as members of 'withs'. A good example of a 'with' is a 'couple' or a 'family party' of parents and children. In a cinema queue, for instance, 'places' may be occupied by 'couples' or by 'family parties', and any individual who is a part of such a unit is accorded the same priority in the queue as any other member. The units that make up the queue, thus, when considered from the point of view of its organization as an interactional occasion, are not individuals but 'participation units', some of which may be 'solos', others of which may be 'withs'.

3

Theoretical Continuities in Goffman's Work

RANDALL COLLINS

Erving Goffman, in my opinion, is the greatest sociologist of the latter half of the twentieth century. This may seem a bold assertion. Goffman certainly did not present himself as such. He did not put himself forward as a major theorist, nor did he trumpet his intentions at all. His style was nearer the opposite extreme: recurrent disclaimers about the value of what he was doing, assertions that he was doing no more than delving into a minor field of small-scale events. Nevertheless, it would be a mistake to take his intellectual self-presentation at face value. Modesty, for Goffman, was a weapon of attack, and his overall stance was an aggressive, even haughty one.

The best way to put it is that Goffman is deep. His writings have levels, and the more intellectual sophistication one brings to them, the more brilliance one finds there. Goffman was a very elitist writer; if you were not already one of the cognoscenti, he was not going to open the door to his inner meanings for you. In this respect, Goffman was very different from other prominent sociologists. Talcott Parsons, for instance, is all on the surface. This is not to claim that he was a clear or easy writer, but Parsons was always as explicit as he could be about what he wished to say, and he not only trumpeted his intentions, he thundered and echoed them. (Is it possible that Goffman, writing early in his career against the dominance of Parsons, deliberately chose his style as a form of genteel one-upmanship?) Or Harold Garfinkel, another writer whose meanings are on the surface: no one would claim that Garfinkel is easy to read, but he starts out from the very first words to press on you the point he is trying to make. Garfinkel may be difficult, but he has no hidden intentions.

Goffman, though, hid away what he was doing. It is not for nothing that this is the man who made famous the frontstage *versus* backstage model of everyday life, and who later elaborated layers of frames within frames. One might think, at first glance, that Goffman is a debunker, stripping away the falsities of social life. But that is far too simple a stance for this master of subtleties. The debunker is a well-known social type, and s/he presents a reality that has two levels. One false, one true. Goffman was willing to play with this style; his early public fame, arising from *The Presentation of Self in Everyday Life* and *Asylums*, is no doubt due to his appeal to this ready-made popular image. But Goffman as Machiavellian cynic is only a surface.[1] Goffman knew how to be popular and dramatic, but he wore this as a mask for deeper intellectual intentions. Also belonging to the surface levels is Goffman's reputation as an underground sociologist: the specialist in esoteric forms of deviance, purveyor of the secrets of con artists, the man who lived out (more or less) the popular fantasy of having oneself committed to a mental hospital in order to find out what it was like from the inside. Goffman did, of course, make important contributions to the field of deviance. *Asylums* was perhaps the most influential statement for labelling theory (at least it was taken as such), and it helped to create the conviction that mental institutions were self-defeating, and to generate the resulting wave of decarceration. But read more closely and Goffman's arguments turn out not to be of that sort at all: he is not protesting the plight of the individual against the institution, but demonstrating a theory about the inevitable processes of social organization and the self.

One path into the depths is to realize that Goffman was always intellectually serious to the very strongest degree. Goffman wished to reveal the nature of social life in its most basic forms; it was not part of his intention to shock, to entertain, to make exposés and protests or even to offer practical advice. He was, in short, a scientist, perhaps an ethnographer of undiscovered terrains, and a theorist. His intellectual lineage is usually assumed to be symbolic inter-actionist. After all, he was trained at the University of Chicago in a notable cohort of SIs; he wrote about the nature of the self and the processes of face-to-face interaction. It was natural to assume that Goffman was merely continuing the themes of Mead, Thomas and Blumer. Yet if one examines Goffman's works closely, one sees scarcely a reference to these figures, and what is there is slighting or negative. Goffman was in fact an enemy of any glib processualism or reality constructionism in everyday life. He always asserted the primacy of structural constraints, and one might say that his originality was to push this social determinism down to the micro level as far as it could go, even willing to dissolve the self in the face of the structured situation. Goffman of course had to make compromises on this chosen battleground; but the multiple realities that he charts, as we shall see, are themselves structured in such a way as to bring situational process and reality constructionism within as much constraint as possible.

I am asserting that the deepest layer in Goffman's works, his core intellectual vision, is a continuation of the Durkheimian tradition. There is some external evidence for this. Goffman's most important teacher at Chicago was not one of the symbolic interactionists, but W. Lloyd Warner, for whom Goffman was research assistant while Warner worked on the ritual aspects of American social classes. Another Durkheimian social anthropologist, C. W. M. Hart, had already impressed him with this intellectual tradition when Goffman was a student at the University of Toronto (as Goffman himself once wrote to me). And there are crucial references to Durkheim in Goffman's early works (e.g. Goffman 1959: 69, 1961a: 152). Most importantly, once one has this key, one can trace the essential themes of Goffman's arguments throughout his life's work; though he amassed new empirical materials, took on new topics and confronted new theoretical camps, Goffman always defended an essentially Durkheimian position. I will try to show, in the argument that follows, that Goffman's last major works are more elaborated versions of his early, rather explicitly Durkheimian statements.

This is not to say Goffman's only intellectual concerns are Durkheimian. He had a very strong streak of empiricism; he liked to see himself, not without justification, as an anthropological fieldworker whose 'tribe' was the unnoticed world of everyday interaction under our own noses. A good deal of Goffman's work was taxonomic, the primitive effort to bring his newly discovered species into some kind of order. Much of Goffman's work, especially from his middle period onwards, looks like a micro-sociological Linneus, laying out classifications and modestly waiting for some later Darwin to bring these materials into an explanatory theory. But I think this was only one side of Goffman's intellectual persona; he couldn't help making theoretical arguments, albeit veiled ones, and these arguments always went back to the Durkheimian core.

GOFFMAN'S EARLY DURKHEIMIANISM

What is the Durkheimian tradition in sociological theory? Reduced to its most important elements, it proposes: social reality is at its core a moral reality. Society is held together by feelings of right and wrong, emotional sentiments that impel people towards certain actions, and into righteous revulsion against certain others. Durkheim also proposed, especially in his great last work, *The Elementary Forms of the Religious Life* (1912), a mechanism by which these moral sentiments are produced and shaped into specific social forms. That mechanism is *ritual*. Its nature is easiest to understand by examining explicit rituals with very strong moral sentiments; hence Durkheim focused on religious ritual, especially as performed in isolated tribal societies. But the mechanism thereby revealed is a very general one; in its various modifications, it is found in all societies, and in forms which are merely implicit rather than explicit – what I have called 'natural rituals' as well as formal rituals (Collins 1987). Goffman himself was to provide a major impetus for this generalization, by discovering the class of taken-for-granted ritual in modern everyday life which he called 'interaction rituals'.

The ingredients of ritual are as follows:

1 The group (which may be as small as two persons) is assembled face to face. Ritual is thus a micro-situational phenomenon, though it has macro, trans-situational consequences.

2 The participants develop a mutually aware focus of attention. They focus on the same thing, action, or thought; and they become aware that each other is focusing upon it, and that each is aware of this awareness. The content of a ritual is arbitrary, in the sense that whatever action, object or thought can sustain this mutual focus, is sufficient grist for the mill. The stereotyped action found in formal rituals is important only because it provides an easy and habitual common focus.

3 The participants share a common emotional mood. Again, the particular emotional content is arbitrary, since any mood held in common can sustain a ritual: reverence, fear, thankfulness, anger at one's enemies, love, and so forth.

4 If these ingredients are present, an intensification takes place. The mood becomes heightened. Bystanders at a funeral, entering into the spirit of the occasion, find themselves grieving intensely, if

temporarily; just as the mood of reverence intensifies in a religious ceremony, or of righteous anger in a punishment ceremony, or (as Goffman pointed out) of shared humour or dramatic involvement in a conversational ritual. I would suggest that both (2), the mutual focus of consciousness and (3), the common emotion, feed back upon themselves and upon each other, so that a successful ritual progresses over time to become a kind of socially induced trance as well as an encompassing emotion.

5   The consequences of such ritual interactions are to shape the subsequent behaviour, thought and feelings of those who took part in them. The social pressure which exists in its most intense form during a ritual is impressed upon the consciousness and the emotions of the individual. Rituals thus produce (and reproduce) moral sentiments in individuals. Whatever the content of the ritual, arbitrary though it may have been initially, it becomes a symbol of the experience in which it originated. It carries a charge of emotional energy and a sense of the interpenetrating consciousness that was manifested in the mutually aware focus of attention during the ritual. The physical and mental world, in short, becomes populated with objects that symbolize society. Internalized and carried around in the minds of individuals, these symbols become the steering mechanisms by which people recognize co-members. By means of these symbols people feel where to gravitate for support, where are the centres of power they must respect. On the negative side, they recognize the boundaries of their groups by the lack of respect for their own sacred symbols; and they feel the impulse to punish deviants within their groups who demean them symbolically.

It is important to recognize that the Durkheimian model is a mechanism which produces variations. It is not a social absolute, a kind of functional necessity which is automatically provided in every and all societies and which results in an inevitable state of social integration. It is, rather, a set of causes; where they are present in a given configuration, they work upon those present to generate certain results. If the conditions are absent or weak, the results will be absent or weak. Further, the model is micro-empirically grounded. There is not (usually) some grand ritual in which every member of society participates, and thereby becomes constrained alike into a grand society-wide consensus. Most rituals take place within fairly small groups; it is quite possible, in a large and complex society, for ritual interactions to divide people into morally exclusive communities along lines of class stratification. Or the lines may be even more personalized, so that each individual goes through his/her own unique set of interaction rituals (especially counting the 'natural rituals' of everyday life), and thereby acquires his/her own specialized symbolic reality. We are all offshoots of society; but it is possible, especially in a complex interactional world like our modern one, for us to be individualized and idiosyncratic offshoots.

Such are the main points of Durkheimian theory as I conceive them. I have sharpened up certain aspects, and stated them more formally than did Durkheim himself or his immediate followers, and I have deliberately tried to detach this part of the theory from the functionalism and macro-holism with which this tradition has usually been connected (see Collins 1985). But I believe this provides us with an analytical key for seeing what Goffman did in his early work. Everyday life is ritual: this is a direct extension of the Durkheimian argument. And the primary sacred object, elevated to symbolic status by the way rituals are structured in everyday life, is the self.

Ritual in Everyday Life

Goffman's work indicates that the entire structure of society, both work and private sociability, is upheld by rituals. Furthermore, it shows that this structure is ritually stratified. These implications are usually missed because Goffman tends to direct our attention to the individual self as one passes through these rituals. This is what has given the impression that Goffman is a symbolic interactionist. The basic model, though, is that the self is socially enacted through rituals on frontstages, supported by backstages. One's homes, and especially bedroom and bathroom, serve as backstage areas for hiding the less impressive aspects of self: for getting rid of dirt and garbage (literally), for putting on a frontstage self in the form of clothes, makeup, and hair styling. These same places also are psychological backstages, where one can plan, brood and complain about frontstage social relationships of past and present, as well as act spontaneously without concern for the proper impression one is making. Conversely, part of the frontstage self is the mood one tries to get into, the facial expressions that one wears, the style of one's talk.

This regionalization of the self has implications for social relationships. Interpersonal ties are more intimate to the extent that they take place on backstages rather than frontstages. Moreover (although Goffman does not go into this), one can readily see that there is a hierarchy of frontstages and backstages: workers out of sight of their boss are on one kind of backstage, while the same individual at home with family is on a more intimate backstage, and what transpires between husband and wife in bed is still more intimate. Nevertheless, the most intimate of situations still has a ritual structure to it, and Goffman comments (1959: 193–4) that even sexual intercourse is in some sense a staged performance.

Goffman analyses situations as rituals centred on the self. Conversation is itself a ritual. 'Natural rituals' (my term rather than Goffman's) are found even in the most casual and ordinary interactions of everyday life. There is the assembly of the group (most commonly, two people); the shared focus of attention (the intention of doing the talking itself); and a shared mood, which builds up as the participants become drawn into the topic. Initially, the mood may be only a shared desire to be sociable; subsequently, if the conversation is successful and as people become engrossed in it, it is enhanced into whatever tone of humour, anger, interest or anything else which might emerge with the flow of talk.

The result of this conversational ritual is to create a little temporary cult, a shared reality consisting of whatever is being talked about. This is a major respect in which humans differ from other animals: we can take leave of our immediate physical surroundings and invoke a symbolic world of ideas referring to elsewhere, or to abstractions or fantasies which have no real physical locus. Goffman points out that once the conversational ritual is in full swing, it builds up its own pressures which control its participants. The topic has to be respected, at least temporarily believed in; it has become, for ever so short a time, a sacred object to be worshipped. Goffman describes this by saying that the conversation is a little social system with its own rules, which acts to protect its own boundaries, keeping the mundane surrounding world outside. Another way to put it would be to say that the circular reaction among attention and common mood builds up, so that the topic becomes more impelling as a focus, and the mood becomes successively stronger. A humorous conversation becomes funnier along the way, so that almost any remark, introduced with the right timing, becomes an occasion for laughter. Complaining about one's boss, one's job, political enemies, or the like becomes a ritual affirmation of the point of view shared by the talkers, so that sins are magnified and every detail becomes viewed in darkest perspective. The conversation as a ritual reality now demands that the individuals respect the mood that has built up. Its criterion is not whether what one has said is correct; in fact, one violates the ritual if one too bluntly questions a point, takes a joke literally, or fails to go along with the proper mood of sympathy in listening to someone's bragging or complaints. Goffman goes so far as to describe a conversation as a psychosis-like state, temporarily entered into, in which the only reality that counts is that which will keep the relationship going among the talkers: '. . . talk creates for the participant a world and a reality that has other participants in it. Joint spontaneous involvement is a *unio mystico*, a socialized trance. We must also see that a conversation has a life of its own and makes demands on its own behalf. It is a little social system with its own boundary-maintaining tendencies' (Goffman 1967: 113).

Interaction Ritual and the Cult of the Self

For Goffman, the self is not so much a private, individual attribute, as a public reality, created by and having its primary existence in public interaction. His first important paper (written in 1955 and reprinted in Goffman 1967) is 'On face-work: an analysis of ritual elements in social interaction'. The implications of the argument come out when this paper is seen in conjunction with his next article, 'The nature of deference and demeanour' (written in 1956 and reprinted in 1967), which leads off by referring to Durkheim's theory of the soul. Most religions have a conception of the soul, a sacred part of the individual. The individual soul is regarded as akin to the gods or totems, or as created by them, and is spiritual or immortal and goes to join them after death. According to Durkheim, this represents the fact that the individual's consciousness (and especially his/her moral sentiments) is created by society, and that society is constantly within him/her. Goffman (1967: 47) summarizes: 'the individual's personality can be seen as one apportionment of the collective *mana*, and . . . the rites performed to representations of the social collectivity will sometimes be performed to the individual himself.' In modern society, these rituals centre especially around the 'worship' of the self. The 'line' one takes, the 'face' one presents, does not have to be realistic, but it has to be consistently maintained so that other people will be able to know what to expect and how to react to it. Hence ritual codes exist, requiring individuals to maintain a consistent face and also to help others in maintaining their own faces. Although there can be competitive and deceptive elements in interaction, these depend on a more basic *ritual co-operation* in upholding the enactment of a shared reality.

In other words, people accommodate to each other's constructions of their social selves. They tend to accept the way they define what they are. The politeness of everyday interaction is largely oriented towards protecting these self-definitions. The ritual code calls for people to avoid threatening topics in conversation, and to avoid questioning claims that people have made about themselves; to show tact in overlooking errors in what one's conversational partner has said. What Goffman calls 'face work' in conversation includes not insulting others, not getting into disagreements but rather covering up differences of opinion by polite assent or ambiguous expressions, and avoiding lulls or 'embarrassing pauses' which would reveal a lack of interest in the other person's line.

In 'The nature of deference and demeanor', Goffman uses evidence from a mental hospital to prove his point by comparison. What we consider to be mental illness, Goffman argues, is the violation of the ceremonial rules of everyday life. Extreme and consistent violation of these rules is what gets one committed to a mental hospital in the first place. The worst violators are put in the 'back wards', while those who are considered less 'ill', or on the road to recovery, are placed in a 'good ward', where the ceremonial rules of ordinary interaction are better observed. Moreover, the staff of the mental hospital defines the mental health or illness of its inmates according to what kind of *self* they have, although the actual behaviour they use to rate mental health is patients' adherence to ceremonial rules. This indicates that interaction is seen as an expression of one's self. Persons on the back wards, who tear off their clothes, defecate on the floor, drool, growl, curse or otherwise violate the ceremonial standards of polite society, are also showing no regard for the self-image they are expected to display. By this comparison, Goffman shows that the self depends on – one might also say, is created by – the acceptable use of the ritual of ordinary social etiquette.

Interaction is a process of exchange between ritually enacted selves. Each person defers to the other's demeanour self, and in return receives deference which helps them to uphold their own demeanour. One's personal self is partly based on other's reactions via deference to one's demeanour. Each individual relies on others to complete one's picture of one's self.

All this constitutes a ritual, non-utilitarian dimension of social behaviour. Goffman (1967: 73) quotes Durkheim: 'The human personality is a sacred thing; one dare not violate it nor infringe its bounds, while at the same time the greatest good is in communion with others.' The polite aspects of everyday interaction are rituals in the same sense as the religious ceremonies of the community, only on a smaller scale. Instead of worshipping the whole society or group, as symbolized by its gods and other public sacred objects, however, these everyday rituals express regard for each person's self as a sacred object. Goffman concludes:

> . . . this secular world is not so irreligious as we might think. Many gods have been done away with, but the individual himself stubbornly remains as a deity of considerable importance. He walks with some dignity and is the recipient of many little offerings. He is jealous of the worship due him, yet approached in the right spirit, he is ready to forgive those who may have offended him. Because of their status relative to his, some persons will find him contaminating while others will find they contaminate him, in either case finding that they must treat him with ritual care.
>
> (Goffman 1967: 95)

We may push the implication one step further. Durkheim's sacred objects, the gods of a society, do not really exist in themselves; they are merely symbols reflecting the structure. If the self is the central sacred object of modern society, it is correspondingly unreal. The self in Goffman is not something that individuals negotiate out of social interactions: it is, rather, the archetypal modern myth. We are *compelled* to have an individual self, not because we actually have one but because social interaction requires us to act as if we do. It is society that forces people to present a certain image of themselves, to appear to be truthful, self-consistent, and honourable. But the same social system, because it forces us to switch back and forth between many complicated roles, is also making us always somewhat untruthful, inconsistent, and dishonourable. The requirements of staging roles makes us actors rather than spontaneously the roles that we appear to be at any single moment. The self is real only as a symbol, a linguistic concept that we use to account for what we and other people do. It is an ideology of everyday life, used to attribute causality and moral responsibility in our society, just as in societies with a denser (e.g. tribal) structure, moral responsibility is not placed within the individual but attributed to spirits or gods.

GOFFMAN'S LATER SOCIOLOGY: THE RITUAL GROUNDS OF LANGUAGE AND EXPERIENCE

I am suggesting that Goffman maintained this Durkheimian viewpoint from his early to his latest works. In what follows, I will discuss

Forms of Talk (1981b) first and conclude with *Frame Analysis* (1974), which is the most generalized statement of Goffman's mature period. Goffman's vision is that conversation is always part of a larger frame of interaction. Only if the larger frame is properly handled can the conversation take place; and just how that larger frame is set will determine what kind of conversation can proceed within it. Most of the time we don't notice this larger frame, because it is routine and can be taken for granted; that is why Goffman is at pains to pick out instances when it is not quite routine, and hence intrudes in the form of 'byplay' and the like. But even when there is nothing disruptive about the larger frame, it has to be there to make the conversation possible. (An example would be the privacy and other situational appropriateness necessary for a casual chat). Goffman is saying that talk needs to be analysed 'from the outside in', with the larger frame setting the conditions for what can emerge within it.

Now what determines the larger frame, with which the analysis should begin? There are several layers here, which (making more explicit what Goffman refers to only in passing) we can call (1) the physical world, (2) the social ecology, and (3) the institutional setting.

1   Often talk arises or takes on meaning from the relationship of participants to some event or task in the physical world around them. The talk which occurs when individuals are repairing a car ('There' – pointing to the problem; 'Hand me that'). or playing cards ('Three spades') is not understandable at all unless one knows what is being done physically, and often this requires being right there on the spot. This embedding in a *particularized* physical world is an instance of what the ethnomethodologists called 'indexicality': these statements have a meaning only in that context, which is not transferrable or generalizable. Goffman concludes that the basis of language is not a primal intersubjectivity, a meeting of minds, but rather a common focus on a physical scene of action. The anchoring of the mind is outside ourselves, and communication at its most primitive derives from the way several people anchor themselves to the common physical world in which they are acting.

This does not mean that Goffman is a 'physical reductionist', with a purely external, behaviourist view of talk. Rather, he is saying that mental levels are emergent from this most fundamental, physical frame, and are always anchored to it through one or more trans-formations. There is a mental level, but it is not a free-floating realm, and it is not the primary reality but a derived one.

2   The social ecology that Goffman takes as the social basis of any conversational situation comprises the physical bodies of the people who happen to be present, whether they are actually all talking to one another or not (i.e. bystanders must be included). This might be called an 'ecological' perspective, since Goffman is looking at human beings the way a biologist would look at birds or mammals who are in range of each other. Goffman asserts that people must always pay attention to other human beings in their presence; each one needs to check out the others, if only to see if it is safe to ignore them.

One piece of evidence Goffman brings to make this point is the kind of utterance that he calls 'self-talk'. These are the outcries, mutterings, and so forth that people utter in the presence of others but without being in conversation with him. For example, it is embarrassing to behave incompetently when there is someone else around. Hence one makes a 'ritual repair', implicitly directing it towards the other people. Talking to oneself (thinking out loud), and then suddenly discovering there are other people present, calls for just such a ritual repair. It violates the social demand that we should show ourselves as competent and self-controlled persons; hence one needs to do something to re-establish oneself, by communicating to the bystanders.

This might be referred to as a kind of 'ecological order'. As Goffman puts it, even 'when nothing eventful is occurring, persons in one another's presence are still nonetheless tracking one another and acting so as to make themselves trackable' (1981b: 103). Human beings, as sheer physical bodies, share an animal level of inter-awareness: each is potentially dangerous to another, as well as potentially someone who might be of aid (by calling out in common danger, for instance). Hence we are 'primed,' perhaps even bio-logically, to pay attention to how each other are behaving. Whenever someone does something that is abnormal, they set up a flicker of attention among the people around them, because they are giving off a sign that they are not quite under control, and may in fact be dangerous. Hence, to reassure others and ward off their possible fear of our 'craziness', we communicate little ritual repairs disavowing our mistakes, and thereby rendering ourselves normal bodies walking down the street, whose behaviour can be taken for granted.

Goffman, like Wittgenstein (see Bloor 1983), denies that private experience is primary; the social is always the centre of the action and of attention. Whenever something happens which takes us temporarily out of the social realm (e.g. when we are turned on sexually so that we pay no attention to anyone else) or when we fall short of expected competence (by feeling pain or muscular strain), the return to social awareness always triggers a need to re-establish contact, and to explain to other people why we have taken leave of them (if only for an instant). Hence these expressive cries, grunts, and groans. Goffman's theory depends on the empirical pattern that we make such noises mainly in the presence of other people, not when we are alone. But it does seem to be true that we also can make these noises in solitude. Goffman's argument implies that these solitary instances are derivatives of the social ones, that we can cry by ourselves, or grunt in muscular effort, because we are performing before an imaginary social audience. Presumably, if a person had never been socialized, they would not only be unable to talk: they would also be unable to make these kinds of 'non-linguistic' expressions.

3   The institutional setting is a frame which arises inside these two outermost frames: the physical world and the ecological co-presence of physical human bodies. We can see the significance of the institutional setting by looking at the variations in the kinds of micro-conversational events which can take place. In informal talk, the participants themselves must arrange, or negotiate, who takes which turn in a sequence of turns. But there are other kinds of inter-actions, organized by different turn-taking rules. There is the lecture, which not only gives one speaker a certain amount of time to talk, but also may have a chairperson who calls upon the persons who are allowed to ask questions. There is the theatre or the musical recital, which have their own ways of alloting turns. There are formal rituals, such as a church service or wedding, in which the turns (and for that matter what is said in them) are rigidly programmed in advance. There are also situations of hierarchical authority (an army drill, a corporate board meeting, and so forth), in which there is a ranking according to who is allowed to initiate conversation, by giving orders, asking for reports, and so on. These institutional frames determine the kind of talk that can take place within them. Notice that a free, casual conversation does not escape the institutional model, but is itself constituted by certain institu-tional conditions: namely there must be a situation which is *away from* the more formal types; there are certain arrangements that call for informal talk – such as being invited to a party; there may also be prior sociable relationships among the persons involved, as when

talk is called for when running into an acquaintance on the street. These institutional frames have further levels of complexity within them, which Goffman explicates via his discussion of 'frame space' or 'footing'.

From Stages to Frame Space

Goffman proposes that the constraints on how one speaks and replies are not in the formalities of language, but in the realm of social relationships, in how one must display one's self with respect to others. Instead of turns, talk is organized into 'moves', each of which may take a good deal more, or less, than a full turn as speaker. Austin's and Searle's theories of speech acts are pointed in the right direction, but Goffman argues that the essence of speech acts is not captured by analysing single utterances for their illocutionary force. These are only particular kinds of moves in a social situation. A performative (like christening a baby) may take much more than one utterance or turn at speaking, and the speech act is not really finished until the move is over. Alternatively, one might make several speech acts within the same utterance, packing one's 'turn' with several different moves.

Goffman makes turns derivative of speech acts, and both are derivative of social moves. Social action, in short, is more basic than talk. Speech is embedded in interaction ritual, and one moves through talk by displaying a self to others. Goffman's late works are continuous with his early model in *The Presentation of Self in Everyday Life* (1959). Though his terminology has changed (frames and frame space, instead of frontstages and backstages; footings instead of presentation of self), his later arguments are more sophisticated elaborations of his earlier ones. There are two main components: self and stage. We will take stage first, since self depends on it.

Any situation, as it has become organized through social moves up to that point in time, constitutes a frame, a socially defined reality (which itself is a transformation of some prior or more basic reality). Take for instance a public lecture, which Goffman once analysed before a packed auditorium while giving a lecture. In the lecture, there are 'multiple selves in which the self of the speaker can 'appear' (1981b: 173). There is the self as enunciating its own current beliefs or desires; but also there is the self as a figure within the talk; and further, the self as animator – the self who delivers a performance in the situation (the lecturer as lecturer). When some-one reads someone else's lecture for them, it is clear that the animator is not the same person as the self as enunciator; but that is only a reminder, because even when you are reading your own lecture, it is one self that is the reader, and another self whose voice is making a statement. The lecturer as lecturer has certain staging requirements to worry about: speaking loudly enough, making sure the microphone doesn't tip over, and so forth, while the enunciator is simply involved in making his/her points. These roles are embedded in each other, and one can distance oneself from various of them, as well as inadvertently breaking frame (for instance, when one stops lecturing to say 'I'm running out of time so I'll skip the next page').

Total deception is not necessary for attention to be drawn into the reality which is being constructed. Audiences are usually aware of mundane physical contingencies, in case there is a fire in the theatre. And primal social monitoring always goes on, checking the solidarity or hostility of the human animals around them. Humans have the capacity to be aware of transformations and emergent levels of reality, and even to enjoy multi-level alternations. This is perhaps their distinctive humanness. An important theoretical point emerges by examining the conditions when these alternations feel clumsy and distracting: perhaps it is losing rhythm between audience and speaker, the crucial ingredient in maintaining any social ritual. Goffman thus seems to be showing what is meant by the key feature of 'focus' in interaction-ritual theory.

Goffman elaborates this analysis by examining the errors made by radio announcers, who often become inadvertently hilarious by the way they break frame to apologize for a mispronunciation or *double entendre*, and then make the situation worse by committing still further frame breaks in trying to correct their previous breaks. Goffman is not merely describing radio shows or analysing the source of humour. His theoretical point is that frames build on previous frames, so that even errors do not so much destroy the social situation as give rise to a new situation, a transformation of the old one. The complexity of reality (and of talk) comes from this 'emergent' quality. Further, the radio announcer illustrates a 'frame space' which is tightly prescribed, so that errors in it are both highly visible and create a lot of anxiety when they occur. The comparison between this extremely 'staged' situation, and the informality of everyday conversation, highlights just of what that 'informality' consists: the freedom of frame space in which we ordinarily move. Friendly talk allows for a maximal amount of reflexive frame-breaking.

Goffman is telling us more precisely the difference between front-stages and backstages in his earlier model. Formal situations (or frames) are ones in which the structure is very consciously and deliberately manipulated by performers to have a certain effect on an audience. The words to be said may be tightly scripted (as in a radio show, or a wedding ceremony), but that is not crucial (since ad-libbing may also be scripted in). More fundamentally, there is a pre-planned set of slots in which certain speech acts are supposed to take place: an announcement, an introduction, a sermon, a joke, and so forth. The more formal the situation, the more the performer tries to hide any notion of the performance process itself, so that attention will be concentrated only on what is on the stage. This is, so to speak, the most intense state of a Durkheimian ritual, in which only the sacred object produced by the ritual commands the audience's attention, and the fact that it is a ritual is forgotten. Such 'extreme frontstages' are hence most vulnerable to embarrassment by frame-breaking.

From here, we can go down through a continuum of increasing informality, allowing for more collusion between performer and audience in putting over the performance, and hence more tolerance for frame breaks. At the other end are personal conversations, in which both participants more or less interchangeably take the stage, as well as sympathetically participate in what the other person is trying to put on. For this reason, informal talk need not maintain much 'successful' structure, and it can be full of interruptions, mis-speakings, speech acts which change course in mid-stream or fail to come off. Such is the 'backstage', which we can now see consists of performers' shop talk about the more formal performances they have put over on other people, or their comments on the performances they have witnessed (and perhaps wanted to puncture) as audiences. This does not mean that friendly talkers are exempt from problems of framing or staging. It still remains necessary to dramatize one's point of view in order to get it across, and to perform ritual repairings when things go wrong. The informality consists of mixing together the performer and audience so thoroughly that neither has many secrets from the other – that is, secrets in the problems of performing (whatever information about other things they may be hiding from the other). There can be plenty of performance failures here: in fact the sharing of such failures as they actually transpire is what makes up the 'informality' of the talk, and the sense of ease and intimacy of selves that goes with it.

Goffman argues (1981b: 240) that 'frame space' is a more precise referent for what older sociological theory called 'norms'. Social constraints are not encoded in the form of verbal prescriptions, but are something deeper. These are not rules that people have learned to carry around in their heads, but are ways in which situations unfold, so that participants feel they have to behave in a certain way, or make amends for not doing so. It is the frames that are the constraints. Even when they are broken, the situation that emerges remains constraining in a predictably transformed way. Similarly, Goffman (1981b: 321) sees 'role' as an imprecise concept; on finer examination, it (e.g. the role of the lecturer, or of the radio announcer) really consists of multiple voices and a way in which changes in footing are managed.

We come, finally, to self as conversational motivator. We have already seen that Goffman regards the idea of a unitary self as a myth. Nevertheless, something analogous to this is involved as a motivational principle, to account for the way people move through frame spaces. Goffman states this as it applies to talk, beginning with a criticism of Chomsky for assuming there is only a single, verbal 'deep structure':

> The underlying framework of talk production is less a matter of phrase repertoire than frame space. A speaker's budget of standard utterances can be divided into function classes, each class providing expressions through which he can exhibit an alignment he takes to the events at hand, a footing, a combination of production format and participation status. What the speaker is engaged in doing, then, moment to moment through the course of a discourse in which he finds himself, is to meet whatever occurs by sustaining or changing footing. And by and large, it seems he selects that footing which provides him the least self-threatening position in the circumstances, or, differently phrased, the most defensible alignment he can muster.
>
> (Goffman 1981b: 325–6)

The 'self' that selects the 'least-self-threatening position' or 'footing' in the interaction as it unfolds is the core motivational unit. It is a thread through all the various selves which are enacted, which can be exalted or threatened by the way the performances are carried off. But the content of this self probably cannot be discovered. Since all these interactional frames are a series of embeddings upon the primal reality of living creatures in the physical world, we could argue that the underlying 'self' is simply the awareness residing in one's physical body, as one tries to deal with the other physical bodies around one. But this in turn spins off many levels of self-presentation, performative exigencies, frame breaks, transformations, and so forth, which differentiate the stances of many 'selves', most of them quite temporary. The underlying, motivating 'self' has no enduring description, but is simply the human capacity for negotiating all these performances and transformations.

Frame Analysis: the Anchored Construction of Multiple Realities

Frame Analysis (1974) establishes a way to mediate between the mentalism and hyperrelativism rampant in the intellectual world today and the objective determinism of conventional sociology. Goffman operates on the same turf as the symbolic interactionists and ethnomethodologists, structuralists and deconstructionists, and in some ways he is extending their analyses. But he is also explicitly critical of them. Goffman argues that exclusive emphasis on definition of the situation, on Schutzian reality construction and local production, is too radical. These reduce the world to whatever the human mind happens to construct at a particular time. On the contrary, Goffman defends the 'realistic' view that the physical world exists and has a primary reality. Society, too, is external and prior to the individual. Even situations have a structure to them, a set of contingencies and constraints that may enter into the definition of the situation, but which are not merely created by the defining process. They are something that participants arrive at, rather than merely construct.

Goffman also criticizes the reality construction/definitional view for not going far enough. To speak of *the* definition of the situation, in the manner of the symbolic interactionists, misses the multidimensional and layered nature of situations. It is not just that different people might have different definitions of the same situation, but that each participant can be in several complex layers of situational definition at the same time. (The fact that these layers have a structure in relation to one another is one of Goffman's reasons for arguing that they are not simply created by the observer.) Similarly, Goffman (1974: 26) attacks Schutz and his followers for giving primacy to the 'natural attitude' of 'everyday life', as if this were a single 'reality that people construct. For Garfinkel, the everyday commonsense world may sit over an abyss that people try to avoid seeing, but as long as people keep up standard interpretive procedures, the world has a banal unity to it. Goffman wishes to show that everyday life is not at all simple, yet people are capable of dealing with complexities as a matter of ordinary commonsense.

Goffman's *frames* are designed to support both these points: avoiding complete relativism, but showing multiple realities. This is done by a set of levels, each of which is built upon another. The multiple nature of realities comes from the way frames can be built upon frames, while the whole is anchored because some frames are more fundamental than others. These levels begin with 'primary frameworks': the natural world of physical objects in which people live, including their own bodies; and the social world of other people and their networks of relationships. At a higher level, a strip of activity in these primary frameworks can be transformed into make-believe, contests, ceremonials, or technical redoings (enactments carried out so that the activity itself can be tried out, practised, or observed, without being seriously committed to it).

Other, more complicated and arcane 'keyings' of ordinary activities can occur. Quite possibly there are no limits on how far such transformations might go. Transformations can be made of transformations: for example, someone might be practising for a make-believe play, which is about a wedding ceremony, which the participants are really only going through as an experiment. This gives us four levels of transormation embedded in each other (and the physical activities of the people involved gives us a fifth frame). Reality, in short, can become very complicated. Yet, Goffman wishes to point out, people rarely have trouble with this kind of multiple reality. They know what frame is related to what, and they can easily fall back into a more primary reality if any trouble arises. They know how long they have to practise, and how to stop the play if a fire breaks out in the theatre.

Another order of transformation occurs in what Goffman calls 'fabrications'. These are cases where people try to induce false beliefs about what is actually going on. Examples range from spying and military espionage, through the more mundane frontstage-setting of jobs and of status impressiveness in sociable life. These add layers of reality on to ordinary activities, both because ordinary appearances are made to represent something that they are not; and also because the participants can now have several layers of reality to which to pay attention (Goffman 1969, 1974: 156–200). At a minimum, someone who gives a deceiving appearance must be aware of (a) what their appearance is supposed to look like, and (b) what they are actually hiding and how they have transformed it. Matters become further complicated when the opposing observer becomes an active part of the game, who tries to penetrate the 'cover' and discover what is actually going on. Now the reality multiplies to include (c) what the observer actually knows about (a) and (b), and perhaps (d) what the perpetrator believes the observer knows. Higher-level complexities here can sometimes be added. For the most part, though, these kinds of mutual deceptions have a limit. Goffman (1969) concludes that conflictual trickery is hard to carry through, just because of the cognitive strains involved in managing all these layers of monitoring and impression management. Conflict is self-limiting because human actors do not have much capacity for it; this reinforces his earlier arguments that social reality is constructed for the most part in an accommodative way.

Yet another kind of reality is produced by 'out-of-frame activity' and 'frame breaks'. What I have listed above are ordinary multiple realities encountered in social life. The human being is thus something like an actor, concerned about staging a performance. But things do not always, or even usually, go flawlessly. This does not bother us much; we are used to this staged nature of much of social life, and we make allowances for people's difficulties as actors. When something happens that disrupts a performance or just does not fit within the frame we are trying to be in at the time, we usually ignore or speedily repair it. When a dog wanders into a wedding ceremony, someone quietly tries to shoo it out while others ignore the frame break. When children interrupt adults' conversations, the latter may attend briefly to the kids and then pick up where they left off. Sometimes, however, extreme troubles disrupt a frame entirely; the performers become flustered, or the setting breaks down so badly that the performance cannot go on. This is considered very disturbing, often scandalous, but it testifies to the power of more primary realities over the contrived ones.

Why is this analysis of frames important? Several reasons may be given. Goffman's examples often deal with the lighter, more frivolous parts of life; entertainment, playing, ceremonies, sociability, the arts. But this cultural realm is distinctively human, a level of consciousness in which animals do not participate. A key characteristic of the realm of human culture, then, is precisely this feature of transforming ordinary actions into things seen in a different light. Even the nature of language itself might be interpreted in this way (although Goffman does not raise this point). Talking or writing, seen from the level of primary frames, is merely making certain physical gestures with the mouth and tongue, or certain marks on material objects. Culture transforms these actions, sounds and sights into meanings, an emergent level which wholly supersedes the primary, physical level.

Framing permeates the level of ordinary social action. We live in a world of social relationships, in which roles are acted out, with various keyings and deceptions played upon them. This is the core of practical activities and occupations, of power and stratification. Here again, Goffman leads us to the brink of seeing the micro-reality upon which macro-structures are based, though he shies away from the theoretical implication.

A third reason for the importance of framing is that people's most common activity is talking. And the nature of talk involves a complex shifting of frames, as people set up topics of conversation, manoeuvre over the implied relationships among the conversation-alists, make jokes and insults, bargain, engage and distance them-selves with their words and each other (Goffman 1974: 496–559).

Social life, then, is permeated by the use of frames and their trans-formations. We move through numerous layers of experience in the course of a single day, and probably during most of the minutes within it.

Goffman's Middle Course between Relativism and Objectivity

Despite his criticism, Goffman adopts many of the points of the reality constructionists, while extending them in a new direction. He even defines 'frame' as an element out of which definitions of situations are built up (Goffman 1974: 10–11). At the same time, 'frame' is made equivalent to the phenomenologists' bracketing of the contents of experience in order to look at the devices by which we give it a certain reality status (Goffman 1974: 3). One might say, too, that the frame (or nested set of frames) puts greater detail into the 'contextuality' within which Garfinkel stressed human perceptions always occur.

Goffman however wishes to make all this more structured. Definitions of situations, precisely because they are built up by transformations, have to respect the other frames out of which they are built. They have to move to 'adjacent' frames, so to speak, rather than arbitrarily defining any situation any way at all. *Vis-à-vis* the ethnomethodologists, Goffman rejects the more extreme implications of indexicality and reflexivity. Contexts are not merely an inexplicable taken-for-granted; they can be spelled out, by specifying the surrounding frames. The reflexive nature of our reflections on social reality are merely another frame to pay attention to, not a place to become transfixed so as to keep us from seeing anything else about these various levels (Goffman 1974: 11–12).

Goffman connects the levels of higher mental life, of conscious transformations into constructed realities, 'downwards' to the physical frame in which they occur. His model goes in the other direction as well. Any physical or social activity can be transformed 'upwards', by reframing it. There is no intrinsic upper limit to the amount of self-conscious reframing that can be done. It is for this reason that extremely high-level transformations can be reached (like Garfinkel commenting on his 'breaching experiments', as well as other intellectuals commenting in turn upon Garfinkel's comments, and so on). Human life has a creative, open-ended quality – but only at the 'upper end.'

I would suggest that many problems are cleared up if we see that different analysts are referring to different parts of the framing continuum. The ethnomethodologists examine the world of social routine at its most commonsensical. This is where the 'natural attitude' prevails. Garfinkel argues that most people try to avoid becoming conscious of the cognitive practices which lie behind the production of this ordinariness; for to be conscious of these practices would throw one up to the highest level, where everything becomes arbitrary. Garfinkel ignores the way that each level is grounded in an adjacent one. But whereas people are reluctant to make a huge leap across several levels of framing, a gradual ascent is possible. For example, intellectuals can entertain their analysis at the highest level of reflexive consciousness, because they have worked their way up through progressively more sophisticated levels of awareness. Hence their theorizing does not impair their ability to operate in the world.

Symbolic interactionists are little concerned with the mundane world, but concentrate on the dramatic shifts which can occur in definitions. But this power of actively intervening in defining situations only occurs against a background of a certain routine, at the medium–high levels where situations have already been dramatized as especially exemplary of some larger reality. Goffman stresses, to the contrary, that if one drops back to much lower levels of framing, situations become much less amenable to anyone's definitional activity.

Goffman's own ambiguities about the nature of the self (e.g. 1974: 573) can be seen in this light. Goffman typically stresses that the human self is multiple and dependent upon the kinds and levels of situational activity that are happening at the time. Here, I think,

Goffman is mostly pointing to what happens in highly transformed bits of activity: complex stances that can be taken in talk, in performances, in self-reflection or psychiatric contexts. Moreover, given the fact that the sequence of transformations is opened-ended 'at the top', the search for the 'ultimate self' will never come to an end in that direction. However, if we go in the opposite direction, back towards the human actor as a physical being in a social world of other human bodies, we can come to a core self in the living organism that is trying to orient through these successive laminations.

In my opinion, Goffman's model of emergent levels of realities offers a breath of fresh air on the current intellectual scene. We tend to concentrate on the highest, most reflexively transformed end of the framing continuum, and ignore how these levels themselves emerged out of the physical and social world. We seem to be living in an age of sophists, who regard the previous generation's interest in objective science as so much superstition.

It would of course be undesirable to return to naive positivism, which sees only a single-levelled world 'out there', ignoring issues of human subjectivity and the way it shapes what is seen of the world. But there is a better alternative than the current hyper-constructionism which leaves us trapped in our own discourse. Without going back, Goffman offers a way out. These are some reasons why Goffman is the greatest of recent sociologists. The potential implications of his work extend not only to the future of social thought, but to its philosophical foundation as well.

NOTE

1 Among those who misinterpret Goffman in this way are Habermas (1984: 90-4); MacIntyre (1984: 115-17); and Hollis (1985: 226).

4

Understanding Goffman's
Methods

ROBIN WILLIAMS

The death of Erving Goffman in 1982 inevitably quickened the pace
of commentary on his work, and also provided the opportunity to
assess the nature and influence of his contribution to the development of sociological knowledge.[1] Nobody has found this latter task
effortless, since it raises difficult questions not only concerning the
status of Goffman's own work, but also concerning the status of
sociological knowledge as a whole. In addition, certain features of
Goffman's professional practice have made it difficult to follow the
conventional tracks of institutionalized influence. He seems to have
entirely eschewed the ritual apparatus of institutional continuity:
never editing collections of papers by his students or imitators; never
contributing a prefatory endorsement of another's book; discourag-
ing the growth of commentaries and secondary studies of his work;
and until 1981, never publicly responding to published criticisms.[2]
Such negative practices make it inevitable that consideration of the
influence of his work is forced to concentrate on its cognitive rather
than its institutional effectiveness, thus neatly removing one of the
conventional props of scholarship in the history of disciplinary
development.

Stanford Lyman's review of Goffman's *Relations in Public* contained
the assertion that:

> In particular, crucial aspects of his methodology are unacceptable
> . . . his mode of exposition strikes one at times as strange, and often it
> is at the very least, uncongenial. On the other hand one finds oneself
> compelled to affirm that his mode of exposition is simply brilliant
> and, what is more important, attains results that are intrinsic to it and
> not to be attained by any imitator. Indeed nearly every one of his
> works abounds in important new theoretical ideas and the most subtle

observations . . . Altogether then, even when he is on the wrong path, he fully deserves his reputation as one of the foremost thinkers, a first-rate stimulator of academic youth and academic colleagues.

(Lyman 1973: 361)

Perhaps the final sentence provides a clue to the fact that these are not Lyman's own words; they are instead, comments made by Max Weber about Georg Simmel. Lyman was concerned to draw attention to the parallels between Goffman and Simmel, a point made by many other commentators on Goffman. The point that needs emphasizing, however, is not that there are parallels between what the two writers produced, but the fact that the critical reception of their work seems to have been so similar. Anyone reading Lyman's text without prior knowledge of the original source of the quotation would, I'm sure, have had no difficulty in reading it as referring directly to the work of Erving Goffman himself. That combination of admiration and unease that Weber expresses rather well, is so often found in contemporary appreciations of Goffman, that it has come to represent something of a critical orthodoxy. In this paper, I want to examine some features of this orthodoxy for the light they throw on what I consider to be Goffman's positive achievements within the human sciences.

It may be instructive to begin by considering the view taken by Simmel and Goffman themselves concerning their influence in the light of the criticisms made of their work throughout their respective careers. Simmel commented that:

I know that I shall die without spiritual heirs (and that is good). The estate I leave is like cash distributed among many heirs, each of whom puts his share to use in some trade that is compatible with his nature but which can no longer be recognised as coming from that estate.

(Frisby 1984: 150)

While Simmel's analogy is a poignant one, the statement as a whole has a strong optimistic ring to it. Goffman, was, if anything, rather more pessimistic about his influence within sociology – not only on his successors, but also on his contemporaries. Consider a remark in his presidential address to the American Sociological Association:

My concern over the years has been to promote acceptance of this face to face domain as an analytically viable one . . . a domain of

study whose preferred method is microanalysis. My colleagues have
not been overwhelmed by the merits of the case.

(Goffman 1983b: 1)

It is impossible to tell of course whether such a statement was a true
expression of his belief. Professional modesty might be thought to
play a part in such a self-assessment, yet other sections of the same
address exhibit little sign of such sentiment. Such is not, however,
my primary interest here; what is of interest is the question the
comment implicitly raises about the kinds of such 'cases' that might
be successful in sociology in general. There is a standard story here:
successful styles of work in sociology are made up of several
elements, most particularly, the fact that they are capable of
producing stable findings arrived at by the use of some reliable
methods on topics of some theoretical relevance. But of course, the
standard story begs several questions; what are stable findings, what
are reliable methods, and what are topics of theoretical relevance?

Despite the lack of communally agreed answers to these rather
intransigent questions, at least the standard story provides a focus
of attention for this paper. The focus will be on the methodological
aspects of Goffman's work, and the part played by those aspects in
his success or otherwise; but it is impossible to pursue this without
some consideration of the character of his substantive interest. His
investigations were entirely concerned with the nature of face-to-face
interaction. His view of what he termed the 'interaction order' was
most elegantly summarized in his presidential address already
referred to, and is the subject of a number of other papers in this
volume. What is worth emphasizing from the perspective of this
paper, however, is the deliberate and insistent stress that it be
studied 'in its own right' and his reasons for emphasizing that point
– 'in its own right' – are worth noting. Like Simmel before him,
Goffman argued that the treatments normally accorded to face-to-
face interaction in sociology were markedly different to what he was
proposing. There were two predominant ways of attending to the
stuff of interaction in sociology, both of which were to be rejected.

First, there were types of sociological analyses – social structural
in their focus – in which accounts of what happened in the course of
face-to-face interaction were used for largely illustrative purposes: to
provide evidence for claims made about social institutions like the
family or bureaucratic organizations; as part of an examination of
the way in which social class determines conduct; as illustrations of
major changes in the nature of social organization, etc. It was not

usual, however, to find attention being paid to interactional practices as objects which warranted explicit definition and examination directly. Second, there was an alternative, roughly humanistic-interactionist tradition in which interactions were examined more directly, but seen as the product of individuals taking each other's acts into consideration as they pursued their own pragmatic ends. This latter tradition stressed meaning and motivation, and according to Goffman, took a primarily instrumental view of interaction.

The problem with the first view was that it assumed that the details of the interaction order could be simply read off as reflecting a more real order 'above' it – of the economy, of the legal system or whatever; it therefore failed to conceive of the possibility that face-to-face interaction could have its own ordering principles at all. The problem with the second view was that, although it did invoke ordering principles, these were largely individualistic principles of calculation and of the cognitive and informational processes used by individual actors – as if the interaction order was determined from below. This neglected the fact, as Goffman put it, that we not only take other people into consideration when we act, but that we also give consideration to others.

For Goffman, the key to the nature of the interaction order was that it was a ritual order. [4] And I think he uses this term in two ways, to refer firstly to the 'moral' character of interaction, and secondly to the 'standardized' character of interaction, the latter then perhaps better described as 'ritualization'. These two senses clearly intermingle, but they can be teased out a little. In *The Presentation of Self in Everyday Life* for example, it is the moral character of interaction that is given considerable, but generalized, treatment. The view taken in this text is that social life is organized on the principle that an individual who possesses certain social characteristics has a moral right to expect that others will treat him/her in an appropriate way. In return, any individual who claims to have certain characteristics ought, in fact, to be what he/she claims. In consequence, then, when a person projects a definition of the situation and thereby makes a claim to be a person of a particular kind within it, a moral demand is made of others, obliging them to value and treat him/her in the manner persons of that kind have the right to expect. But before writing these general remarks about morality and ritual, he had shown considerable interest in the formalization of interaction sequences. He had, for example attempted to characterize the nature of all face-to-face engagements as necessarily involving the alignment of participants to one another, to the situation and to themselves.

> Just as there is no occasion of talk in which improper impressions could not intentionally or unintentionally arise, so there is no occasion of talk so trivial as not to require each participant to show serious concern with the way in which he handles himself and the others present.
>
> (Goffman 1967: 33)

This 'concern' is itself subject to organizational production and recognition. Ego has to know how to produce it, and alter has to know how to recognize it. At each moment in a conversational engagement then, participants are required to be sensitive to the consequences of their conduct both for themselves and for others. Such sensitivity, argues Goffman, is difficult to maintain with exactitude since, while it is necessary to convey sufficient respect for others (for example, by providing and demanding attention proportionate to one's own importance, by the way one handles interruptions, delays and conversational lulls), at the same time, these accomplishments are expected to be carried through without apparent effort, and without becoming material for the participants directly to consider. Such competences rely on knowledge of the ritualized forms of interaction.

Much of Goffman's effort was devoted to the development of concepts to describe the units and entities of this interaction order, but the description of this substance is beyond the scope of this paper.[5] In turning to questions of method, it may be useful to consider Goffman's intention in contrast to established traditions of inquiry in sociology and social psychology, since just as his substantive interest is defined in opposition to previous practice, so too is his methodological position. Consider these comments by Goffman on what he calls 'traditional research designs' for the investigation of face-to-face interaction.

> The variables that emerge tend to be creatures of research designs that have no substance outside the room in which the apparatus and subjects are located, except perhaps briefly when a replication or a continuity is performed under sympathetic auspices and a full moon. Concepts are designed on the run in order to get on with setting things up so that trials can be performed and the effects of controlled variation of some kind or another measured. The work begins with the sentence 'we hypothesise that. . . .' goes on from there to a full discussion of the biases and limits of the proposed design, reasons

why these aren't nullifying, and culminates in an appreciable number of satisfyingly significant correlations tending to confirm some of the hypotheses. As though the uncovering of social life were that simple. Fields of naturalistic study have not been uncovered through these methods. Concepts have not emerged that re-ordered our view of social activity. Understanding of ordinary behaviour has not accumulated; distance has.

(Goffman 1971: 20-1)

There are other more positive accounts of 'naturalism' (Goffman's own 'slogan' for his preferred research method), both by Goffman and by others; but this one at least tells us one thing about the approach he recommends – that the method has a dual purpose, consisting in the requirements both to uncover fields of study and to make possible the emergence of concepts. The method is then both empirical and theoretical. Now the problem with examining Goffman's method has been the relative absence of his own attempts to deal with this issue directly. The quote used above is one of the few that are available from his texts, and it is hardly more than suggestive about what he wants to do; it certainly provides no detail on how 'naturalism' might be done. Add to this his reluctance to write about methodological matters, his sensitivity about others' attempts to summarize his method, and one may sense the source of the difficulty that commentators have experienced in dealing with this aspect of his work. His statements could be simultaneously clear and unhelpful: 'Methodological self-consciousness that is full, immediate and persistent sets aside all study and analysis except that of the reflexive problem itself, thereby displacing field of inquiry instead of contributing to them' (Goffman 1974: 12).

In order to draw out what I think are the salient features of his method, I propose to make use of work which has drawn attention to its problematic nature, and only after having done this, return to what I consider are the strengths of what he has produced. The critical orthodoxy of Goffman commentary has drawn attention to three vulnerable features of his work: (a) the problem of arbitrariness in his selection and development of topic; (b) problems in the management of concepts; and (c) problems in the management of data.

The problem of arbitrariness is a feature to which Goffman himself has drawn attention. Some examples:

To begin with, I must be allowed to proceed by picking my span and level arbitrarily, without special justification.

(Goffman 1974: 8)

An exercise will be undertaken in marking off the material on stigma
from neighbouring facts . . .

(Goffman 1964: preface)

I assume that a loose speculative approach to a fundamental area of
conduct is better than a rigorous blindness to it.

(Goffman 1963: 4)

So I ask that these papers be taken for what they merely are:
exercises, trials, tryouts, a means of displaying possibilities, not
establishing fact.

(Goffman 1981b: 1)

This apparent celebration of arbitrariness and unconcern for
cumulation is sometimes expressed in relation to several parts of the
same volume. For example:

The six papers that form the body of this book deal with a single
domain of activity and were written to be published together.
Moreover, they are sequentially related . . . Yet . . . each develops
its own perspective starting from scratch. And taken together the six
do not purport to cover systematically, exhaustively, and without
repetition what is common to them.

(Goffman 1971: 11)

Goffman's clear awareness of issues of arbitrariness and cumulation
in his work, has, however, not prevented critics treating his attitude
as an indicator of weakness or carelessness. Suggestions have been
made that he is an essayist rather than a systematic theorist, and
remarks like these are very common:

My main difficulty with Goffman's work has to do with the
relationship of part to whole. Open each of his books and read them
as entirely self-contained entities and you will find that they each
consist in a well-made essay, elegant, structured, sardonic, insightful,
coherent and well written. Read those same books as part of a unified
intellectual production and you will likely begin to find yourself
wondering what is going on – though there is a considerable overlap
between them, each of them is written as if the others never had been.

(Sharrock 1976: 332)

The apparent lack of cumulation in Goffman's corpus would of
course be a significant shortcoming in any attempt to build upon it
following his own death. The issue of the reality of this appearance
will be addressed later.

The second vulnerability, also the subject of criticism, is the problem of Goffman's concept management. Here, there are two recurrent issues: concept imprecision and concept appropriation. Concept imprecision first: the predominant way in which he introduces concepts is by assembling some combination of several commonsense expressions which themselves suggest certain commonly known but technically undefined associations. Thus commonsense concepts and their associate clusters of meanings are permitted to enter the theoretical vocabulary without apparent care. An example is the way in which he introduces and utilizes the concept of 'secondary adjustment' defined by him as 'any habitual arrangement by which a member of an organisation employs unauthorised means, or obtains unauthorised ends, or both, thus getting around the organisation's assumptions as to what he should do and hence what he should be' (Goffman 1961b: 189).

This is a very informal definition, and not untypical of many of his conceptual inventions. Not long after it is introduced, a series of distinctions are made between different types of secondary adjustment, and these are listed for the reader. The strategy seems to be to introduce the concept, give it a holding definition and put it to work immediately. A few pages later, in order to make a further distinction, he elaborates his original concept, deriving two terms as a result: 'disruptive secondary adjustments' and 'contained secondary adjustments', the latter (the type of adjustment in which he is really interested) being defined as those that fit into an institutional framework without introducing pressure for radical change. In a comment on these 'contained secondary adustments', we can see the second, frequently mentioned problem in concept management. He refers to the fact that the literature source for knowledge of these phenomena are studies of industry and prison life, and comments that in the latter case, they are known as 'conways' or 'informal adjustments'.

Notice what has happened here: he has first appropriated, then for no apparent reason, reformulated these other concepts and the observations that relate to them. His tendency to raid other concepts, change them, re-name them, recast them in what may seem to be quite pointless ways has, unsurprisingly, been the subject of persistent complaint. As one writer nicely expresses it, 'other people's concepts have their names changed' (Phillips 1983: 114).

The third vulnerability in Goffman's method is the problem of data management. All his readers know the range of material he jumbles together in his book: participant observation field notes;

newspaper clippings; sections of fictional accounts; and many more scraps are pressed into service as data. Perhaps the most notorious, and the ones which usually receive the most critical comment in some circles are made-up data – imaginary examples of interaction and speech which are then dealt with by the conceptual scheme, usually and unsurprisingly, with conspicuous success. His own comments may illustrate this:

> The illustrative materials used in this study are of mixed status: some are taken from respectable researches where qualified generalisations are given concerning reliably recorded regularities; some are taken from informal memoirs written by colourful people; many fall in between. In addition, frequent use is made of a study of my own of a Shetland Island (subsistence farming) community.
>
> (Goffman 1959: xi)

His move in the last few years of his work to utilize carefully recorded conversational data may appear on first sight to represent some adjustment to the frequent complaints made about these problems of data sources, but the way that he used such material remained unsatisfactory from the point of view of most of those who work exclusively with transcriptions of naturally occurring conversation. Insofar as the data continue to be used illustratively, the problem is then shifted from that of quality to deployment. Jameson (1974) raised this quite sharply in his review of *Frame Analysis* in which he claimed (in his example), that the concept of 'keying' is not validated by the difficulties and problems it can be shown to resolve, but rather the reverse is the case – that the examples and illustrations are used by Goffman merely to show how wide is the range of the applicability of this term or 'figure'.

These three lines of attack – on the lack of cumulativeness in his work, the cavalier nature of his definitions, and his deployment of data – represent in outline a critical orthodoxy in Goffman commentary. Perhaps one other feature of this orthodoxy deserves notice: rarely, if ever, are these weaknesses described by critics in order to undermine Goffman's whole endeavour. More often, the criticisms serve to legitimate the parcelling out of some part of Goffman's work and make it possible for this part to be pressed into service for the critic's own project.

I want to use these vulnerabilities differently; not to legitimate the appropriation of those aspects of his work which may best serve a slightly different research programme, but rather to illustrate the essential features of his success within the terms of his own research programme. My argument is that he is successful not *despite* these vulnerabilities, but rather *because* of them. His discoveries depend on them, and furthermore, that while they may be the subject of criticism, there is no reason to see these criticisms as doing serious damage to Goffman's enterprise as he conceived it. Note one thing, however, the upshot of the critical orthodoxy is to throw doubt on the credibility of Goffman's substantive discoveries – the criticisms are of method, but ultimately have their effect on substance.

At the beginning of an important, but largely neglected paper, W. W. Baldamus (1972) suggests that there are real difficulties in deciding whether we can call some piece of sociological work a discovery or not. Much of our difficulty arises, he argues, from the nature of the basic material with which sociology deals. The data of the social sciences consist entirely of 'interpreted facts' – that is to say, events, actions, reported experiences, which are already the product of common conceptualizations in everyday life. As Baldamus puts it:

> If we realise that our raw data – our observations on elements of practical knowledge – have potentially a validity of their own, deriving from the pragmatic contexts of everyday life, we can understand how it is possible that mere observational facts have a power to assert themselves. They perpetually generate theoretical interpretations of the world that compete, as it were, with the researcher's own theories, hypotheses, concepts and analyses.
>
> (Baldamus 1972: 281)

The history of attempts to deal with this ready availability of understandings and interpretations of the events and nature of the social world is the history of sociology itself. But whatever proposals have been offered, they all necessarily share a common strategy, which is to disclose a regularity or an organization of some kind, present but unannounced within this realm of already known objects. Sociological discoveries are not then about the anticipated or unanticipated discovery of previously unknown facts; they are much more about the attribution of different significances to what is already known. If sociological discoveries are about re-ordering what is already known, then sociological methods must be those which permit that re-ordering to take place as efficiently and reliably as possible.

Baldamus's observations of the implicit character of sociological theorizing and researching as activities largely involving the reordering of available information resonates remarkably well with many of Goffman's general statements concerning the status of his investigations. Consider the following quotation:

> The dramaturgical perspective . . . can be employed as the endpoint of analysis, as a final way of ordering facts. This would lead us to describe the techniques of impression management employed in a given establishment, the principal problems of impression management in the establishment and the identity and inter-relationships of the various performance teams which operate in the establishment. But, as with the facts utilised in the other perspectives, the facts specifically pertaining to impression management also play a part in matters that are a concern in all the other perspectives.
>
> (Goffman 1959: 240)

The relevance of the 'traditional' scientific ideal to the design of enquiries oriented to the issues raised above seems questionable – that ideal of gaining knowledge through a deductive sequence involving the derivation of testable propositions from axiomatic ones, the formulation of hypotheses from those propositions, the making of observations, and finally testing hypotheses and drawing conclusions. If the observational process itself is capable of generating valid knowledge in its own right – by inspection as it were – then the adoption of the sequential procedure seems pointless. In Richard Rorty's words: 'If the explanandum can come up with a good vocabulary for explaining its own behaviour, this saves us the trouble for casting about for one ourselves' (Rorty 1982: 200). But if formal methods are not helpful, what else have we got to help us develop or use frameworks that will do the job we have identified, that of de-trivializing abundant facts or observations? Baldamus (1972: 295) argues that there is one predominant but unofficial practice for achieving this, and he calls this practice 'articulation', which he provisionally defines as an analytical process whereby an initially vague and vacillating image of a complex framework is perpetually redefined so as to produce an increasingly definite and stable structure.

Later in the same paper he expands this description of the process of theorizing as involving a continuous restructuring of conceptual frameworks whereby a specific technique of what he calls reciprocal or double-fitting is employed.

> This may be envisaged by imagining a carpenter alternatively altering the shape of a door and the shape of the door frame to obtain

a better fit, or a locksmith adjusting successively both the keyhole and the key. In one sense such a technique looks like deliberate falsification: the investigator simultaneously manipulates the thing he wants to explain as well as his explanatory framework.

(Baldamus 1972: 295)

The point about the procedure is that it contains a directional element. It is, argues Baldamus, not an activity that goes on in some random fashion; rather it is progressive, in that a kind of product emerges from the innumerable trial-and-error actions. The procedure has no particular requirement about its starting-point for theorizing. Beginning from a small observational base, one may move towards more and more comprehensive conceptual frameworks for the description of that base. On the other hand, the level of abstraction can remain constant while the number of phenomena seen to be interrelated can be increased. It is these two features working in common – the rise in the level of abstraction and the increase in complexity – that make the whole apparatus seem more stable:

> Taken together, they bring about a gradual improvement in the stability of the total process. In other words, both the emerging conceptual frameworks and the clusters of eclectic discoveries will appear in the end less arbitrary, less fluctuating, more established and more structured than they did initially.
>
> (Baldamus 1972: 299)

Can we use Baldamus' device to clarify Goffman's procedures and preferences in the construction of his rather unique texts? I think we can, and furthermore, that what were characterized in the critical orthodoxy as weaknesses in Goffman's method turn out to be quite otherwise when located in their deployment as part of this overall strategy.

Before dealing with these issues in detail, however, it should be possible to see the character of Goffman's work as constituting the kind of emergent framework which Baldamus describes by comparing two statements Goffman made about his work: the first, in his doctoral thesis in 1953, the second in 'The interaction order' in 1983. Together, they span the 30 years of his work:

> The aim of the research was to isolate and record recurrent practices of what is usually called face-to-face interaction . . . I was especially concerned with those social practices whose formation and analysis

might help to build a systematic framework useful in studying interaction throughout our society. As the study progressed, conversational interaction came to be seen as one species of social order. The social order maintained through conversation seemed to consist of a number of things: the working in together of messages from different participants; the management by each participant of the information about himself conveyed in his messages; the show of agreement maintained by other participants; and other things.

(Goffman 1953: 1)

Social interaction can be identified narrowly as that which uniquely transpires in social settings, i.e. in environments in which two or more persons are in one another's response presence. . . . When in each other's joint presence individuals are admirably placed to share a joint focus of attention, perceive that they do so and perceive this perceiving. This, in conjunction with their capacity to indicate their own courses of physical action and to rapidly convey reactions to such indications from others provides the preconditions for something crucial: the sustained intimate coordination of action.

(Goffman 1983b: 2)

Notice the differences between these two statements: the abandonment of conditionals ('might', 'seemed') in favour of definitives; the replacement of a list of a number of 'things' in conversation by a more carefully integrated set of formalized concepts such as 'focus of attention', 'response presence'; the complexity invoked by the reference not only to perceived perceptions, but to the perception of perceived perceptions – and the implicit claim that his work can deal with such a phenomenon; and the lack of closure in the early expression indicated by the use of 'etc.' in contrast to the completeness of the later expression.

These are of course only summary statements, and it might be argued that the effective demonstration of this process of substantive accumulation necessitates examination of the details of Goffman's work. This is not undertaken in this paper, but other papers have demonstrated that Goffman did develop and consolidate a stable core of basic concepts for the analysis of social interaction; that this core had a highly integrated hierarchical structure of interlocking definitions and usages; and that this conceptual system was continually being worked at and refined by Goffman throughout his years of work.[6] It ranged from the concept 'occasion' used to define the overall structuring context of action through to the most basic unit of 'move' used to refer to 'everything conveyed by an actor during a turn at taking action'.

How does an orientation to process of 'articulation' as described by Baldamus help us re-consider the complaints generated by the critical orthodoxy? First, there is the problem of arbitrariness. It can be asserted immediately that the problem of the arbitrariness of the starting-point is insoluble: there can be no non-arbitrary starting-points for enquiry, and it is hard to believe that anyone working in a discipline so fully penetrated by the premises of Weber and his neo-Kantian contemporaries could ever hope to establish a truly foundational substantive starting-point for social inquiry. What, perhaps, is a more serious issue in Goffman's case is that his later work so often appeared to be re-starting or re-covering analyses that had already been undertaken in earlier publications. There is, however, little cause for complaint about this appearance if we simply notice that in each of the monographs Goffman consistently sets a series of problems or puzzles for the emergent framework – the conceptual system – with which to deal. The puzzle may be a paradox of some kind, a problem for participants in some setting or alternatively, a proposal for analytical development. Two strategies especially recur: the first is to raise issues of perspective itself – what happens if we look at social life as a game, drama, territorial conduct, etc? Here, his interest has been not only with the fecundity of some perspectival device in permitting the re-ordering of data, but also, and very importantly, in the assessment of the limitations of any particular device. The second strategy is to consider the question of how participants deal with degradation, conversational lapses, potentially discreditable information, and the rest. Here, the direction of interest is reversed; where the first strategy gives priority to the analyst's focus of attention, the second gives priority to that of the participants. Of course, both strategies are most successful when they are conjoined. The selection of what to find puzzling remains unpredictable; it is what the puzzle is used to do that is important.

It may be a puzzle that generates the need for new concepts. In which case, an attempt will be made to build or borrow 'suitable concepts'. By suitable here, I mean both able to effect a plausible redescription and also able to be integrated in some way into the general scheme. Or, it may contribute new observations but not pose the necessity for new concepts, the available framework having provided sufficient to deal with the observations on the basis of their similarity to observations drawn from other contexts. In this case, then, the framework can be shown to be able to deal with an increasingly complex and extensive set of observational material. Since there is a premium on discovery in Goffman's work, it is clearly likely that new monographs will contain new concepts, but it is worth remembering that they will largely augment rather than replace those that are at the core of the framework, while both addition and replacement at the periphery occurs more frequently.

Turning secondly to problems in concept management, when we consider this problem with the help of Baldamus's model, the first thing to notice is that the two issues separated out in the earlier section – that of appropriation and that of imprecision – are now seen to be closely related. When Goffman uses other analysts' concepts, that is where we find critics complaining of appropriation; when he uses ordinary members' concepts, the preferred critical term has been 'imprecision'. Both are of course, interrelated. An example of a detailed argument about such an issue might clarify matters. In a recent review of *Forms of Talk*, David Helm (1982) discussed particularly the paper entitled 'Radio talk' much of which is concerned with the concept of speech faults, making some use of work by Schegloff, Jefferson and Sacks on error and its correction in conversation. Helm complains of being irritated by Goffman's substitution of the concept 'faultable' for Schegloff's 'repairable' to refer to speech production problems, a replacement which according to Helm does not enhance his analysis. The point that Helm has missed here, and it is a general point despite the apparent triviality of the example, is that if Goffman is making his analytical decisions in the context of the demand for reciprocal double-fitting, then whatever concept he is using, and whatever observations he makes, will be oriented to the demands of that progressive development. Now although it is true that the data in this paper are recordings of naturally occurring talk, the interest that Goffman displays in this data is very firmly located in that part of the framework which is concerned with the presentation of self, most particularly with issues concerning the appearance of interactional competence. The use of the term 'fault' here is part of a vital link to this concern. It may be recalled that a rather elderly term in his vocabulary is that of 'faulty person', an individual who brings offence to interactions, causing others to feel ill at ease (a term incidentally, given a chapter to itself in his 1953 thesis).

> . . . acceptable individuals sometimes become faulty persons for a brief period of time. A temporary disorder in communication equipment would render a person unable for a while to participate as smoothly as usual during interplay. Laryngitis, extraction of teeth preparatory to obtaining false ones, intoxication, nasal disturbances

causing one to wheeze, a stiff neck – all these were common reasons
for temporarily transforming the individual into a faulty person.

(Goffman 1953: 264)

Apart from being a subject of that chapter, the idea of faults also
served as the focus of the paper 'Alienation from interaction' which
was concerned with the nature of spontaneous involvement in interaction and its vulnerabilities. The point here is that the analytical
moves made in 'Radio talk' have to be related to the formulation of
issues in his dissertation of 1953, as well as to 'Alienation from interaction' not simply to serve the purposes of arid scholasticism, but in
order to reveal the reason for Goffman's preference for the concept
'faultable'. The change from 'repairable' is not wilful, and it is not a
sign of some personal idiosyncrasy: there is a purpose to it, and this
purpose lies in the requirement for the further articulation of his
conceptual framework. The scope and applicability of the concept
'faultable' are both tested and extended by being put to work on the
more complex and detailed observations made possible by using
recordings of naturally occurring radio talk.

Finally, in the matter of the critical orthodoxy, let us turn to the
problem of the management of data. It is important to recognize that
at many points in the course of development of a theoretical
apparatus, one will find oneself concerned with the nature and scope
of the classifications that it makes possible. We know, following
Wittgenstein, that one of the best ways to evaluate a classification is
to describe cases of its application or use, and try to discover what it
is that makes them instances of the classification or the concept
which serves as the ground for that classification. There may of
course be no one element common to all instances of the application
of certain concepts. Wittgenstein has, after all, been quite
persuasive on this point regarding the kinds of concepts in which
philosophers have been interested – like truth, knowledge, thought,
etc. – but even these might have a certain physiognomy in common,
and the understanding of this physiognomy enables us to understand
what 'truth', 'justice', etc., are.

While a philosophical interest might perhaps be limited to the
analysis of existing concepts, sociological interest is additionally
concerned with the invention or adaptation of new concepts. Now in
cases where a new concept is formed, giving us a new ground of
classification, the uncovering procedure would be the same: we
describe cases of it and see what makes them so. Obviously this will
involve filling out the context of the occasions on which the concept

is applied to something. Schatzki (1983) argues that this method for the attainment of understanding (in philosophy in his case) simply parallels the ways in which we learn a new language. When acquiring a language, we are, he argues, acquiring the ability to recognize the phenomena to which particular terms might appropriately be applied. We are simply unable to legislate in advance for what would count as the right kind of phenomena to which any such term would appropriately be applied. An important part of a method for developing such skills is the description of imaginary situations and seeing if one would intuitively call them cases of *x*. What one does is to use one's practical understanding of the concept to test whether something qualifies as a case of *x*. The skilful use of this practice permits the collection of an array of both actual and imaginary phenomena that is more effective than an array of actual phenomena alone in leading one to see the physiognomy which links the possible cases of whatever is the focus of interest. This, it seems to me is the rationale for the deployment of imaginary data at various points in the Goffman corpus. It is not supposed to ground the concepts in a secure way, but rather demonstrate the scope of their application. Jameson's (1974) talk of validation is simply irrelevant here.

Goffman uses two techniques in particular as part of this strategy: one may be called 'the projected logical sequence' while the other might be termed 'the projected logical set'. First, the projected logical sequence: the most basic unit in his analysis of talk is what he called 'the move', defined as 'everything conveyed by an actor during a turn at taking action' (Goffman 1967). The concept is subsequently used intermittently in a number of papers, especially in *Strategic Interaction* (1969), but it is given its most thorough treatment in 1976 in 'Replies and responses' (see Goffman 1981b) where it is defined more fully as 'any full stretch of talk or of its substitutes which has a distinctive bearing on some set or other of the circumstance in which participants find themselves' (another nice example of the progressive articulation of concepts in the scheme). But the point here is his recommendation about a technique of analysis for dealing with such an object. In one revealing passage in an earlier paper, he advises the analyst as follows:

> to get at the significance of a move, play through the interchange not only as it actually (or purportedly) happened, but also as it would have happened had all the participants acted in the most routine fashion imaginable, or contrariwise, the most cuttingly; then

compare . . . to appreciate the significance of a move, look for the effects it has on anticipations as to how the interchange in which it occurs was to unfold.

(Goffman 1971: 209–10)

The second kind of projection occurs many times in a number of texts. Here as a single illustration is a reference from the essay 'On face-work'. 'Face-work' is a name given by Goffman to a set of remedial actions taken to deal with events that offer actual or potential threats to the positive social value a person claims for himself in the course of some interaction.

> Each person, subculture and society seems to have its own characteristic repertoire of face-saving practices . . . the particular set of practices stressed by particular persons or groups seems to be drawn from a single, logically coherent framework of possible practices. It is as if face, by its very nature can be saved only in a certain number of ways, and as if each social grouping must make its selections from this single matrix of possibilities.
>
> (Goffman 1967: 13)

The paper continues with a description of this matrix of possible practices, many of which are outlined but not given empirical instantation. Goffman then moves on to take up a number of further issues about their use, concluding with a series of remarks about the relationship between the ritual order and the nature of human nature. Now the investigation of this matrix is done in a very characteristic way in this paper; its description is obviously the result of a combination of both intuitive and empirical materials in a complex way. It is obvious in reading the descriptions that they are under-determined by data – descriptions such as the following, of which there are many in the paper: 'Once the person does chance an encounter, other kinds of avoidance practices come into play. As defensive measures, he keeps off topics and away from activities that would lead to the expression of information that is inconsistent with the line he is maintaining' (Goffman 1967: 16). The statements have no clear empirical referent. Which person? What encounter? etc? But it would be wrong to criticize him for this practice unless it were all that he ever does. The projected logical set – the matrix of possibilities – has the function of allowing for the creation of categories that *might* be filled at some future point. Categories that are not empirically filled, as long as they do not comprise the majority of categories in a categorial scheme, constitute interesting cases in and of themselves.

Thus far, this paper has attempted to describe how Goffman operates an informal method for producing sociological discoveries – a simultaneously theoretical and empirical method. It is this method that encourages him to borrow, beg and build concepts, encourages him to look for interrelationships between them; at the same time, it is a method which he uses to make discoveries consisting of new ways of organizing data. Or in a more Geertzian way, the discoveries consisted of thicker and thicker descriptions. Goffman's ways of dealing with concepts and with data have seemed to others to be wayward or idiosyncratic practices; but this is the result of a failure to locate them by reference to the central methodological device described above. His perpetual re-starts, his faults in concept management and his problems of data quality control are far from being defects in his method: rather they serve quite definite functions in the context of the implicit trial-and-error characteristics of the practice of reciprocal double-fitting.

But what of the end result of the application of the methods described above? The end result, according to Baldamus, is to ensure that both the conceptual framework and the discoveries which it makes possible will seem to be more established and more stable. The more successful they both are, the more they will appear to carve the world at its joints. It is crucial to the understanding of Goffman's view of sociological knowledge, however, to note his awareness of the fact that this success is an artefact of the method itself. The *apparent* success of a conceptual scheme in achieving such correspondences as it is able to achieve, while seductive, remains deeply problematic, and this realization was absolutely central to Goffman's whole sociology.

The stabilization of a conceptual framework does not result directly from the recognition of the intransigence of particular phenomena, nor does it result from the imposition of *a priori* concepts on to the unknown realm. Nor is it a matter of the happy co-incidence of concept and object. It results from an intelligible display of analytic work on the part of the investigator–author. The importance of Goffman's work lies not merely in its conceptual cumulativeness (though others continue to treat it as a repository of a kind); his work is important precisely because it is concerned with the limitations of any such framework of interrelated concepts and observations. Manning (1986a) has drawn attention to the underlying tension between form and formlessness in Goffman's texts – their form being the result of the application of categorical devices of various kinds, while their formlessness is achieved by his interest in exceptions and vulnerabilities. And in a further paper (Manning 1986b), he extends his analysis of the way in which Goffman managed to pursue his interest in the deployment of procedural programmes alongside an interest in what any such programme necessarily absents from analysis.

This distinctive aspect of Goffman's method is not given separate expression in his work, although few of his published studies fail to raise the issue at some point or another. In 'Replies and responses' (Goffman 1981b) he pursued the analysis of conversational dialogue. In the long passage that concluded the work he teased the reader with the promise that his text promised nothing less than a complete mapping of the forms and routinization of talk. However, just at the point where he is beginning to open his catalogue of these forms and routines, he also begins to distance himself from such a claim: what begins as a catalogue of results turns into a warning about the nature of such results. What was first described as a system of constraints became something to honour, invert or disregard, depending on how the mood strikes:

> Every conversation, it seems, can raise itself by its own bootstraps, can provide participants something to flail at, which process in its entirety can then be made the reference of an aside, this side remark then responsively provoking a joking refusal to disattend it. The box that conversation stuffs us into is Pandora's. But worse still. By selecting occasions when participants have tacitly agreed to orient themselves to stereotypes about conversation, we can, of course, find that tight constraints obtain . . . But there are other arrangements to draw on . . . In these circumstances the whole framework of conversational constraints – both system and ritual – can become something to honor, to invert, or to disregard, depending as the mood strikes. On these occasions it's not merely that the lid can't be closed; there is no box.
>
> (Goffman 1981b: 73–4)

Such reminders – that there is a fundamental distinction between abstraction and the concrete world, between form and formlessness in Manning's terms – constantly recur throughout his work, though usually done without pomposity and with some wit. In the text of a lecture given in 1976 (Goffman 1981b), he deploys a similar irony to that referred to above, this time writing as if to demonstrate the existence of an independently structured world that is obdurately fixed, and available to the sight of those skilled enough to make out its shape. Only in a further paragraph does this demonstration become a mere presupposition, a polite fiction of the occasion of lecturing itself. The lecture over, like the text read, 'speaker and audience rightfully return to the flickering, cross-purposed, messy irresolution of their unknowable circumstances'. The constitution of 'interaction order' is an analyst's fiction – useful, as all heuristics aim to be, but nevertheless an arbitrary abstraction.

This view of the vulnerability of sociological analysis also plays a part in the way in which Goffman inserts himself as author directly into his published texts. The normally de-authored speech of the disembodied social scientist is constantly toyed with in Goffman's work, although for serious reasons. An example:

> We cannot say, however, that role distance protects the individual's ego, self-esteem, personality, or integrity from the implications of the situation without introducing constructs which have no place in a strictly sustained role perspective. We must find a way then, of getting the ego back into society.
>
> (Goffman 1961a: 107)

The use of this active voice – the 'what we can and cannot do, what we must do' – is the practice to which I want to draw attention. Simply a convention of writing of course, but not the standard scientific convention, and one which serves to remind the reader that there is a specific author at work rather than the working out of some preformulated algorithm. Sometimes he conveys a sense of authorial difficulty, an analyst *almost* defeated by problems in conceptualizing or dealing with data: 'this is a difficult matter to deal with . . .' when he is writing about the observation that his basic remedial cycle – 'remedy followed by relief', or 'remedy followed by relief followed by appreciation' – is as much honoured in the breach as in the observance.

This realization causes difficulties, Goffman argues, because allowing this reduces analytical control over the material: 'exceptions becomes grounds for confirming the value of the argument and this is bad. Nevertheless, some argument must be made' (Goffman 1971: 183). The author wearily picks up his pen again: 'Perhaps the best thing that can be done at this stage is to try to be clear about the kinds of variations that take their meaning from the basic form' (1971: 183). This appearance of the analyst in his own text can be both engaging and disturbing since it contributes to the complexity of arriving at a judgement of the text's veracity and plausibility. Of course the narrative line, the display of concepts in the course of articulation, and the presence of a distinctive authorial voice all contribute to the sense that an analysis is being built up in response to issues posed by the necessity for concept development, application and data management. Yet at the same time, drawing attention to these features also gives the same analysis an equivalent sense of vulnerability. Not only are its origins arbitrary, but its construction is clearly the result of a mass of practical as well as theoretical difficulties – as much a response to pragmatic concerns as to conceptual ones.

It would be legitimate to ask the following critical question here: if it is the case that Goffman's method is to use a common and notoriously flexible device in order to make his sociological discoveries, and furthermore, to raise questions concerning the vulnerability of the knowledge thus obtained, surely he has an obligation to deal with a series of fundamental epistemological issues raised by such practices of sociological work? In particular, should he not deal with the basic issues of concept formation and of obser- vational certainty that have for so long preoccupied the study of sociological analysis? I think his answer to that question would have been a negative one. Goffman was unconvinced by the suggestion that the problem of the foundation of knowledge has a solution. Ryan's complaint about Goffman offers a useful summary of Goffman's position. In a footnote to a paper on Goffman's dramaturgical perspective, Ryan writes that:

> . . . the bulk of the paper was intended to offer something to which Professor Goffman, who was at the meeting, and philosophers not primarily interested in the philosophy of the social sciences might find relevant. It emerged, however, that, like other social scientists, Professor Goffman found philosophical discussions useful as a source of empirical hypotheses, or as sketches of mechanisms to be found in social life, but that again, like most social scientists, he was not much concerned with problems in the logic of explanation, not much concerned to distinguish one kind of explanation from another. To that extent, therefore, the hope that one could so to speak try out a first draft on Professor Goffman, and clear one's mind in the process, was not fulfilled . . . I have simply tried to make this essay as lucid as I can.
>
> (Ryan 1978: 65)

Goffman's sociology is one which attempts to develop without secure epistemological foundations, but it should be clear that he does not regard this as a shortcoming. Those who are disturbed by such a position would do well to consider a nasty possibility that the success of any sociological programme actually depends on just that – that its practitioners, by ignorance or intent, manage not to get caught up in attempts to solve basic epistemological problems. Of course attempts have been made to ground sociology in one kind of epistemological certainty or another; but these have unable to attain such certainty even while they were successful at doing sociology. The examples of Parsons and Schutz are relevant here. Who could successfully argue that any sociological perspective, or even any human-science discipline, rests on unequivocally firm epistemological foundations. The image, of course is easy to conjure: the accumulation of knowledge over time with the abandonment of disproven theories along with an increasing mastery of the world through a more and more certain knowledge of its features. But who can point to such knowledge in sociology, or even to sociological theories that have convincingly been subjected to stringent observational tests? Theories move in and out of favour, but the grounds for these shifts are not clearly known. Current work in the philosophy of the social sciences which has consistently raised questions of such certainty has, if anything, been deeply destructive of the attempt to construct firm foundations on either *a priori* or empiricist grounds – Wittgenstein (1972), Foucault (1974), Rorty (1980), Bergner (1983) and Bershady (1973) have all contributed to this critique.

To summarise crudely and assertively: the critical orthodoxy of Goffman commentary, which claims that he says interesting things but has no apparent procedure for directing what he says, is fundamentally misleading. He does deploy a stable procedure for establishing his particular sociological discoveries; the use of this procedure does not constitute any strong epistemological claim, nor does it rest on any. It would be difficult to point to any sociology that had managed to sustain such foundational claims anyway.

Goffman's project succeeds not *despite* its vulnerabilities but *because* of them. His work simply displaces prescriptive epistemology from its privileged position within the field of knowledge. The requirement for a fixed foundation which can establish the rules according to which sociological knowledge should be assembled is an irrelevance. Should a decision concerning the 'correctness' of a particular epistemological position ever be established, that achievement could only come about as the result of substantive disciplinary successes rather than constituting their precondition. Viewed as one discipline among many, rather than the discipline of disciplines, the particular regulatory conceits of epistemology are hard to sustain. There are of course many thinkers who express this more forcefully than Goffman. Richard Rorty is perhaps the most influential of these. But Goffman did not seek to enter that debate himself, and I do not think he would necessarily have had much to offer as a direct contribution to it.

Of course there are many issues that arise once the unavailability of secure epistemological foundations of inquiry is given serious consideration. The multiplication of frameworks of analysis in the human sciences is the most obvious one, but 150 years of epistemological legislation has hardly managed to confine them anyway. Such questions are, however, beyond the scope of this paper which has been concerned with the contribution of one analyst to one corner of this whole field of study.

At the beginning I mentioned Simmel's idea of the estate that he left behind him. Goffman too had the opportunity to talk of inheritances and bequests in his presidential address. He framed his inheritance largely in terms of a particular spirit of inquiry, and the wisdom of not looking elsewhere but to our discipline to ground such inquiry. A suitably Weberian sentiment. Weber's notion of the history of the social sciences as one of a continuous process passing from the attempt to order reality through the construction of concepts, the dissolution of these concepts through shifts in the horizon and their replacement by others, is as good a description of sociology now as it was a prediction in the first decade of our century. Goffman's spirit of inquiry will continue to play its part in that difficult and endless project.

NOTES

This paper would not have been completed without the help of Erica Haimes and Irving Velody. I also benefited from conversations with Bob Roshier before the York conference. I gratefully acknowledge comments and criticisms offered by Tony Wootton, Paul Drew, Phil Strong and Karl-Peter Markl following the paper's presentation. The further editorial work of Paul Drew and Tony Wootton has helped to improve what began as a very scrappy text. It should be clear to readers of this paper that I have found the work of Peter Ashworth, Jason Ditton, Philip Manning and Gregory Smith particularly useful in formulating my view of Erving Goffman.

1 See for example Hymes (1984), Lofland (1984) and a series of papers in *Theory Culture and Society*, vol. 2, no. 1 (1983).
2 See Goffman (1981a).
3 An excellent and detailed treatment of the relationship between Goffman and Simmel can be found in Smith (in press). See also Frisby (1981) on Simmel.
4 Phil Strong's paper in this volume deals with these issues better than I am able.
5 Goffman was very good at that. Susan Jane Birrell, writing on Goffman in 1980, took the trouble to make out a separate index card for each concept which he had explicitly defined and utilized as part of this project – she needed more than 900 index cards.
6 See Williams (1980).

5

Goffman and the Analysis of Conversation

EMANUEL A. SCHEGLOFF

Last night there was a debate in the Arts Club on a political question. I was for a moment tempted to use arguments merely to answer something said, but did not do so, and noticed that every argument I had been tempted to use was used by somebody or other. Logic is a machine, one can leave it to itself; unhelped it will force those present to exhaust the subject, the fool is as likely as the sage to speak the appropriate answer to any statement, and if any answer is forgotten somebody will go home miserable. You throw your money on the table and you receive so much change.

William Butler Yeats (1926)[1]

I

In this essay I mean not to canonize or celebrate Goffman. Rather I mean to continue a fight with him, and thereby to keep alive a tension with his legacy that may continue to yield dividends. For we have undoubtedly not yet finished learning from the work which he has left us.

The critical stance which I shall take up is, then, not for lack of appreciation of his contributions, both to social science in general, and to conversation(al) analysis (henceforth CA) in particular.

There is, for one, his contribution, almost single-handed, to sketching and warranting analytically the boundaries and subject matter of a coherent domain of inquiry – that of 'face-to-face inter-action'. Although explicitly taken up largely in his prefaces (and, most decisively, on special occasions: cf. 1964b, 1983b), it seems to be an underlying theme of much of his work. Although there are not many, even among his students, who have pursued this path and taken up this study, it is especially in point for this essay, for CA can be seen, variously, as following that path, or further developing it, or exploring what it might entail and how, or transforming it.

There are his observations, which some might think are more successful than his prefaces and other theoretical discussions in establishing a field of inquiry. In registering certain events and aspects of events as worthy of notice and available to acute and penetrating interpretation, Goffman materialized almost out of thin air the realization that there was a subject matter there to study. One is tempted to say that he rehabilitated a field, except that he seemed actually to have habilitated it.

It is easy to forget how startling and novel Goffman's work was in 1956*/1959 when *The Presentation of Self in Everyday Life* was published. That he habilitated this field initially through a dramaturgic metaphor is not surprising, for if anyone had seen this vision before it was the dramatist, for whom the most telling way of getting at the human and the social was to put several people on stage and have them talk together, and otherwise conduct themselves, for the observation of others. But it was not only dramaturgic imagery which Goffman made accessible to sociology. It was often he who first understood the harvests to be reaped for sociology in other fields – the environmental psychology of Roger Barker and Herbert Wright (1954), the game theory of Thomas Schelling (1960), the work of the ethologists (before there was a socio-biology), what could be read as ethnographic literatures on the handicapped and disfigured, pickpockets and prisoners and other persons in special circumstances – and introduced them in his writing (e.g. *Stigma, Asylums, Strategic Interaction*) or through his teaching.

Goffman's observations habilitated a domain of inquiry not so much via the analytic and conceptual apparatus which they prompted him to develop; its fate seems to me more uncertain than the domain of inquiry itself. That domain Goffman helped constitute by noticing, and by knowing how to provide the first line of descriptive grasp of what he had noticed. He risked what his critics would call 'mere description'; he saw how important it was, and how hard it was, to get ordinary behaviour descriptively right. He let us see – those who *would* see – that there were investigable things here, and important ones; and that it was possible to get an uncanny grasp of the head and the heart of sociality by examining

* Editors' note: *The Presentation of Self in Everyday Life* was first published in 1956 as Monograph no. 2, University of Edinburgh Social Sciences Research Centre.

these occurrences. How many readers, and hearers, felt revealed and exposed, gave out embarrassed giggles at the sense of being found out by his accounts.

And there are, of course, the several sets of analytic resources which Goffman introduced for the understanding of the organization of interaction – whether of dramaturgy, stigma, interaction ethology, frame analysis, or others in his corpus of work.

So the fight I take up with Goffman here is not for lack of appreciation of the contribution of his work; it presupposes it.

If I may introduce a somewhat personal note, there is something metaphorically oedipal in this 'fight'. Goffman was one of the most consequential of my teachers. It was from him that I, then a classically trained graduate student interested in social theory, the sociology of knowledge and culture and deviant behaviour, first understood about the viability of studying events on the scale with which he was preoccupied. In that sense, he could be seen as at least partially the progenitor of the work I came to do. But, as in the life of families, offspring find a way of being both in the vicinity of what the parents stood for and sharply divergent from it, so sometimes in the life of the mind. Sacks and I, who studied with Goffman together, both appreciated his achievement and meant our own efforts to build on it in some respects, though not in others. But we never set ourselves in opposition to it – not in the way we set ourselves in opposition to much of mainstream professional sociology. So that is not what is oedipal here – not some patricidal impulse.

It was Sacks, actually, who remarked once that we nowadays think of the Oedipus story as a story about patricide, but that it was in the first instance, of course, a case of intended infanticide. Prophesies and oracles aside, it was his father who first left Oedipus to die, and not the other way around. Although it had a non- or semi-public history going back some 10 years earlier, the fight with Goffman which I take up here came publicly to a head with the 1976 publication of 'Replies and responses', and then flickered intermittently, alternating with receptivity and approbation, through the posthumous 'Felicity's condition'. By the time of 'Replies and responses' Sacks was already dead, and we had decided early on that there was little use in public responses to attacks. So it was left to lie unanswered, together with Goffman's other critiques, overt or tacit, loving or nasty, phrased by him or by his students.

Invited now to reflect on matters of concern common to Goffman's enterprise and CA, some replies and responses to 'Replies and responses' make one claim on my next turn in the

dialogue with Goffman. Much in that critique is based on misunderstanding which needs to be set right. But there are other themes to
be addressed as well, ones which capture some of the more general
issues and commitments on which Goffman's undertaking and CA's
differ. One of these can be captured by the distinction which
Goffman draws between 'system' and 'ritual' requirements, constraints or considerations (1981b [1976a]). Involved here are the
sorts of analytic and theoretical issues which we should take as the
central preoccupations of this domain of inquiry. Another of these
more general themes, not unrelated to the first, concerns the sort of
data which will be needed to address the central questions in this
area, and the modes of analysis which we should bring to bear on
such data on behalf of these issues, and leads to a review of this
aspect of Goffman's work.

More of this comparative treatment than I like takes the form of
discursive writing which is the common idiom of theoretical *responsa*
in the contemporary social sciences. What matters in the end, by
contrast, are the analytic practices which emerge as the stock-in-
hand of practitioners. It is the way we do our work and thereby
shape our product, our contribution to the stock of knowledge, that
should provide the assessment of this discussion. So, at the end, I
examine an episode of interaction chosen for its similarity to a
vignette treated by Goffman. I prefer to think of the following
sections of this essay as a series of discursive preparations for the
empirical analysis which follows. Indeed, many of the matters raised
discursively in earlier sections of the discussion were originally
prompted by, and must finally be understood by reference to, the
differing ways Goffman and CA go about noticing, capturing,
formulating, analysing, and understanding the organization and
import of what they take to be the significant detail of ordinary interaction.

What I called at the start 'a fight', is, of course, a kind of
dialogue, with one voice stilled; actually with two voices stilled, for
Sacks is a party to this dialogue as well. It is an eristic dialogue – one
in which the parties mean to convince not one another, but a third
party who will serve as judge – you, the readers, others who will
work in this area.

Such a mode of discourse is not meant to be 'balanced'. I will be
addressing Goffman from one CA position; there are others. And I
will of necessity be ignoring some of the several Goffmans, for
example, the dramaturgic Goffman. But the Goffman I am addressing is the Goffman that Goffman pushed in his later years. That

Goffman was increasingly preoccupied with talk-in-interaction (a term which I shall prefer to 'conversation') and with the analytic stance toward it taken up by 'conversation analysis' (a term which, having become a name, I can do less about). These increasing preoccupations are expressed through the topics of his last half-dozen papers, their citations, and more revealingly, their tacit incorporation of terms and topics from CA work. If the Goffman I address is not the only one, he is the one he came to.

Nor do I mean this to be an overall assessment of Goffman and CA's relation to him and his work. It is a partial, but strategic, joining of some issues. Because his vision was fresh and original and pointed to new territory, it is still alive. Because it pointed to something beyond itself, it is no longer the cutting edge; in my judgement, it is no longer the way to work in this area. This essay is concerned to sharpen our understanding of the difference between what Goffman did and what he (among others) made possible. It is partial and polemical, rather than balanced and judicious. It is meant not to close the books, but to keep them open.

II

In one of his most telling aphoristic *dicta*, Goffman declared at the end of his preface to *Interaction Ritual* (1967: 3), in which he had sketched a proper focus for the study of interaction, 'Not, then, men and their moments. Rather moments and their men.' That declaration resonates voices from the past. It can be seen to recommit inquiry to the view of the ancient Greek tragedies. They, the classicist John Jones (1962) reminded us some years ago, did *not* treat the tragic hero as decisive, though western culture has come to think of them that way, probably under the influence of Christianity. Rather, the key for the Greeks was the tragic *situation*. Central was not the figure of Oedipus, or some tragic flaw in his character; central was the situation in which he was enmeshed. Oedipus figured only to underscore that if a son of kings could be so inescapably ground up by the situation, how much more so an ordinary person. The structure of a situation, not the individuals who happened to be caught up in it on any given occasion, was what was of enduring import for man's fate. Not, then, men and their moments; rather, moments and their men.

Although in various respects engaged in distinct undertakings, in the commitment to this position there is some initial common ground for Goffman and CA. Earlier in the same preface (1967: 2), Goffman had written: 'I assume that the proper study of interaction is not the individual and his psychology, but rather the syntactical relations among the acts of different persons mutually present to one another.' And the 1973 Schegloff/Sacks paper 'Opening up closings' described the programme of work from which it drew as concerned 'to explore the possibility of achieving a naturalistic observational discipline that could deal with the details of social action(s) rigorously, empirically and formally'. Neither enterprise was focused on talk particularly; indeed, the CA enterprise did not insist on *interaction* particularly. For both, talk-in-interaction became a convenient and attractive research site.

But Goffman himself recognized (in the same preface) that the papers collected in *Interaction Ritual* (and, I would argue, in much of his work) did not conform to his declaration. Accordingly, he defended the need for a psychology of the individual to support the study of interaction. 'What minimal model of the actor is needed', he asked (ibid.: 3), 'if we are to wind him up, stick him in amongst his fellows, and have an orderly traffic of behavior emerge?'. But he surely recognized that such a traffic is the product not only of the drivers, but of the properties of the vehicles, the roadways, the fuel, the traffic system, etc.

Yet, despite his explicit commitment, it seems to me that too often, perhaps even on the whole, Goffman did not escape the study of the drivers and their psychology to focus on the traffic of behaviour or the syntactical relationship between the acts. There are parts of *Encounters* (1961a), of *Behavior in Public Places* (1963), and others (especially 1964b) in which the traffic, the syntax, the moments, get the spotlight. But, it seems to me, the perduring entanglement with 'ritual' and 'face' kept him in the psychology. It was the programme of *Frame Analysis* (1974) which began to free him. Perhaps the clearest emergence is the paper on 'Footing' (1979), from which ritual has virtually disappeared, and which may fairly be said to be concerned with the syntactical relations between acts. But that was almost the last substantive thing he wrote.

From his earliest writing on interaction, Goffman's focus on patterns of talk and action was tied to ritual and face, and resisted 'secularization' to the syntax of action. As early as 1955, in introducing the 'interchange' as an object for description in 'On face-work', he treated it not as a formal unit in the organization of acts, but as 'the sequence of acts set in motion by an acknowledged threat to face, and terminating in the re-establishment of ritual equilibrium'

(1967[1955]: 19). Goffman was indeed bracketing for description a particular sequence found naturalistically in ordinary human interaction.[2] He wrote of the unit (ibid.: 20) as a 'basic concrete unit of social activity' which 'provides one natural empirical way to study interaction of all kinds'. But in his actual analysis, it remained tied to a particular job, a job defined by the contingencies of ritual organization and face preservation. It was not treated as the more formal, generic unit implied by the 'syntactical relations among acts'.

Goffman's continuing identification of this unit, under whatever name, with ritual work is made manifest in its reappearance in two of the essays in *Relations in Public* (1971), 'Supportive interchanges' and 'Remedial interchanges'. There is here a differentiation of the earlier notion, but both specifications are still focused on the maintenance and restoration of actors' 'right relation to the rules', or ritual propriety. It is manifest in 'Replies and responses', which finally is an overt attack on the effort to develop, or recognize, a formal unit of the organization of action *per se*, in this case turns at talk doing various actions.

On this reading, the greatest obstacle to Goffman's achievement of a general enterprise addressed to the syntactical relationship between acts was his own commitment to 'ritual', and his unwillingness to detach such 'syntactic' units from a functionally specific commitment to ritual organization and the maintenance of face.

The focus on ritual and face provides for the analytic pursuit of talk or action in the direction of an emphasis on *individuals* and their *psychology*.[3] Although this is a very different psychology than the conventional ones, it is a psychology of individuals nonetheless. 'Face' occupies the same theoretical niche in Goffman's work as individual 'material' interest does in utilitarian social theory; it is its ritual or 'expressive' (see below) counterpart.

To claim this of so great an admirer as Goffman was of the anti-utilitarian Durkheim of *The Elementary Forms of the Religious Life* may appear quixotic. Still, putting 'face' at the centre of interaction drives Goffman's account toward the individual and the psychological at two levels. On the one hand is the recurrently invoked direct account for, and understanding of, conduct by reference to a concern for preservation or demeaning of face (either own or other's). On the other hand is the depiction of an organization of interaction which is driven by, whose *raison d'être* is, the individual and his/her interest – namely 'face'. Interaction is seen, to be sure, to be organized, but to be organized to secure the individual's ritual needs. It is in this sense that Goffman's emphasis is persistently on the individual and the psychological.[4]

We can discern this theme of contrasting theoretical and analytic commitments when we track the usage of the term 'ritual' to contrast with others, as for example in the essay 'Replies and responses' (1981[1976]), where it is contrasted with 'system', as in the contrast between 'system requirements' and 'ritual requirements' in talk-in-interaction.

Goffman offered (ibid.: 14–15) some eight classes of such system requirements and system constraints, saw these as 'what would appear to be the sheer physical constraints of any communication system' (ibid.: 15), and considered work on this to be 'dealing with talk as a communications engineer might, someone optimistic about the possibility of culture-free formulations' (ibid.: 14). Many CA concerns are included here, concerns with the distribution of turns, with evidence that messages are getting through, devices for attracting, retaining and displaying attention, for participant identification, forms for dealing with trouble in the talk – all these are described in a dismissive idiom as of no special interest, and as the subject matter for some other discipline than sociology or anthropology. In the same early portion of this essay, where he is purportedly making the case *for* 'dialogic analysis', he sets beside these system requirements a concern for ritual requirements, which he illustrates largely from his own work, including the earlier-mentioned account of ritual interchanges.

A similar contrast informs his paper on 'Radio talk' (1981c), which is his version of dealing with the phenomena of 'trouble' and 'repair' in talk. In discussing the consequences of an individual's competence or breakdown thereof, he discriminates between two sorts, which he terms 'substantive' and 'expressive'. The former concerns the contribution of the actor to some ongoing activity, presumably including talking; it concerns the *actions* the individual is performing. The latter concerns the consequent judgements concerning 'the *individual's* competency and *his moral character* as a claimant to competency' (1981c: 198–9). This contrast echoes the one between system and ritual: on the one side, the environment for and organization of action; on the other, the individual and his psychology. Although working with a collection of bloopers – major troubles in talking, Goffman largely eschews treating these themselves, and with them the underlying systematic organization for dealing with trouble, and focuses primarily on the forms of ritual restoration of face. Again, and now very late in his career, the 'ritual' leads Goffman to the psychological and keeps him from the 'traffic'.

But this is no mere theoretical accident. That Goffman was persistently more interested in the individual than in the structure of interaction and its syntax can be seen in his choice of these very data. Though the talk is 'recipient-designed' or audience-sensitive, it is not interactional in another sense; there is obviously no provision for interaction between speaker and audience (a fact which Goffman remarks on several times but makes nothing of). In fact, ordinary conversational data, or data on other forms of talk-*in-*interaction, do not have (in my experience) the elaborate apparatus of ritual face restoration in the aftermath of troubled talk which is the main focus of Goffman's treatment.

But it is such ritual restoration that Goffman is interested in. Given the choice between studying trouble in *ordinary* talk-in-interaction *without* this ritual work, or highly specialized, *non-*interactive talk which *includes* it, Goffman opts for the latter. Could it not be argued that the need to go to idiosyncratic materials for this ritual talk suggests that, from the point of view of ordinary interaction, the ritual concerns attached to trouble in the talk are an occasional, context-specific overlay or lamination, to use Goffman's term? Whereas the restoration of *the talk itself*, the *repair* proper, what is the '*substance*' in Goffman's term, what is a *system* requirement (however much it can be made a vehicle for ritual concerns) – that is somehow more central to the viability of talk-in-interaction as a context for human action.

This is, I think, a central point. For Goffman, what he calls 'ritual' is the heart of the sociology in studying interaction; the 'system' is somehow pre-sociological, engineering, biological, whatever. Here I think him seriously mistaken. There are other ways, various ways, of allocating opportunities to participate in interaction, and to constrain the length of those opportunities. There are various ways of making distinct parts of the talk cohere with one another into sequences. There are various ways of dealing with, or ignoring, trouble in the talk. Some of these are embodied in various 'speech-exchange systems' (Sacks Schegloff and Jefferson, 1974: 729ff.). Others are readily imaginable. If there are 'uniform engineering requirements' for 'communication systems' involved here, there are in principle various ways of meeting them. The organization of turn-taking, of sequences, of repair, to take three kinds of organization which I believe are generic to talk in interaction – i.e. which will have some version in operation whenever talk is going on – these organizations are *social organizations* of talk-in-interaction. They constitute as fundamental a social organization as there is: the one that underlies the very constitution and co-ordination of social action, arguably anterior to concepts such as 'propriety' and 'ritual' as components of serious social theorizing about talk-in-interaction. Let me suggest only one way in which such an argument might be specified.

There is a notion that turn-taking – the provision of a single speaker at a time, with minimization of gap or overlap, has to do with politeness, etiquette or civility. In part this view is related to our treatment in western culture, and in particular in Anglo-Saxon culture, of violations of ordinary turn-taking practices as impoliteness or lack of civility.

But there are serious difficulties in proceeding in this way. Such notions as impoliteness or rudeness need to be recognized as parts of the *vernacular culture* which is the mark of competent membership in the society. They are parts of the apparatus of social control, used for the treatment of occasional violations, lapses, violators, the prospects of which are used to socialize new members to avoid the behaviour which will earn them, and their families or social groups, such epithets.

But the vernacular culture's proper business concerns the *running* of the society, not the building of a discipline for its rigorous description. 'Impoliteness' and 'incivility' may work as vernacular accounts of *occasional lapses* in the turn-taking order (and other orders), but do not serve as an account for the existence and character of *the orders themselves*. The fact that violations of some normative structure may be labelled in some fashion does not account for why there was a normative structure there in the first place, or why *that* normative structure.

If, in a *gedankenexperiment*, one imagines a society with *no* turn-taking system, it would not be one that was especially impolite or uncivil. It would be one in which *the very possibility – the assured possibility – of co-ordinated action through talk had been lost*, for example, the sense of one action as *responsive* to another.

Our sense of civil society, in the Hobbesian or other social-contract sense, is in contrast to a state of nature. That state of nature, it seems clear, presumes the existence of already constituted, or constitutable and recognizable, action (as in Hobbes' 'fraud'); what is at issue is the security of persons in such a world, the propriety of various deployments of these already constitutable and recognizable actions.

But the constitution and recognizability of action are, or ought to be, no less problematic for social theory. And it is this domain of problems to which turn-taking, and other generic organizations in talk-in-interaction, should be seen as relevant. Goffman may have been correct in understanding them to be discriminated from the domain he addressed under the term 'ritual', but not in what he made of that discrimination. That the problems of security and propriety were central for him seems hardly to be doubted; a quick perusal of *Behavior in Public Places* and *Relations in Public* might none-theless surprise the reader for the frequency of the imagery of the problem of security. But these problems are foundational for the *political* problem of order, however much it plays itself out ultimately in scenes of interaction. There is another, one could argue *anterior*, problem of order, for which the *constitution and recognition of courses of action per se* are the central problems. In his last writings, Goffman came to recognize them and increasingly to address himself to them, but somehow always with the suspicion that they were not his, not sociology's, business.

At a crucial point in the posthumous 'Felicity's condition' (1983a: 32) Goffman writes, 'Here, clearly, philosophy and linguistics must give way to sociology'. Here, at the end, is the same split between system and ritual. Goffman has assigned the constitution of action to philosophy, its implementation in talk to linguistics, and the proprieties of its expression to sociology. But these assignments are arbitrary. No, worse. They do not recognize that the constitution of some form of talk as some recognizable action can involve its sequential placement, its selection of words by reference to recipient design considerations or its correction mid-course (Jefferson 1974). What could be more social than the constitution of social action, and its implementation in interaction?

What is made of these contrasts between system and ritual, between substantive and expressive, between cognitive and normative can be the source of much mischief. They go back to a root distinction which Goffman (in common with others, e.g. Parsons 1951, or Bales 1950) inherited from the past, which under-lies all these and other elements of his work, between the 'instru-mental' and 'expressive'. In his own work it informs such useful, if not always discriminatable, distinctions as the one between 'giving' and 'giving off' information. Goffman leaned heavily on the side of the expressive. The giving of information may have seemed to him straightforward enough; it was the more piquant (because officially 'unintentional'?) giving *off* of information, and other forms of 'expressive' behaviour, which were his special penchant.

This imbalance needs redressing. To do that, we must focus not only on the face which individuals cultivate by doing what they do;

we must focus on *what they are doing*, on *how they are doing it*, on the *demonstrable uptake of that doing by co-participants*, and on *how the participants together shape the trajectory of the interaction thereby*, and *vice versa*, that is, how the trajectory of the interaction shapes the participants. These, it seems to me, are some of the issues inescapable in addressing the syntax of actions across participants, the traffic of behaviour in interaction – the moments, not the men.

III

For the questions which I have suggested need to be taken up to address the structure of interaction as the focal topic, different data and different ways of dealing with data in analysis may be needed than were characteristic of Goffman's enterprise. For example, if the trajectory of interaction is to be at issue, a single act or utterance in putative context will not be much help. We need then to reflect further on these aspects (data and analytic method) of Goffman's way of working, in part informed by CA ways of working as a contrast. Here, and in the next several sections, these reflections take the form of discussions of Goffman's texts; then the contrast in ways of working is exemplified in a sample of comparative analysis.

It is common now to refer to the sort of work Goffman did, and that CA does, as 'microsociology', and to remark about the level of empirical detail characteristic of the analysis. Indeed, Goffman himself often referred to 'microsociology' and 'microanalysis'. It is worth remarking, however, that although there is an understandable comparative basis for these terms, both of them imply a reference to entities smaller than the norm in their domain. With respect to interaction, however, if the direction pursued in common by Goffman and CA is correct, then relative to their domain they are *not* 'micro', and the elements of conduct taken up in their analyses are not 'details', i.e. small relative to the normal size of objects in that domain. They are just the sorts of building blocks out of which talk-in-interaction is fashioned by the parties to it; they are the ordinary size.

But it is crucial to keep in mind that for social scientists concerned with other domains of the social and cultural, and for those who bring a vernacular sensibility to this work, it continues to be appreciated for its level of empirical detail, for its subtlety, etc. And indeed it was a singular achievement of Goffman's to see the relevance of this world of events, to hone an analytic sensibility for it, and build it up as a legitimate field of inquiry. Still, we must step back and see to what degree analysis trades on the wonderment of the vernacular appreciation of objects which are analytically, technically, much more prosaic.

One has the sense after reading Goffman that, if one grants him his sense of 'empirical', (that is, if one does not insist on quantitative or other standard social-science senses of that term), his work is densely empirical. But really it is not. There are many observations, and interpretations of them; but there are many conceptual distinctions as well – perhaps as many. But one always suspects that the observations are drawn from a much more densely empirical work elsewhere. For example, he refers intermittently to his field work in Shetland Isle, reported in his dissertation (1953); surely that is the densely empirical ethnography elsewhere drawn on. But it is not. It has much the same texture, and most of the same topics, as his later corpus. Nor is the field work in St Elizabeth's hospital anywhere written up in dense detail. It is drawn on interpretively in *Behavior in Public Places, Asylums, Stigma*, and elsewhere, but nowhere described more densely than that. So how do we readers come to treat the work as so empirical?

Goffman is the master of the darting observation, in a kind of analytical pointillism. His method seems to involve 'sociology by epitome'. It is a powerful method; it yokes the reader to its purposes; it impresses the reader's mind and experience into its service. It works in something like the following way.

His observations achieve their sense of typicality, however exotic their scenes may actually be, by using but a stroke or two, an observation or two, a detail or two, to indicate the scene which we as readers are to call up from memory, personal experience or imagination. If he succeeds, that is if *we* succeed in calling such a scene to mind, our very ability to do so from his detail or two is 'proof' of its typicality. The typicality of the scene or action has not only been 'shown', but has been enlisted and exploited, and the adequacy of his description, the bit or two of characterization, has *ipso facto* been demonstrated.

If he, and we, should fail, not much is lost. Any 'case' is likely to be no more than a sentence or two; anyway, it's probably *we* who got it wrong, for we know how subtle an observer he is; anyway, there are lots of other cases in point, clippings, instances, illustrations. It is both the plethora of cases, and our getting access to much more 'detail' than he ever mentions when we bring to mind the scenes he ordered up by his typifying detail, that provide Goffman's work with its sense of being chock full of detail.

Take, as a case in point, Goffman's exercise in illustrating the various ways some ' "same" event' (1981b [1976]: 68) such as a particular utterance could be taken – an object lesson in the relevance of context. At the end of 'Replies and responses' he presents a catalogue of some 12 or more different ways of taking the utterance 'Do you have the time?', illustrated by some 30 distinct imagined next turns. Indeed, apart from a quite abstract and technical characterization of the several 'reinterpretation schemas' involved, these putative next turns are all we are given as a basis for conjuring up the setting. Thus, 'Do you have the time?' 'Stop worrying. They'll be here'. Or 'Do you have the time?' 'Why the formality, love?'. Or 'Do you have the time?' 'Bitte, ich kann nur Deutsch sprechen'. Or 'Do you have the time?' 'What dime'. Each of these mandates us to fill in the scene, and we do. We think, 'Yeah, there's another one I wouldn't have thought of'.

There is perhaps no more striking demonstration in the literature of the ways in which an utterance can invoke and in that sense 'determine' its relevant context, rather than *vice versa*. For here the contexts are summoned up exclusively by citing what was putatively said. Goffman uses this single feature to invoke a whole scene, with its congeries of aspects supplied by the reader. The method I described before is in full operation here.[5]

What is most striking is not how many and how varied are the classes of uptakes that Goffman suggests, and how fertile and acute the imagination which conjures them, but how transparent and plausible, how 'acceptable' in the linguists' sense, they all are. What is *most* striking is that there are *no implausible* ones, as if implausible uptakes do not occur, or do not need to be dealt with. And as if plausible uptakes need to be dealt with (and can be taken to discredit other people's work) even if they do not actually occur. This is sociology by epitome with a vengeance. It will not deliver the field which Goffman has helped bring us to the verge of, both because analysis proposed about such material is of equivocal relevance when confronted with hard empirical detail, and because of the sorts of occurrences which never come up for analysis at all when proceeding in Goffman's way.

First, when we capture on tape scenes such as he summoned up with a telling detail or two, and we ask what is to be said about them, it is not clear that his detail or two *can* be said, or are in point. For example, in 'Felicity's condition' (1983a: 33), Goffman calls to mind (sic!) the following scene: one sees some dramatic event in a public place in the presence of a stranger, and says, 'Oh God!', '. . . to which the other properly responds by displaying that they have not been improperly addressed . . .', for example, they shake their head or say 'Fantastic'. Now if we had a videotape of such a scene, with such actions and utterances, it is not clear to me that one would properly analyse these bits of response as 'displays that one was not improperly addressed'. From the instance as described, it is unclear what basis there would be for such an analysis, aside from a Goffmanian stipulation of its relevance.

On the other hand, when addressing a scene as recorded, we encounter stubborn, recalcitrant, puzzling details that will not go away, which we must entertain as possibly relevant without quite, or at all, knowing how, but which never arise in a world whose scenes are summoned up by invocations of typical, and therefore usually transparent, details. In Goffman's texts we rarely get puzzling data, actions which have not been solved. For them to get into his text, he has to have seen in them some resonance with a point or theme in the analysis he is building. They only present themselves in his text as 'domesticated'.

Most problematic of all is the import of some initially anomalous appearing material in Goffman's analytic modality. When encountering some 'non-standard' strip of conduct in a recorded scene (as in the utterance 'I know. I decided that my body didn't need it.', which occurs in the data fragment examined later in this paper), one can work at it with the aspiration that a 'solution' will contribute to our grasp of the ways of interaction, conversation, language – some generally operative natural/cultural formation we are out to understand. When we encounter something apparently strange that has been invented (such as the utterance 'Oh. That. Not that I know of.', avowedly invented by Goffman to complement a real exchange reported by Shuy, and discussed in the next section), we do not know what we are investigating. About the former we can ask, what might its speaker have been doing in talking that way. About the latter we cannot, for we do not know what underlies 'that way': an arbitrary decision by the analyst on how to represent an intuited utterance type? a decision to put the utterance just that way for purposes of the analyst's argument? a way someone actually talked? a misremembered version of the latter? what *are* we investigating, and what type and level of account is in order?[6]

This state of affairs may be quite acceptable if what is wanted is a rough indication and justification for a field of study, and for some sense of the immense capacities which ordinary persons bring to ordinary interaction. This job it has done extraordinarily well. It is the materializing of a potential field which we all celebrate.

But if what is wanted is an empirical account of how it is in inter-action actually, there must be some reservations. For then what is needed must include the capacity to analyse particular spates of talk, and, in principle, any such spate. For this, Goffman is of equivocal help. He rarely, if ever, shows us a spate of real talk, he does so only in respects which illustrate some point he is making in a larger argument uncontrolled by that data, and he generally makes only that point about it.

Here, the tendentious juxtaposition with CA cannot be avoided. CA work is applicable, in principle, to any spate of talk in interaction, and a variety of aspects of any such talk are accessible in principle to such analysis. Furthermore, the data being analysed are made available in a form which allows the reader independent access and thereby the possibility of independent competitive reanalysis. It provides as well unsolved puzzles, and even materials on in-dependent problems. In some measure, this is the case because of the technology of recording. In some measure it is because the 'system requirements', the generic sequential organizations of talk-in-interaction, are (if they *are* generic) present and analysable whenever talk is.

When we 'revisit' Goffman's scenes and contexts with this technology – both material and analytic, and with the constraints it now allows us to impose on analysis and meet, his observations are often elusive, and, to skeptics, illusory.

IV

Clearly, the differences between Goffman's 'data' and CA's are decisive rather than marginal, however indiscriminably 'detailed' they may appear to those who work on differently sized worlds. Although he is reported to have, in private conversation, endorsed recording as now the way to work, he never did so publicly, and never systematically incorporated recorded data into his own work.

Goffman's attitude toward 'real data', in the sense of actual observed occasions, whether taped or not, was equivocal at best, and has not been fully appreciated. Consider, for example, that in 1971 he could write in *Relations in Public* the following striking footnote to the first appearance in his text of something which looked like a transcript (p. 140, fn. 31):

> The interchanges in this paper are drawn from notes taken on actual interaction, except where quite stereotyped or apocryphal interplay is cited. I have done this because it is easier to record interactions or cull them than to make them up. In all cases, however, *their intended value is not as records of what actually happened, but as illustrations of what would be easily understandable if they had happened and had happened with the interpretive significance I give them.* (emphasis supplied)

The last sentence is uncharacteristically convoluted and difficult to interpret. I make it out to say, 'If events happened with the sense I describe, then my description would be correct'.

Nor was this view merely the consequence of concerns about prosody, physical movement, facial expression, unspoken aspects of social situation, biographical context, and the dangers of retroactive resolution of the indeterminacy and contingency of utterances (1981b [1976]: passim). When, in 'Radio talk', he worked with recordings which arguably present all of what made those events what they were, he did not use the detail thereby made accessible in a markedly different way than previous references to data.

Still, by the time of 'Felicity's condition', he could write as one conclusion (1983a: 23–4) that 'certainly discourse can be taped, the occasion of its production filmed, and the whole result subjected to repeated close examination. But the record itself will not always be enough.' Presumably, then, one might have thought, sometimes it *will* be, perhaps for *some purposes* it will *generally* be, perhaps the burden should ordinarily be on the one who wishes to claim that it is not enough. Presumably, if it is an empirical discipline being built, this record will give us more, even if it is not always enough, than its absence will.

Nowhere is Goffman's discomfort with actual observations, recorded in detail, more evident than in a brief discussion in 'Replies and responses' which is as stunning in its way as the footnote quoted above from *Relations in Public* is in its. He provides in the text (1981b [1976]: 55) a four-utterance exchange:

Doctor	Have you ever had a history of cardiac arrest in your family?
Patient	We never had no trouble with the police.
Doctor	No. Did you have any heart trouble in your family?
Patient	Oh, that, Not that I know of.

About this exchange he remarks in a footnote, 'The first two lines are drawn from Shuy, and are real; the second two I have added myself, and aren't'.[7]

This is one of the few places in Goffman's corpus of which I am aware that he undertakes a sustained analysis of a single fragment of interaction, real or imagined (where by 'sustained' I mean more than an observation or two on several consecutive moves in a spate of interaction). What is so striking is that the 'detailed' analysis which he undertakes is not of the claimedly real utterances taken from Shuy, but of the additions which he made up.

Two different causes for concern are presented. First, his renderings are empirically not accurate. For example, he remarks about turns which are addressed to misunderstandings, such as the third in the excerpt above, that 'misunderstandings lead to a two-move turn, its first part signalling that trouble has occurred, and its second providing a rerun' (ibid.), and he goes on to treat such a turn as an 'elision and contraction' of a sequence.

As it happens, work on turns like this one (in which 'third position repair' is done; cf. Schegloff, Jefferson and Sacks 1977; Schegloff 1979a) shows that, although such two-part formats *do* occur, the full format of such turns has *four* components. The parts Goffman does not discuss do important jobs, and contribute to our understanding of the parts Goffman does discuss. For example, in one recurrent part the speaker of the misunderstood talk rejects the incorrect understanding, in a usage of the form 'I don't/didn't mean X'. In certain sequential environments, omission of this component can specifically decline to withdraw the understanding which the speaker is trying to replace (in a kind of 'be that as it may' operation). Further, the last parts of turns such as this, in contexts like this, are almost always framed by the phrase 'I mean'. Surely, one may think, this is beside the point, a quibbling over details, picking a fight. But how is that known? Why is it that most misunderstanding repairs have the 'I mean', even though Goffman's version seems as viable? And if we already know what makes a difference and what does not, why study this domain at all?[8]

Note, first, then, that Goffman offers as a claim about the world, as a theorizing about conversation, something which is warranted entirely by a bit of talk which he invented to allow that claim, and, secondly, invented not quite right. And this analysis, in detail, of hypothetical utterances whose detail he invented, is extended to the fourth utterance in the excerpt, with a component by component 'gloss' (his term) of 'Oh', 'that', and 'not that I know of', which are, after all, entirely stipulated bits of utterance.

Surely these were strategic slips on Goffman's part. He ought not to have risked this kind of somewhat extended and detailed analysis of invented data. But, first, as far as I know, no one has challenged him on this before; the scholarly community has been willing to accept both his stipulations about how the talk is done, and then the theorizing from it. And second, there is no reason to think that more *abbreviated* analyses are empirically more on the mark, or that bits of talk which are only *characterized* are more solid foundations for analysis than ones whose weaknesses are revealed by being explicated in verbatim form.

Just as Goffman's focus on ritual and face was no accident, but reflected a special *metier*, so were his choice of data and method of work. He did not exploit the details of real events when he had them in the 'Radio talk' data, he pointedly avoided them in the Shuy data, his sustained 'detailed' analysis is not on target.

Why does that matter? One way it matters is that it may have seriously undercut any chance of Goffman coming sustainedly to focus on the moments, not the men. I suggested earlier certain questions which seem unavoidable if one is to take up the syntactical relationship between acts. I want to return first to a brief discussion of those questions, and then to a consideration of one way of providing answers, and Goffman's objections to it.

V

One common tack in Goffman's writing is the presentation of some putative utterance or other move, with an account of what its producer might be doing with it, and then suggesting that it can be done in some 'keying' which radically transforms it, for example into a mock act of that type, and then adds another lamination, yet again metamorphosing the action we are to imagine and understand.

Although there are exceptions, ordinarily two matters remain unaddressed in such treatments, and in important ways they are critical for understanding how interaction comes to have the trajectory it does. In important ways, they *are* the analysis.

First, do other participants in the interaction understand the utterance in the manner which Goffman proposes – as a mock version? as a serious deployment of an apparently mock version? For example, he writes (1981b [1979]: 153),

> Innuendo is also a common candidate for playful transformation, the target of the slight *meant to understand* that a form is being used unseriously – a practice sometimes employed to convey an opinion that could not safely be conveyed through actual innuendo, let alone direct statement. (emphasis supplied)

Only '*meant* to understand'? What grounds are there for asserting that other participants have so understood the utterance or move? How is it revealed in the interaction? This is, of course, hard to address if the materials being discussed are imagined, and one also imagines the responses. But it is crucial, for if it is only Goffman and his readers who appreciate the subtle analysis, how can the utterance so understood be, or have been, consequential for the sequel in some actual interaction?

Second, how does the speaker (whether animator, author or principal) *do* it? That is, how does a speaker bring off (to draw for examples on 'Replies and responses', 1981b [1976]: 54–7) 'How much did you say?' as a 'standard rerun signal' as compared to a remark that the price is out of line? And, if the putative speaker is doing the latter, how is s/he doing it differently with this utterance as compared to 'You gotta be kidding'? How does 'you forgot', an apparent 'assertion of fact', get to be 'understood as blame-giving' (ibid.: 58, and the data analysis section below)? What is it about the conduct of a participant in interaction that brings off these actions in these understandings, or that opens them to such understandings? Are not these among the basic practices by which actions in interaction are achieved? And are they not what underlies the actual trajectory in which courses of interaction are progressively realized? For it is by recognizing what someone is doing from how they are conducting themselves (e.g. talking), and acting on the basis of that understanding, that the several participants, one after the other, build the actual development of the course of interaction.

For these questions, one needs real data, for we do not know in advance in what ways these, or other, effects will show up. Or in what hitherto unnoticed or unsuspected detail some recipient understanding is made manifest, or some speaker project procedurally enacted.

These questions – does the analysis capture what the participants were demonstrably up to for/with one another? How are such courses of action and interaction achieved? How are they combined temporally and sequentially? – are close to the core analytical differences between Goffman and CA. For CA (or at least this practitioner), the interest in findings about such things as adjacency pairs is not just in having extracted a general practice, or organizing format, or domain of such practices or phenomena from a swarm of unique episodes. There is the further payoff, and constraint, that the results afford us the capacity to return to singular cases, singular strips of talk and other conduct, and be able to explicate what is going on there, and how, and be able to do so better with the use of these tools, because what are the analytic tools for us were for them – the participants – the actual practices of conduct.

It is to deal with questions such as these, on data such as these, that notions like the 'adjacency pair' were introduced. Goffman found much to object to, both in this unit of sequential organization and in the mode of analysis from which it developed. Before using that notion in the analysis of an interactional episode, it is appropriate to examine some of those objections.

VI

Although the term 'adjacency pair' is now sometimes used in the literature without explication, some readers may not be familiar with it. The basic notion was this (Schegloff and Sacks 1973: 295-6):

> Briefly, then, adjacency pairs consist of sequences which properly have the following features: (1) two utterance length, (2) adjacent positioning of component utterances, (3) different speakers producing each utterance.
>
> The component utterances of such sequences have an achieved relatedness beyond that which may otherwise obtain between adjacent utterances. That relatedness is partially the product of the operation of a typology in the speakers' production of the sequences. The typology operates in two ways: it partitions utterance types into 'first pair parts' (i.e. first parts of pairs) and second pair parts; and it affiliates a first pair part and a second pair part to form a 'pair type'. 'Question–answer', 'greeting—greeting', 'offer–acceptance/refusal' are instances of pair types. A given sequence will thus be composed of an utterance that is a first pair part produced by one speaker directly followed by the production by a different speaker of an utterance which is (a) a second pair part, and (b) is from the same pair type as the first utterance in the sequence is a member of. Adjacency pair

Emanuel A. Schegloff

sequences, then, exhibit the further features (4) relative ordering of parts (i.e. first pair parts precede second pair parts) and (5) discriminative relations (i.e. the pair type of which a first pair part is a member is relevant to the selection among second pair parts).

Lectures by Sacks (1965–72) and papers by Jefferson (1972) and Schegloff (1968, 1972) had already shown that larger sequences could be built from adjacency pairs, for example, by prefacing the first pair part with a preparatory sequence, or by inserting talk between the first and second pair parts. Subsequent papers (e.g. Schegloff 1980; Davidson 1984; Jefferson and Schenkein 1977) describe additional expansions.

Goffman's evaluation of this analytic unit is rendered equivocal by his casting of it in different moulds from the very outset of his discussion (in 1981b [1976]). Thus, he begins by taking as prototypic of adjacency pairs 'question–answer' sequences. He finds this formulation inadequate on various grounds, and it is transmuted into the presumably more adequate 'statement–reply' format. But then various second utterances in such sequences are seen not to fit well to the notion 'reply', this being seen as a defect of *adjacency pairs*, and not of Goffman's adoption of the term 'reply' earlier in the same essay. The problem is fixed by replacing 'reply' by 'response'. And then various problems are found with the notion 'statement', once again serving to undercut the viability of adjacency-pair analysis, rather than the 'set up job' in replacing 'first pair parts' with 'question' and then 'statement' in the first place. The solution to the problems with 'statement' as a formulation of the first parts of such sequences is to continue the metamorphoses: from 'first pair part' to 'question' (though Goffman never does this one explicitly), to 'statement', and finally to 'reference', leaving us with 'reference–response sequences', which have their own vulnerabilities. Having thus dismembered the caricature he constructed in the first place, he triumphantly declares the enterprise futile.

But, if anything here is futile, it is the enterprise which Goffman originated in trying to treat question–answer sequences as prototypic. The point of introducing the notion of 'adjacency pairs' is, in part, to circumvent the problem of treating some particular type of sequence unit as a serious prototype. In offering question–answer, greeting–greeting and offer–acceptance/refusal as three instances of pair types, three quite different types of relationship between first and second pair parts were included. 'Greeting–greeting' involves an exchange of cognate objects (even the same greeting term). 'Question–answer' involves complementary turn types, but relatively unspecified ones (i.e. it is compatible with a considerable range of relationships between the two utterances). Offer–acceptance/refusal involves a limited number of determinate, alternative response types. Nor do these three instances necessarily exhaust the sorts of relationship which can obtain between first and second pair parts. In declining to privilege any one of these sequence types over the others, a claim was being made about the presence of certain robust sequential relationships that operate across such differences between sequence types, and which characterize the more abstract or formal unit being introduced as the 'adjacency pair'.

Now this claim may be wrong; there may not be such sequential relationships which transcend differences between particular types of sequences. But arguments to this effect should be made directly, and ideally should be supported by analyses which exemplify the differences which render the more generally formulated unit problematic. The argument should not be made implicitly, by identifying all adjacency pairs with a single type, and finding problems in treating that type as generic. By proceeding in this fashion, Goffman has indirectly offered some of the arguments *for* developing an analysis of a more generic unit of sequence organization instead of working with more specific types, rather than the argument against which he seems to have been pressing.

Setting aside the equivocality introduced into Goffman's discussion by this rhetorical strategy, one major misunderstanding appears to underlie a whole host of consequent confusions in his treatment of the adjacency pair and of CA more generally. This misunderstanding is expressed in two forms or at two levels: First, it appears as a confusion of the *relationship of adjacency* between successive turns at talk on the one hand, with *adjacency pairs* as units of sequence organization on the other. This, in turn, reflects a more general failure to distinguish between the organization of turn-taking and the organization of sequences. Here I can only address a few of the misunderstandings manifested in 'Replies and responses' (and in occasional writings by others) which appear to result from not insisting upon these distinctions (surprising for Goffman, so much of whose writing is preoccupied with making distinctions between different levels and domains of analysis).

1   Recurrently Goffman's text shows him to believe that use of the notion of adjacency pair commits the user to the view that every

utterance is either a first pair part or a second pair part. Thus, he formulates a 'deep complaint' about the 'statement–reply formula' (1981b [1976]: 29): 'Although many moves seem either to call for a replying move or to contribute such a move, we must now admit that not all do.' Reccurently, he announces with apparent relish some kind of turn that is neither a first nor a second – a back-channel response, an aside or 'bracket marker' (ibid.: 49–50), 'elbow room to provide at no sequence cost an evaluative expression of what they take to be occurring' (ibid.: 29), or the third turn in three-part sequences reported in classrooms or medical interviews. He seems to feel that even the several parts of multi-unit turns should be understood as the answers to some reconstructable putative questions (ibid.: 9, following Stubbs).

This is all quite beside the point.

First, no serious CA worker has suggested that all turns were either first or second pair parts of adjacency pairs. This is patently not the case, and it is unclear why any such claim should be taken seriously.

Second, no serious claim has been made that all sequences are adjacency pairs or based on adjacency pairs. In fact, there are accounts within CA work of sequential units larger than turns which are not adjacency pair-based, for example, storytelling sequences (Sacks 1974; Jefferson 1978; Goodwin 1984).

Third, as noted above, there is much work within the CA corpus concerned with the ways in which much more extensive spates of talk can be understood as expansions of adjacency pairs. There are pre-expansions before a sequence's main first pair part (Schegloff 1980), insert expansions between the two parts of the core sequence (Schegloff 1972; Goffman's discussion of pp. 7–8 hardly recognizes the scope of such expansions), and post-expansions after the second part (Davidson 1984). Many of these expansions are themselves organized as adjacency pairs, but some (especially in post-expansion position) are not. Third turns which register receipt and/or acceptance of second pairs parts, or which offer assessments, are minimal expansions of adjacency pairs.[9] They are not embarrassments for them.

As for the treatment of each part, or clause, of a multi-unit utterance as some version of an answer to a question, it is unclear what warrant there is for such a view, or what theoretical urgency seemed to Goffman to compel it. The same can be said for his apparent view (1981b [1976]: 48) that 'non-verbal' moves, or expressions responsive to talk, cannot be accommodated within the adjacency-pair format.

2   Goffman makes much of the ways in which adjacency pairs facilitate 'effective transmission.' This is part of his general treatment of dialogic analysis/CA as a kind of communications engineering. In this framework, adjacency pairs are seen as most important for their capacity to reassure speakers that they have been understood.

> Given a speaker's need to know whether his message has been received, and if so, whether or not it has been passably understood, and given a recipient's need to show that he has received the message and correctly – given these very fundamental requirements of talk as a communication system – we have the essential rationale for the very existence of adjacency pairs, that is, for the organization of talk into two-part exchanges.
>
> (ibid.: 12)

This claim reveals clearly the misunderstanding underlying Goffman's discussion. For what Goffman is here discussing is not adjacency pairs, but a weaker, more generic organizational feature, the *adjacency relationship*. The effects which Goffman discusses – of showing that a turn at talk was heard and how it was understood –are most generally the by-products of the construction of a next turn. Next turns show understanding of prior turns, act with respect to prior turns so understood, etc. (unless marked as addressing some other turn than the prior one) *independently of whether they are components of adjacency pairs or not*. The adjacency-pair relationship is a *further organization of turns*, over and above the effects which sequential organization otherwise invests in adjacency, as is made quite clear in the text cited earlier from 'Opening up closing' ('The component utterances of such sequences have an achieved relatedness beyond that which may otherwise obtain between adjacent utterances.')

The *adjacency relationship* operates most powerfully backwards, with next turns displaying their speaker's understanding of prior turn. *Adjacency pairs* have in addition a powerful *prospective* operation, first pair parts making a limited set of second pair parts relevant next. If such second pair part turns are forthcoming, they are seen as specifically responsive. If not, they are ordinarily replaced by turn types which show that the sequentially implicated response has been deferred but is still oriented to and 'is in the works'. Failing such a turn next, the sequentially implicated response is notably absent; its absence is accountable, and may, in fact, be replaced or followed by an account. There are other such features of *adjacency-pair organization which are not features of the adjacency relationship*.

Again, turns which are adjacent – one after the other – regularly have certain properties by virtue of that relationship. Other turns, *not always adjacent to each other* (e.g. if a sequence is expanded internally), constitute a unit of sequence organization and sequence construction of a different order. Adjacency pairs may do especially powerfully some/many of the things which merely adjacent turns do, but they are still quite distinct phenomena.

Note: mere temporal succession (as the product of the turn-taking organization's 'one speaker at a time' feature) produces an *acoustic* fact. The investing of temporal succession with sequential organization is an independent fact, a fact of *social* organization, and not an artefact of engineering contingencies. Adjacency as a sequential relationship is a conversational, an interactional, a social fact. It invests mere seriality with social and interactional import. Adjacency pairs add a prospective, multi-turn, multi-action course of conduct to these other layers.

Obviously, the fact of *adjacent positioning* of turns is virtually omni-present in conversation. It may be this omnipresence of the *adjacency relationship*, left undiscriminated from the *adjacency pair*, which has led Goffman (and others) to the mistaken belief that CA claims that everything is a first or second pair part. Most turns are next to other turns; most turns display some understanding of the turn they are after (though some may be constructed to show themselves otherwise addressed). But it should now be clear that this does *not* entail that most turns are first pair parts or second pair parts.

It should also now be clear that the needs of 'effective trans-mission' to which Goffman refers (if, indeed, there are such functional needs, and if functional needs can account for anything in any case) are satisfied by aspects of the adjacency relationship between successive turns and what that relationship is treated by participants as requiring. These needs do not especially mobilize the resources of adjacency-pair organization, although that organization may also deal with them. And, once we have registered how the organization of turn-taking, adjacency pairs, etc., do satisfy functional communicational needs, we must go on to note that they regularly do so as a by-product, and are otherwise focused. Adjacency-pair organization in particular is directed to the organization of action in various respects.

3   The distinction between turn-taking organization with its adjacent positioning of turns and adjacency pairs and their expan-sion into larger sequences can be brought to bear on other difficulties which Goffman believes confront dialogic analysis/ CA. For example,

Goffman suggests (ibid.: 28) that back-channels (e.g. 'uh huh') interpolated by a recipient into another's turn constitute an 'embarrassing fact'. But it is not clear why. For the most part, back-channels seem to be actions related to the organization of turns and turn-taking; they are ways recipients/hearers have of showing that they understand that an extended turn-at-talk is in progress and is not yet finished. They seem to be *not* a way of responding to a turn, but of allowing a turn to continue to completion, at which point it will be responded to (Schegloff 1981; Jefferson 1984). In this sense they do not change the character of the ongoing talk as a 'single speaking'; they show an orientation to it precisely as that. They do not ordinarily count (for the parties to the talk) as a turn (Schegloff 1981: fn. 16; Duncan and Fiske 1977). They have no particular bearing on adjacency-pair organization.

When Goffman's discussion does not run turn-taking and adjacency-pair organization together, it sometimes poses false dilemmas in requiring a ranking of their relative primacy. For example, with respect to turns with two units or 'moves' in them, one of which belongs to one sequence, the other to another, he writes (ibid.: 24), 'We are still required to decide which concern will be primary: the organization of turns *per se* or the sequencing of interaction'.

But we need not decide this question. The organization of turns and turn-taking on the one hand, and of sequences on the other, are both generic organizations in talk-in-interaction. Both are present all the time. The talk can be organized to achieve varying relations between them. Sometimes the parties will talk in a manner which momentarily elevates the relevance of one or another organization (for example, raising the voice to insist on completing a turn in the face of an early start by recipient on the response). But this is not something 'we' as analysts are required to decide with respect to primacy, only something which is ours to describe when it appears as a practice in talking.[10]

By the time of writing 'Felicity's condition' Goffman appears to have recognized the difference between the adjacency relationship and adjacency pairs (though he does not make this explicit), and it contains (1983a: 49–50) the same sort of attack on the former as 'Replies and responses' mounted on the latter. He seems to want to say, 'but everything is so much more complicated'. For example, he writes (ibid.),

> It is true that prior turn is very likely to provide some of the context in terms of which current utterance will be interpreted . . . But . . .

prior turn can never be the only such condition current speaker will
be required (and allowed) to employ as a frame of reference . . .

and he goes on to list others.

Now why would Goffman (or anyone else) understand CA writers
to be claiming that it is *only* prior turn which conditions the
production and understanding of next turn? Perhaps it is this. CA
workers examine some utterance or string of utterances in its
sequential context, or examine instances of some phenomenon, each
in its sequential context, and recurrently find prior turn being
relevant in this or that way, because for the participants it was
relevant in this or that way. For CA, as for them, 'this *versus* that
way' matters. The different ways in which one turn figures in the
organization of another, the different ways in which speakers are
responsive to what has just been said and show that in their talk, are
the stuff of CA work, and differences are consequential. For those
whose enterprise is not committed to the analysis of the details of talk
in its sequential context, these differences do *not* matter in the same
way. From that perspective, CA papers appear to conduct analysis
by reference to prior turn again and again – as if that was all that
mattered.

But it is critical to recognize that CA inquiry is examining *data
fragments* as representations of singular strips of talk in interaction,
subjected to repeated detailed scrutiny in their singularity. Such
inquiry tries to make sense of how these strips of talk are organized,
what their participants are doing moment by moment, how the
episodes come to have the trajectories they have. These segments of
talk-in-interaction are *CA's units of work*. Goffman (as also perhaps
others) is examining *issues*, and trying to enumerate and array them
(how often the phrase 'and then there is the issue of' used to recur in
his discussions). Those are *his units of work*. So all CA's different
instances, with different bearings of turn on turn, all go in the same
basket for him; and he is led to conclude that for CA that is all that
matters.

Similarly for turn-taking and sequence organization; it is not that
they are the only things worth studying, but, being fundamental and
omnipresent, they regularly enter into the constitution of what is
going on in some fragment of data. For those concerned with the
'range of issues' in the several relevant disciplines, they see 'more on
turn-taking, more on adjacency pairs'. But, of course, the fact that
certain aspects of the talk enter into analysis recurrently does not
mean that they alone are relevant. There is no lack of analyses in the

CA mode in which much else besides prior turn is brought into the analysis.

By the end of 'Replies and responses', Goffman has reached a position of considerable ambivalence. On the one hand, declaring that 'the box that conversation stuffs us into is Pandora's', he seems to celebrate the final inaccessibility of this human activity to disciplined inquiry by asserting its potential arbitrariness.

> In these circumstances the whole framework of conversational constraints – both system and ritual – can become something to honor, to invert, or to disregard, depending as the mood strikes. On these occasions it's not merely that the lid can't be closed; there is no box. (1981b [1976]: 74)

There is here a nice twist on the metaphor, but in the service of an entirely premature analytic nihilism. The particular phenomena invoked earlier in this paragraph are *not* beyond description. Goffman chooses to see in them arbitrariness, but he has picked a particular usage – what have been called 'out-louds'; mutterings which leave another free to respond or not – utterances built precisely to allow such 'arbitrariness'. To conclude from this that all is lost is a *non sequitur*.

Balancing the conclusion of arbitrariness and unanalysability in his ambivalence is quite the opposite concern, an almost resigned concession that the tie in conversation between an utterance and the preceding turn

> . . . must be explored under the auspices of determinism, as though all the degrees of freedom available to whosoever is about to talk can somehow be mapped out, conceptualized, and ordered, somehow neatly grasped and held, somehow made to submit to the patterning-out effected by analysis.
>
> (ibid.: 72)

Perhaps it is this prospect that Goffman triumphantly rejects at the end, his analytic nihilism motivated by an assertion of human freedom (a sharp turn from the closing of *Stigma*, where he teases those who would keep a corner of the world, or was it the soul, safe from sociology).

But this metaphysical pathos is as unwarranted as his analytic nihilism. For the organization present in human action is *enabling* as much as it is constraining – at least the organization described by the notion 'system requirements'. The orderliness of the structures of action and talking-in-interaction includes an endless array of options. The organizations of interaction no more confine humans in a deterministic prison than the laws of geometry and physics determine the outcome of a game of pocket billiards. Of course, on particular occasions particular participants may find themselves constrained, oppressed, etc. But surely this is not the result of general and formal organization that makes a participant's contribution organizationally responsible in *some* fashion to what has preceded. We need not reject the very possibility of formal analysis that is nonetheless responsible to the empirical detail of ordinary occasions of talk on this account.

VII

How, then, might one proceed? What is needed is not abstract proposals, but exemplars of other ways of conducting analysis. To preserve a sense of what follows as alternative to Goffman's enterprise, I have selected as the material for analysis an interactional episode directly related to one of his instances. Here is his vignette, drawn from 'Replies and responses' (1981b [1976]: 58), and introduced to make the point that

> . . . just as interchanges can incorporate non-linguistic actions along with verbal utterances concerning these actions, so interchanges can incorporate references to past doings as occasions for now doing praise or blame, thereby placing responses to wider circumstances before or after verbal reference to these circumstances and thus bringing them into the interchange.

I must say, parenthetically, that this discussion is part of the effort of the whole of the paper to show the untenability and unusability of the notion of 'adjacency pair', and that I do not understand how this point, if successfully made, would contribute to that outcome. Still, I wish to make available the context in which Goffman introduces the example to which my fragment of data is similar.

Here is his offering:

> B comes home from work, apparently not having brought what he promised to bring, and shows no sign that he is mindful of his failure.

A_1: 'You forgot!' [An utterance whose propositional form is that of an assertion of fact, but here can be understood as blame-giving]

B_1: 'Yes. I *am* sorry.'

A_2: 'You're always doing it.'

B_2: 'I know.'

That is all. Immediately following this presentation, attention is shifted to other ways in which 'the accuser' can proceed, especially with hedges. What Goffman has had to say about this excerpt, then, is the introductory framing about the incorporation of reference to past doings (actually, although in past tense, 'you forgot' is more an observation about the present situation), and the observation that the initial putative utterance has an ostensible assertion of fact used as a blame-giving, but with no suggestion as to how this can work, whether any assertion of fact could be so understood, or could be so understood in some context, and if so what aspects of context or utterance might be relevant to this usage.

Here is the beginning of the episode in my materials which approximates the vignette reproduced from Goffman.

Sherri, Ruthie and Karen are in their dormitory room, talking with Mark, who has been telling a story. Carol, who may also live there, comes in. She apparently had said she was going to get an ice cream sandwich, but has returned with some other edible. The whole episode begins at line 151 of the transcript with the squeak of the door, and ends with Carol's departure at line 191.

```
151     [door squeaks]
152 S:  Hi Carol. =
153 C:  = H[i::.]
154 R:     [CA:RO]l, HI::
155 S:  You didn't get en icecream sanwich,
```

I want to begin by focusing here on the parallel to Goffman's vignette at line 155, though my discussion will only sporadically be comparative, and will largely treat this fragment in its own terms. Still, I note that this episode begins with a greeting exchange, and Goffman's does not, or he did not provide it, and that this can bear on our understanding of what is going on, as can the termination of the greetings after an initial round – without an exchange of 'howareyou's, for example. So line 155 is not as early as it could be, but may be somewhat pre-emptive nonetheless.

Further, and again without taking this up in any detail, after the greetings, a structural issue is faced that regularly comes up when new arrivals join previously ongoing conversations: whether to assimilate the newcomer to the talk-in-progress, or abandon the talk in favour of something tailored to the newcomer. Line 155 displays an instance of this second practice. What then can we say about the utterance, or turn, or move, at line 155?

To begin with, Sherri *does a noticing*. That may seem obvious enough – both that she does a noticing, and what she notices. But it is not so obvious, or rather, its obviousness is itself to be explicated.

Sherri's *noticing is of a negative event*, something which did not happen. The issue about such observations – by both interactional participants and by professional analysts – should by now be commonplace. Because an indefinitely expandable set of things did not happen (here an indefinitely expandable set of things which Carol did not get), some relevance rule or relevancing procedure must underlie the formulated noticing, by reference to which it is remark-able.

This may lead us to note that the girls might well have forgotten that Carol was to bring an ice-cream sandwich in particular, just as Carol might have forgotten that she was to do so. The patent fact that she doesn't have one, then, by itself, is of equivocal relevance to the doing of an utterance which does such a noticing. The noticing, then, remarks not only on the absence of the ice cream, but on the relevance, and hence the observability, of this absence to Sherri.

So also could Carol have 'forgotten', and it is not given in the scene whether Carol forgot and therefore will be surprised at relevantly not having an ice cream (i.e. although there is not one with her, she may be unaware of relevantly lacking one), or whether she *knows* that she doesn't have one (where this does not refer to being aware, for example, of having lost something). So it is unclear, and not only to us but also perhaps to Sherri, whether this noticing is telling Carol that *Sherri has noticed* 'no ice cream', or whether it is *also informing Carol* of the observation 'no ice cream' itself. Is it, then, just a noticing, or is it also an announcement or a telling?

I might mention, parenthetically, that this noticing occurs in a position in which noticing recurrently is done, namely just after initial exchanges. Noticings are subject to a metric relative to perceptual (here visual) access; someone who doesn't comment during or just after openings about a change in appearance of other or of the surroundings (when, that is, such a comment is apt on recipient design grounds) may be suspected of not having noticed at all. So openings, and just after openings, is a place in which noticings regularly occur (Schegloff 1985). And that is where this one has occurred. (This is the point of my earlier remark that this noticing could have come earlier, but may still be pre-emptive.)

Having noted that the noticing is about a negative event, we can go on to notice that it *formulates a failure*, and particularly something which the recipient failed to do. This observation is especially in point here, for (as will become apparent from subsequent utterances) Carol *has brought* something, something to eat. They could, then, have remarked on what she *did* bring. Making the noticing be one about an absence, and about an absence as a product of Carol's action or failure of action, invites analysis (both from us, and in the first instance from Carol) of what is being done by and through this form of noticing. This, it appears (both here and in other data), is a practice which is regularly used to do *complaining*.

Obviously, some constraints must be added to this observation, for some such noticings can constitute praising – if, for example, the remarked absence is something which is negatively assessed (as in 'you didn't stumble once during the whole speech'). But with such constraints, we may note that one method, one practice by which 'complaining' can be done is by formulating a failure, either by some object (as in 'My car is stalled'), by speaker ('I couldn't write a word today') or by recipient ('You didn' get an ice cream sandwich', or, for that matter, to return to Goffman's case, 'You forgot').

Now it should be clear that the preceding is but the beginning of an analysis of how 'You didn't get an ice cream sandwich' (or 'You forgot') could be used to do complaining, and to be so recognized by co-participants. No evidence has been offered yet that these utterances were so understood. And only the initial lines of a candidate account have been offered of what about such talk provides for its status as a complaint. There has been only the mention of some other instances, with no analysis of them. No more than this sketch of a direction of analysis can be offered within the scope of this essay.

But it should indicate the sort of analysis that is largely missing in Goffman's treatment of action in interaction. Although he does note that what seems to be one sort of talk ('assertion of fact') can be seen to be doing another ('blame-giving'), the observation appears only as a parenthetical quasi-assist to the reader, rather than as the point of the discussion of his vignette. He offers no analysis of what makes

this work, and accordingly what restrictions operate on the observation – clearly, not all assertions can be seen to be doing
complaining; some do other actions (cf. Drew 1984); and sometimes
an assertion is just an assertion. What is needed for such analysis is
not a conceptual working through of 'conditions' under which some
form of talk successfully qualifies as an instance of the action-class
'complaints'. That sort of 'speech-act'y analysis should by now be
understood to be at best a kind of lexical semantics of a certain class
of verbs, giving the conditions under which they operate as
descriptions, rather than a procedural account of action. What is
needed is rather an analysis of actual talking to see how 'complaining' is done, or what 'noticing failure' is used to do, or how *any*
actions which get recognizably achieved do so. And that requires
access to the detailed doings of interactional participants, not per-
spicuous reconstructions by analysts.

Now it is in point to note that the preceding observations about
line 155 contribute to several possible characterizations of it as a first
pair part of an adjacency pair. Linked to these accounts of it as a first
pair part are projections of sequentially implicated second pair parts,
response types if you like. There are two main characterizations
involved, one of the type of action being prosecuted – a possible
complaint; the other about the turn format through which that
action is being effected – a noticing/informing. [11]

A variety of turn types and action types can serve as responsive
seconds to complaints – among them remedies or offers of remedies,
accounts, excuses, co-complaints or agreements or alignments with
the complaint, apologies, and others (of course, not every complaint
will tolerate each of these response types). Among the sequentially
implicated *seconds to noticings/tellings* are registerings (for example,
through what Heritage (1984) calls 'change of state' tokens), claims
of prior knowledge, assessments of the noticed feature, agreements,
and others. If both characterizations we have offered of line 155 are in
point, then both sets of constraints should be relevant, either on next
turn, or deferred in an orderly manner to later in the sequence. [12]

What then, in the case in hand, actually does happen next?

155   *S*:   You didn' get an *i*cecream sanwich,
156   *C*:   I kno:w, hh I decided that my body didn't need it,

As before, only a few observations can be taken up.

Note first that Carol's turn begins with what appears to be an
agreement, indeed a verification, that there is no ice-cream

sandwich. The factuality of that state *does* appear to be affirmed, but surely more is going on. Indeed, if we ask what Carol is *doing*, we might not want to say that she is doing 'agreeing' or 'verifying'. Those actions might be done by an agreement token such as 'no' (an agreement with the preceding negative would take a negative form).[13]

Although the facticity of the noticing may be affirmed as a by-product of 156, the form Carol uses speaks directly to an issue we earlier noted was raised by 155, namely, *whether Carol knew* she did not, relevantly, have an ice cream, or *whether she would be informed* of that by the utterance. With 'I know' she claims that she was aware of this before the preceding utterance was produced. Her turn thus begins with a unit, a 'move' in Goffman's locution, which is addressed to one aspect of the preceding turn – the noticing/informing format which can raise the issue of recipient's knowledge, by taking a stand on it. 'I know' shows Carol to have taken such an issue to have been raised by the format (e.g. did she just forget), and to respond to it. She has, then, not just agreed with the noticing; 'I know' is consequentially different here from 'no'.[14]

The preceding paragraphs are meant to exemplify the second sort of issue generally missing from Goffman's treatment of talk-in-interaction, an absence inseparably linked to the form of data relied on. That issue concerns the locus of analysis of what one participant has done by a turn at talk: is that analysis the academic analyst's and (if convincing) the readers'? Or is it, and in the *first instance*, that of the co-participants in the interaction? And if the latter is claimed, what evidence can be offered in support of that claim? If we are to understand the lines along which the interaction actually developed, what is needed is evidence of the latter, for it is on *their* understandings which subsequent actions (which *constitute* the developing line) are predicated.

I mean in the preceding and following paragraphs to show and to have shown that earlier discussion of Sherri's turn at 155 has introduced aspects of that utterance relevant not only to this academic interest in it, but to Carol's practical interest in responding to it. Once again, these displays of co-participants' understanding of the talk are embodied in aspects of their subsequent conduct which an academic analyst is unlikely to have invented, or would be sore put to defend if s/he had. Indeed, such a defense would require having already in hand just the sort of analysis we are trying to develop.

Note next, then, that the second unit in the turn at 156 offers an account for not getting the ice cream. And recall the earlier analysis that, by formulating a failure by Carol, Sherri had done a complaint, a first pair part for which a variety of seconds were relevant, among them an account or explanation for the failure or absence. So we are noting that this next turn seems oriented to the sequential relevancies projected by its position in an adjacency pair, both with respect to the responsive action it is doing, with respect to the format it is responding to, and with respect to the relationship between the two.

Several features of the way in which this account by Carol is formulated deserve mention, even in this abbreviated treatment, because with these data they can get us to appreciate features of the way talk is conducted by the parties really, which are not likely to be incorporated in the diction by which analysts choose to render it.

Note, for example, what Goffman (1981b [1979]: 146–52) calls the 'embedding' which Carol employs in saying not 'I don't/didn't need it', or 'My body didn't need it' (I will return to that way of putting it), but '*I decided that* my body didn't need it' (emphasis supplied). It seems clear that it is not so much 'embedding' that is relevant here, as a continuing orientation to the possibility raised by the prior turn that the failure to bring the ice cream was a product of forgetting. The 'I know' asserted that, at the moment of the telling utterance (i.e. line 155), she did not have to be told; but it was compatible with having forgotten earlier (as, for example, in 'I know. I remembered on the way up the elevator'). 'I decided that my body didn't need it' marks the 'non-bringing' as an intentional, achieved outcome.

Note next that the terms used by Carol to express this decision build in an allusion to its basis. Specifically, the use of 'my body' to refer to herself, most obviously in contrast to 'I' ('I didn't need it'; 'I decided that I didn't need it'), is a device for focusing attention on her appearance, or her weight, etc.[15] And in that regard, she can be heard to have expressed a negative self-assessment, a self-deprecation, one of the few types of utterance with which it is preferred to disagree rather than agree (Pomerantz 1978).

By the end of the utterance at line 156, then, among other things, there has been a complaint at the failure to bring an ice cream and an account for that failure, constituting a first and second part of an adjacency pair. Of course, there has been more: a working through of the several parties' state of knowledge about this, and a put down by Carol of her appearance, which can make some rejection by others appropriate. But the 'conditional relevance' of some second pair part to the complaint has been met. However, given the range of possible response types to complaints, and given the particular account Carol has offered, it remains to be seen whether or not this response will be treated by its recipient(s) as adequate. At the same time, it remains to be seen how the self-deprecation will be dealt with, if it is dealt with at all.

```
155 S:  You didn' get an icecream sanwich,
156 C:  I kno:w, hh I decided that my body didn't need it,
157 S:  Yes but ours di:d =
158 S:  = hh heh heh heh ⌈ heh heh heh ⌈ ·hhih
159 ?                   ⌊ ehh heh heh ⌊
160 ?                                  ⌈ (       )
```

Sherri's next turn has three components (note that the laughter on line 158 is a continuation of Sherri's turn, placed on a new line as a transcription convenience to allow representation of overlapping contributions by unidentifiable others).

As is commonly the case in such multi-unit turns (Sacks, Schegloff and Jefferson 1974: 722–3), the first unit is back-linking to prior turn (as was the initial unit in Carol's turn at 156). Although 'yes' might have seemed to be a sort of agreement token as 'I know' had, they are clearly quite different. This 'yes' can acknowledge Carol's prior turn without agreeing to the self-assessment as overweight, and without accepting prior turn's account as an adequate response to the complaint. It operates here as a form of 'be that as it may'. This usage here is by no means unusual; disagreements and rejections are commonly delayed in their turns, and among the items used to defer them is, as Sacks (1987 [1973]) and Pomerantz (1978, 1984) have noted, a pre-disagreement 'agreement token'.[16]

The last observations can serve to anticipate the next step, both in the interaction and in this sketchy account of it – namely, a rejection of Carol's explanation as an adequate response to the complaint. When an agreement with or acceptance of, her account fails to occur at the start of next turn (here they could have taken such forms as an information registering 'oh', an acceptance such as 'okay', or other less formulaic uptakes), the possibility of disagreement or rejection can be projected, and is here realized. The very grounds which Carol had offered for *not* getting the ice cream are now invoked as grounds for getting it, and their service as an adequate account is thereby potentially undercut by precisely the strength they presumed to have in their very offering. The complaint which engendered the sequence is thereby left not adequately dealt with.

Note an additional aspect of Sherri's talk, the terms with which she implements the rejection. By saying 'ours' she moves to transform what is otherwise a *multi-person* interaction into a *two party* one – with Carol as complaint-target as one party, and the others as complainants as the other. She thus moves to unilaterally co-opt the other(s)[17] to her rejection of Carol's account, and thereby potentially to her complaint.

Leaving aside for the moment what happens in the remainder of this turn, this rejection could itself be dealt with in various ways. It can, in turn, be rejected, and a disagreement sequence be prosecuted. Or, the account at 156 having been rejected, Carol could accept that rejection and offer another account. Or, an account having been rejected as the response to the complaint, Carol could accept the rejection and offer a different type of second pair part or response to the complaint – for example, an apology, a remedy, or an offer of a remedy. There may be other structural possibilities, i.e. stable types of response turns for this sequence type, that are not yet appreciated. But recall that these alternatives were outlined after having momentarily set aside the third part of the turn, the laughter, which must now be taken up.

First, the laughter can prompt us to make explicit another aspect of the turn-so-far, and that is its character as a 'quick comeback', as a wisecrack of sorts. Wisecracks require placement in next turn because they are done by playing with aspects of prior turn – paralleling it, transforming it, reversing it, parodying it, etc. Sherri's 157 employs several such devices: it parallels and indexicalizes the construction of 156, the indexicals working by virtue of the parallel (i.e. 'ours' referring to 'bodies' and 'did' referring to 'needing it'). And, as noted in a more somber tone a moment ago, the retort turns the prior speaker's own stance against her, making her argument for not getting the ice cream into an argument for getting it, the legitimacy of these grounds of action having just been attested by Carol's invocation of them (a kind of conversational martial-arts principle).

Note also that the talk does not 'dissolve' into laughter. That is, it does not progressively involve laugh tokens or aspirations in its words, gradually turning into unmixed laughter. It is done straight-faced, without even smile voice, and then sharply, abruptly breaks into laughter. What the utterance might be as a serious one is thus given a moment of its own, before that is allowed a possible transformation (cf. Drew 1987).

The laughter, and the qualification of what has preceded as 'joking' or 'unserious', can be understood as bearing on various strategic aspects of this place in the talk, this position in the sequence, which might be seen as in need of such modulation. There is the apparent agreement to the self-deprecation by not overtly rejecting it and even risking an agreement token directly after it. There is the correlative implied and improper self-praise (i.e. if Carol's 'didn't need it' alludes to overweight, then 'ours did' can claim slimness). There is the rejection of the account, and with it potentially the reactivation of the complaint. There is the unilateral co-optation of others as parties to these potential breaches by the use of 'our'.

The laughter can move to transform all of these understandings of 'Yes, but ours did', by inviting treatment of it as a 'joke'. That 'invitation' has direct interactional expression as an invitation to join the laughter and laugh together (Jefferson 1979). And such laughter, should it be elicited, can serve to help remedy the potential offence or offences, by co-implicating the co-laugher in the potential offender's stance (Jefferson, Sacks and Schegloff 1987). The laughter at line 159 is, unfortunately, not attributable with confidence to a particular participant, and no analysis will therefore be pressed here.

There is not the space to continue to take up all the elements of this episode at the level of detail, sketchy as it is, which we have so far settled at. The main additional point which I wish to register is the way in which this sequence, which constitutes the whole of this interactional episode with Carol between the greeting and leave-taking sequences, is organized *as a succession of second pair parts to an initial first pair part*, a succession of responses to the complaint.[18]

In the episode we are examining, one after another of Carol's tacks in response to the initial complaint is rejected, each rejection being met by yet another offered response. By lines 157–8, we had seen the first of these rejections, of the first of these responses. Note that however much the utterance at 157–8 may get understood as a wisecrack and a joke, its import as a rejection of the account/ explanation as a response to the complaint is not necessarily blunted. Indeed, Carol's next turn (at 161–2) begins with an acceptance of what Sherri has done.

155 *S*:   You didn' get an *i*cecream sanwich.
156 *C*:   I kno:w, hh I decided that my body didn't need it,
157 *S*:   Yes but ours di:d =
158 *S*:   = hh heh heh heh ┌heh heh heh ┌ ·hhih
159 *?*   └ehh heh heh └
160 *?*   ⌊(   )
161 *C*:   hh Awright gimme some money en you c'n treat
          me to
162   one an I'll buy you a:ll some ┌too.┐
163 *S*:   └I'm ┘ kidding,
163a   *I* don't need it.
164   (0.3)
165 *?*   (hhh)
166 *C*:   I WA:N' O:N┌E,   [*in 'whine' voice*]
167 *S,R?*   └ehh heh h┌uh
168 *C*:   └hheh-uh ·hhh =
169 *C*:   = No they ┌didn' even have any T*a*:b.
170 *R?*:   └hheh
171 *C*:   This is all I c'd find.
172   (0.2)
173 *R*:   Well then there's ez many *c*alories ez *th*at prob'ly
174   in en ice cream sa:nwich (so) yih jis', yih know.
175   (.)/(φ)
176 *C*:   I know an icecream sanwich is *b*etter, (b't) I d'n
177   feel like going down tuh 'P' an' seeing all those
178   weird people an' have them st ┌a:re at me.
179 *R*:   └In yer slipper┘s,
180   (0.3)
181 *C*:   Yeah.
182   (0.8)
183 *C*:   I don't want them tih see me when I l(h)ook
183a   th(h)is good.
184   (0.4)
185 *R?*: Hhuh ·hhhh =
186 *C*:   N(h)o ┌one des(h)erves ┐ it.
187 *?*   ⌊(   )⌋
188 *?*   (Tch ·hh =)
189 *C*:   I'll see you all later.
190 *R*:   Awri:ght.
191   (1.4) [*door opening*]
192 *M*:   Where were we.

Note in brief: Carol's turn at line 161, which begins ('Awright') with an acceptance of Sherri's preceding turn (which had rejected her account as an initial response to the no-ice-cream complaint), ends with another of the earlier-mentioned, second pair parts to complaints – an offer of a remedy ('I'll buy you all some too'), though, to be sure, this one is made contingent on the recipients' response to a request. That is, Carol's 'awright' is a form of response to Sherri's prior utterance taken seriously; a response to that turn taken as a joke would be a laugh (but recall that the laugh at 159 may have been Carol's). Taken seriously, Sherri's turn had rejected the account as an inadequate response to the complaint. 'Awright' registers that rejection, and proceeds to a different form of response to the complaint – the offer of a remedy.

This turn, then, is organized not only with respect to the preceding turn (at 157), but with respect to the turn at line 155 as well. It is so organized by virtue of adjacency-pair organization, and cannot be properly understood without reference to that (or some such) unit/level of sequential organization.

Then note: in the utterance at line 163, Sherri rejects this second response to the complaint in turn 155. More specifically, Sherri withdraws the serious import of her own prior turn ('I'm kidding'), and insists on its status as a joke. That is, she *rejects* Carol's offer *by withdrawing the utterance which occasioned it*, both by insisting on its non-seriousness and by specifically negating the overt assertion which was its vehicle ('I don't need it').[19] So, after having rejected the account/explanation as second pair part at 157, Sherri now rejects the offer of remedy as a second pair part at 163. Two responses to the complaint, each rejected in turn.

Note next that Carol's turn at 169–71[20] offers *another* account *and* a remedy: it appears she has brought back some sort of 'goody', gives an account for why she has brought it, and offers it. This, then, is yet another response to the initial complaint, combining new tokens of types already tried – accounts and offers. At 173–4, this response is also rejected, although now by Ruthie, and not by Sherri. The rejection displays by its incorporation of the 'ice-cream sandwich' as a comparison base its speaker's understanding that the turn at 169–171 was addressed to the complaint at 155 in which the 'sandwich' was first introduced. Carol concedes the assertion by which this rejection is made at line 176 ('I know an ice-cream sanwich is better'). A third response to the complaint, also rejected, the rejection again accepted.

Carol then (176–8) goes on to offer *another* account, this one again for not getting an ice cream sanwich – 'I d'n feel like going down to P . . .' (where 'P' is the elevator/lift indicator for the 'Parking' level in the dormitory where, presumably, the ice-cream dispensing machine is located). This, then, is her fourth response to the complaint, a fourth second pair part to that sequence initiator. Note that this one is not accepted either, but does not meet with overt rejection.

Ruthie's response (179: 'In yer slippers') offers what can be understood as a preliminary proffer of sympathetic understanding, but can also be understood (as such clarifications often are) as a preliminary to disagreement and rejection. Note then that after Carol confirms Ruthie's candidate understanding of what had motivated her, Ruthie does *not* go on to align herself with this position, to confirm her sympathetic understanding, etc. There is just silence at 182, where such a display should go, a silence which betokens continued rejection and distancing. This disengaging, disaligning silence is maintained through two rounds (at 183 and 186) of ironic self-deprecation, each of which 'properly' should have been followed by disagreement or some other relief. Whether the rejection of this fourth response to the complaint is more or less palpable for being silent is hard to say. But the sequence peters out here, and the episode ends with a two-turn departure sequence in adjacency-pair format (189–90).

I have meant to accomplish several goals with this discussion.

First, I have meant to provide a sense of the sort of sustained and detailed analysis of single episodes of talk in interaction which I think is crucial for work in this area, both as the application test for analytical and conceptual tools and as one of the payoffs that work in this area produces. Such detailed analyses in turn can serve as a discipline on the interpretations of daily social life which other branches of social science make for their own purposes, usually without serious, detailed empirical grounding in the reality being interpreted.

A second goal has been to make clear that it is an almost wilfully narrow reading to treat the notion of adjacency pairs as claiming that all turns are either first or second pair parts, or that they always come one after the other, or that they require that the parts stand in relation to each other as literal answers to literal questions, or that they cannot accommodate other than literal interpretations or non-verbal actions, etc. I have meant to suggest, by exemplification in a particular case, that it can serve as a useful device and framework for structurally parsing a stretch of interaction, a sequence if you will. It is useful for the best of reasons – because it is used by participants for structuring their participation in the talk, not always in a first–second–first–second manner, but in well-structured and describable ways. If this be 'formalistic' analysis, so be it.

Third, I have meant to show that such analysis need not be rigid and deterministic in an oppressive sense, that it can take into account nuances, keyings, etc. Taking them into account, however, involves more than registering their presence. It involves showing how they are done; that the doing of them is seen and reacted to by other participants; and that time does not stop with such subtleties; they must be, and are, taken up in the ensuing action, and woven into the continuing, or discontinuous, fabric of the interaction. Scenes do not just end, as in the movies; and it is the continuing trajectories to some natural boundary that should set the terms of our inquiry.

Indeed, I mean to have suggested that it is along such lines that Goffman's quarry is now to be pursued – syntactical relations between acts, a sociology of interaction as a potentially rigorous discipline.

VIII

One of Goffman's concerns about 'dialogic analysis' was that, even when some turn or move engendered a next, the next might not be the envisioned one, might not treat its predecessor in the terms *its* speaker had in mind, might reframe it in any of a great variety of ways.

That is the fate not only of turns at talk but of turns at bat in the disciplined study of the world. Turns at talk die when not addressed in subsequent talk. 'Subsequent', of course, is a long time, and it happens that talk which seems not to have even been heard when spoken is cited the next week, when someone says, 'Y'know, last week you were saying that . . .'. But, for the most part, turns not addressed next are not addressed at all. And so also with goes at the social-science enterprise.

Goffman tried to carve out and establish an area. That is an effort to provide an institutionalized basis for engendering responses that address what you said. So far, the evidence is mixed, but for now it looks like a success of sorts. But it could be a bitter-sweet triumph; for the field, if one develops, may not be quite as envisioned, and it may address more than one prior turn, Goffman's just one among them, and may address none of them in the way in which they were meant to be taken.

Goffman may well have shown us how far you can go with real-time observation, clippings and vignettes. With them he helped show the direction in which what must surely be a central domain for the social sciences could be found, but something different may be required to actually find it. The moments, with their men, and their women, may be at hand.

NOTES

My thanks to Paul Drew, John Heritage and Jennifer Mandelbaum for help in sorting and taming what this assignment elicited. Remaining failures, whether substantive or ritual (if I may put it that way), are mine alone.

1 My thanks to Ray McDermott for calling these remarks of Yeats to my attention.
2 That itself had little precedent, except perhaps in the source which Goffman himself cited, namely the work of Elliot Chapple.
3 I use the term 'psychology' here in the sense cited earlier from Goffman (as in 'the individual and his psychology'), and not in its contemporary conventional senses.
4 The relevant contrast with CA work will be developed in the ensuing text but may be anticipated here. As against the central concern with face as both an account for action and as the motivating basis for the ritual *organization* of interaction, there is CA's treatment of such sets of practices as (a) turn-taking organization, which allocates, and constrains the size of, opportunities to participate, and is built to do so for participants of varying 'moral' characters, e.g. for both the verbose and the taciturn; (b) adjacency-pair organization, which orders sequences of actions-in-turns and their properties; and (c) the organization of repair, which orders opportunities for actions of a certain sort, namely dealing with trouble in the talk. In each of these instances, the organizational domain – the locus of organization – is that of actions and opportunities to enact them, something which is in principle independent of actors and their expressive behaviour.
5 Of course, we need in the first instance to question the basis for this sort of exercise, in which the academic analyst takes some lexically specified target as an invariant point of reference, and varies the contexts around it. This is how some linguists and philosophers have proceeded, but it is unclear what it has to do with empirical inquiry. The phenomena of inter-

action are rarely identified by lexical stability, so these framings cannot seriously be claimed to be 'potentially applicable to the "same" event' (1981b: 68). Goffman may have been trying to sweep the problem under the rug by putting scare marks around 'same'; rightly so, for the problem is a scary one for his analysis).

6 For a telling discussion of the contrasting ways of working at issue here, see Sacks (1984 [1971]: 25).

This very divergence presents challenging problems for analysis. For there is apparently some lively sense of the world with which Goffman's descriptions resonated, which they tapped, and for which his analyses 'worked', at least at the time. There is thus some robust intuition for interaction, which may well inform the conduct of interaction, but which does not provide the sort of detailed version of exactly how interaction occurs which a formal discipline answerable to empirical detail requires. Like the grammarians' intuition of grammaticality, it may be a real object in its own right, even if it is not, and does not describe, the way people actually conduct themselves. Because it may itself inform people's conduct, and because it casts an omnipresent shadow on empirical analysis, it is an important object for inquiry in its own right. I doubt that studies of 'typification' have begun to get at it.

7 I am not unaware of the ironic keying that can be attributed to this remark, in which it is Goffman's which are 'really real' in a deeper sense, but this is conjectural at best, and wrong at worst.

8 Much more, of course, can be, and has been, said about turns of this sort. And what Goffman has to say about 'unhearings' as compared to 'misunderstandings' is not quite right either, in part because his data on the former are similarly inaccurate. But this is not the place to detail how; a paper on such 'unhearings', or next-turn repair initiation, is in preparation.

9 Jefferson and Schenkein (1977) view these differently, and treat the three-turn sequence as the basic, or 'unexpanded', form.

10 Of course, not all of Goffman's challenges are the products of mis-understanding. Some of his remarks point to interesting problems for analysis, but ones which are to be met within the scope of CA, rather than subverting its viability. Several examples may be mentioned:

(a) Although I impoverish his point by putting it this way, Goffman notes the effects of what he calls 'unhearings' or rerun signals (requests for repetition) and counters (e.g. questioning or insulting in return) in next turn instead of second pair parts, while still working as responses to first pair parts. Since Goffman wrote, there has been attention to this question with respect to the rerun signals (Sacks 1987 [1973]). The 'counters' have yet to be treated systematically, but it is striking that they appear to work by invoking the same adjacency-pair structures back on the original first-pair-part speaker. Although in need of expli-cation, therefore, they seem more to testify to the robustness of adjacency-pair organization than to undermine it.

(b) Then there are the problems of conversations with more than two participants, for example, the case of multiple answers to questions (ibid.: 28), or proposed topic shifts not honoured by a third party, etc. There is indeed an important class of problems here, centring on an organizational issue for talk-in-interaction which concerns the articulation of a turn-taking organization built for n parties (any number of parties) with a sequence structure built on a two-part base. The solution to that problem will take the form of sequential devices, describable from empirical materials, by which these different organizational designs are reconciled in the talk. For example, the 'conference pass' described in Jefferson and Schenkein (1977) may be treated as one such device. Serial answers by several recipients to another's question may be another.

(c) In a number of other instances, Goffman's remarks offer interesting observations, but in his own explication do not pose any serious problem for adjacency-pair organization, although they are phrased in a manner which gives the impression of being troublesome. There is, for example, the matter of 'reach' (ibid.: 40 ff.), i.e. the capacity of an utterance to refer not just to an immediately prior, but to a whole prior sequence, much earlier talk, etc. But Goffman himself writes of these (ibid.: 44),

> A response that casts backward in time beyond the prior statement, or abstracts an aspect of a statement, or focuses on a particular piece of a statement . . . can . . . leave [initial speaker] with the sense that he [responder] has satisfied system constraints, that the response he evoked has done so, too, and, further, that the ritual considerations have been satisfied – or at least not unacceptably violated.

In other words, satisfactory response is achievable in adjacency pairs, across variations in reach. How this is done may be a puzzle, but it is a puzzle about how adjacency pairs work, not one that undercuts their operation.

11 This characterization of action and format cannot be further developed here, but is taken up in other ongoing work (Schegloff 1985).

12 I might add that past work has suggested that where some turn format is used as the vehicle for some action and both are responded to, then the format is responded to first, and the action which was done through it afterwards. To 'would you like some more coffee?' – an offer done through a question format – 'yes, thank you' speaks first to the question format with an answer, and then to the offer with an acceptance.

13 The import of the 'might be done' in the preceding sentence is that a substantial array of data could be presented, were there time and space, in which agreement with, or verification of, a noticing is accomplished by the use of agreement tokens. This is meant as an *empirical*, not a *conjectural*, 'might'.

14 Note as well that the regularity noted in note 11 is re-enacted here – the format aspect of prior turn is addressed first in next turn.

15 That it is so heard is evidenced later in the sequence, when Ruthie says with respect to what Carol *has* brought, 'Well then there's as many calories as that probably in an ice-cream sandwich'.

16 Still, here this usage is especially delicate and tricky, for in the turn after a self-deprecation, the absence of overt disagreement may be taken as agreement. What is tricky here is not so much that 'yes' will be heard to agree, but that the absence of some disagreement will be so heard.

17 At least Ruthie is involved; it is unclear whether Karen is in the room at this point; neither she nor Mark speak in this interaction at all.

18 This is but one of a number of overall expansion formats for long, adjacency-pair-based sequences. Elsewhere (Schegloff 1980, in press (a)), I have described other such formats, characterized by substantial pre-expansion before the first part, insert expansions between the first and its responsive second, and/or post expansion after the second. And others await description.

19 Although the matter cannot be taken up here, such efforts to abort a sequence by withdrawing the utterance which engendered it regularly fail initially, at least for a moment, as does this one; note the momentary extension by Carol's own 'joke' sequence at lines 166–8. The 'No' at the start of 169 is used as a marker of transition from 'joke' to 'serious' (Schegloff 1987(a): 206–8; 212–16).

20 This is a single, multi-unit turn; the 'heh' at line 170 overlaps with the 'didn' ' in line 169.

6

Embarrassment and Interactional Organization

CHRISTIAN HEATH

To conduct one's self comfortably in interaction and to be flustered
are directly opposed. The more of one, the less, on the whole, of the
other; hence through contrast each mode of behaviour can throw light
upon the characteristics of the other. Face-to-face interaction in any
culture seems to require just those capacities that flustering seems
guaranteed to destroy. Therefore, events which lead to embarrassment and the methods for avoiding and dispelling it may provide a
cross-cultural framework of sociological analysis.

(Goffman 1956: 266)

What is important is that in this change, in the inventions and
fashions of courtly behaviour, which are at first sight perhaps chaotic
and accidental, over extended time spans certain directions or lines of
development emerge. These include, for example, what may be
described as an advance of the threshold of embarrassment and
shame, as 'refinement', or as 'civilization'. A particular social
dynamism triggers a particular psychological one, which has its own
regularities.

(Elias 1978: 101)

INTRODUCTION

Embarrassment has received relatively little attention within the
behavioural sciences. Unlike other forms of emotion, it is said to be a
purely human experience, a social phenomenon, and as such less
subject to physiological and psychological explanation than the less
ephemeral forms of feeling. Sociology on the other hand, has paid
relatively little attention to the emotions, considering feelings either

inaccessible to or unworthy of analytic scrutiny. There are of course important exceptions. In their classic writings both Durkheim and Simmel touch on the social organization of emotion and more recently Hochschild (1975, 1979), Scheff (1973, 1977) and Collins (1975) have in various ways explored sociological aspects of feelings. As for embarrassment, in his treatise on the development of western civilization, Elias (1978) shows how changes in courtly standards in the sixteenth and seventeenth centuries transformed the boundaries of embarrassment. And Ricks (1974), although not a sociologist, illustrates in his discussion of the poetry of Keats, the shifting attitudes towards embarrassment from the eighteenth century onwards; the blush and its cosmetic imitations becoming an integral feature of the 'romantic' era.

The significance of embarrassment to social life however does not rest solely with historical changes in conventions and values. Embarrassment lies at the heart of the social organization of day-to-day conduct. It provides a personal constraint on the behaviour of the individual in society and a public response to actions and activities considered problematic or untoward. Embarrassment and its potential plays an important part in sustaining the individual's commitment to social organization, values and convention. It permeates everyday life and our dealings with others. It informs ordinary conduct and bounds the individual's behaviour in areas of social life that formal and institutionalized constraints do not reach. And as with so many areas of ordinary conduct, it is Erving Goffman who directs analytic attention towards the significance of embarrassment to social life and thereby throws into relief the situational and interactional nature of the emotions.

Goffman addresses embarrassment most explicitly in an essay first published in 1956, though the topic and related issues inform a number of his other studies (for example 1959 and 1969). His approach to the phenomenon reflects the analytic framework found elsewhere in his essays, especially those written before *Frame Analysis* (1974). Drawing observations from a broad range of literary and scientific sources he examines embarrassment in relation to the interactional nature of self and identity within the framework of situations and face-to-face encounters.

He suggests that participants in interaction have a moral obligation to sustain their own and each other's claims to relevant identities and that embarrassment emerges 'if expressive facts threaten or discredit the assumptions a participant has projected about his identity'. Goffman argues that embarrassment involves an individual losing composure, and its characteristic signs such as 'blushing, fumbling and vacillating movement' undermine a person's ability to participate in the topic or business of the encounter; embarrassment threatens the line of activity in which the participants are involved. He concludes that face-to-face interaction requires 'just those capacities that embarrassment may destroy' and provides us with a framework with which to consider how persons ordinarily avoid and dispel such difficulties. It should be added that Goffman's analysis informs more recent empirical work on embarrassment and emotion including Gross and Stone (1964), Lyman and Scott (1970) and to some extent Hochschild (1975).

In this brief paper I wish to draw on Goffman's pioneering work to explore the interactional organization of embarrassment. Unlike previous work on embarrassment and the expression of other forms of emotion, the observations are based upon the analysis of actual instances of the phenomenon drawn from naturally occurring interaction.[1] In the manner suggested by Goffman the paper begins by addressing the social organization of embarrassment and then considers the ways in which this particular form of emotion is avoided and dispelled.

The data employed in this paper are drawn from a substantial collection of video-recordings of naturally occurring medical consultations, collected as part of a research project supported by the Economic and Social Research Council. The project is concerned with visual and vocal behaviour between the doctor and patient and, like a number of other studies of medical interaction conducted from various perspectives, the research is strongly influenced by the analysis and observations found within Goffman's writings, as well as substantial empirical studies generated within conversation analysis. Current work on the project is concerned with the interaction between the doctor and patient during the physical examination and it was in this rather delicate area of social life that we became interested in embarrassment and emotion and its relation to ordinary conduct.

Drawing upon Goffman's observations and those of other scholars concerned with embarrassment and related topics, for example Darwin (1979), Elias (1978) and Ricks (1974), the video-recordings were reviewed to unearth instances which revealed one or other of the participants exhibiting the characteristic signs of embarrassment, in particular a loss of composure and an inability to participate, if only momentarily, within the encounter. In fact such occasions prove relatively rare and one is led, like Goffman, to consider the ways in which embarrassment is avoided. More importantly, however, in locating actual instances of embarrassment embodying the characteristics described by Goffman and others, it transpires in more detailed analysis that rather than 'flooding out', the individual's behaviour is systematically organized with respect to the surrounding configuration of action and activity. Repeatedly unearthing an interactional systematics to embarrassment undermined our confidence in the way in which the phenomenon has been characterized and conceived by Goffman and others.

A MOMENT OF EMBARRASSMENT

An individual may recognise extreme embarrassment in others and even in himself by the objective signs of emotional disturbance: blushing, fumbling, stuttering, an unusually low- or high-pitched voice, quavering speech or breaking of the voice, sweating, blanching, blinking, tremor of the hand, hesitating or vacillating movement, absent-mindedness and malapropisms.

(Goffman 1956: 264)

It has been mentioned that actual outbursts of embarrassment during the medical examination are relatively rare. If they do occur however they tend to happen as the participants prepare for the examination rather than as the doctor actually inspects the patient's body. It is of course following the doctor's request to examine the patient that undressing takes place, not infrequently in front of the doctor; and it is here that the patient reveals his or her body to the doctor for the first time – at least during the current consultation.

The following fragment is drawn from the juncture between the request to examine the patient and the actual inspection of the body. In this case the examination has been delayed whilst the doctor answers the telephone. The patient waits, undressed to her bra, for the examination to begin. We enter the consultation as the doctor finishes the telephone conversation and turns to the patient. Details of the transcription system can be found in Atkinson and Heritage (1984) and Heath (1986). Of particular importance here are the length of the silences captured in tenths of a second and the rows of 'h's, which represent inbreaths if preceded by a degree sign (°hhh); outbreaths if not.

Fragment 1 Transcript 1

    Dr   Slip your::: (.2) gear off: (.) an lets::: have a look

    .

    .   [*intervening phone conversation*]

    .

    Dr   O:::kay thanks::   [*to caller*]
    P   °hhh (.) hhhhh kh:: (.2) °hhhh keh kh:hm:
          (.8)
    P   khh
          (2.3)
    Dr   °hhhh now then: (.2) lets have a li:sten

The actual episode of embarrassment begins towards the end of the silence following the patient's coughing and breathlessness. As the doctor turns towards her, the patient becomes momentarily flustered and appears to lose control of her behaviour. A more detailed transcript including visual as well as vocal elements will be helpful. Unlike the previous transcript, the action is laid out across the page. The gaps are represented by dashes, each dash is equivalent to 0.1 of a second. The visual behaviour of the patient is transcribed above the line used to capture the silence and vocalization, the doctor's below. The gaze of the participant is captured immediately above or below this line and a series of dots represents one party turning towards the other, commas represent turning away. A continuous line or dash represents one participant looking at the other.

Fragment 1 Transcript 2

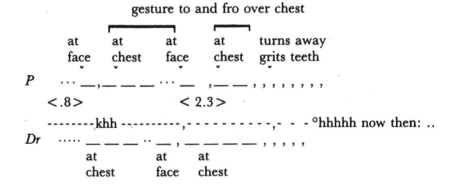

On finishing the phone conversation the doctor turns towards the patient and the patient reorientates towards the doctor. The moment her gaze arrives the patient turns from the doctor to her partially naked chest. There she begins to gesture rapidly, passing her open hand back and forth over the surface of her chest. Whilst gesturing she blinks and shakes her head. After a moment or so the doctor looks up from the chest and the patient follows, turning once more towards the doctor's face. By the time her gaze arrives, the doctor has returned his gaze to the chest. Finding the doctor looking at the chest the patient turns to the object of his gaze and once again begins to gesture, waving her open hand rapidly back and forth over the naked chest. Again the gesture is accompanied by the patient blinking and looking here and there. Less than a second passes and she turns away from her chest to one side, lowering her eyelids and gritting her teeth. The episode subsides as the doctor follows the patient and turns to one side, a second or so later the participants rearrange their seating positions as they begin the examination.

Drawing 6.1 – (a) showing immediately before the episode begins, and (b) during its course – may help provide a sense of the action. This brief episode embodies many of the characteristic signs of embarrassment. The patient's apparently haphazard movements, the flustered gestures, the shifting gaze and blinking eyes coupled with the head movements, and towards the end of the episode, the lowered eyelids and gritting of the teeth, capture behaviour described both by Goffman and other scholars who have addressed this form of emotional expression. For example, Goffman speaks of 'blushing, fumbling, stuttering, tremors of the hand, hesitancy and

(a) (b)

DRAWING 6.1a and b (FRAGMENT 1)

vacillating movement' as signs of embarrassment and continues by describing the associated physiological elements such as the acceler- ation of the heart beat and its effects on the circulation and skin colour. In the case at hand, the patient appears momentarily to lose composure and to become 'mentally confused'; she 'floods out' and undermines her ability to participate in the business at hand, the preparation for the physical examination.

In this as in other examples of embarrassment, the person's behaviour appears bizarre and idiosyncratic, unrelated to the interaction and business at hand, a moment in which the participant is overcome by a flood of emotion and unable to retain control of his/her actions. Yet however extraordinary the behaviour of the patient might appear, the moment of her emotion and its expression is systematically related to the actions of her co-participant. For example, the patient's embarrassment does not arise 'anywhere' within the developing course of the consultation but is co-ordinated with the local environment of activity. As the doctor finishes the telephone conversation and turns to the patient she too turns towards the doctor. As her gaze arrives, the patient finds the doctor looking at her chest rather than her face. She immediately turns to the object of his attention and begins to gesture. A moment or so later the doctor looks up and the patient ceases her gesture and returns her gaze to the face of the doctor, only to find him once more looking at her chest. Her embarrassment re-emerges as she once again begins to gesture and looks intermittently at the object in question.

It is the doctor's glance which gives rise to the patient's emotion and his glance which rekindles her difficulties for a second time. The glance is 'physically' equivalent to many of the looks the doctor gives the patient during the medical examination, yet at this moment within the proceedings it fires the patient's embarrassment. The source of the difficulties arises from the state of involvement during this phase of the consultation; the juncture between the request to examine the patient and the actual inspection of the body. It is one of the few occasions during the encounter where there is no jointly co- ordinated activity in which the participants are involved; no common focus of attention. It is a sort of 'no man's land' in the interaction, a phase which frequently entails a fragmentation of involvement in which the doctor and patient attend to their distinct but related concerns in preparing for the examination. In such circumstances a glance at the body of another can gain a significance it might not otherwise have. Unlike glances exchanged between persons during the production of an activity, either talk or the examination itself, the doctor's looking does not form part of a legitimate stretch of activity to which the participants are mutually committed.[2] Rather, the doctor's glance lies alone, divorced from the business of the consultation and, in this way, can be interpreted as 'looking at' the other, momentarily bringing the patient's chest to the forefront of mutual attention.

Thus it is not simply the temporal structure of a look which transforms glance into stare, but rather its relationship to the local configuration of activity. The doctor's looking renders the chest of the patient' 'noticeable' and 'accountable'. As Sacks suggests in his discussion of some very different materials, being observed is intimately related to embarrassment.

> For Western societies, at least, being noticeable and being deviant seem intimately related. The notions that one is suspect whose appearance is such that he stands out, and correlatively that the sinner can be seen, have the deepest of foundations. Indeed, in Judeo-Christian mythology, human history proper begins with the awareness of Adam and Eve that they are observable. The next bit of social information thereupon we learn is: to be observable is to be embarrassable.
>
> (Sacks 1972: 280–1)

In the case at hand the doctor's glance brings the patient's chest to the forefront of mutual attention and initiates a stretch of activity – the patient's brief episode of emotion. Whatever feelings the patient or anyone else associates with the revelation of particular parts of their body, it is a specific action, the looking, that renders the object embarrassable.

On finding the doctor looking at her chest, the patient produces her flustered gesture and the associated movements of the eyes and head. Though seemingly chaotic, the patient's gesture, like other movements which occur in face-to-face interaction, may be carefully designed with respect to the local circumstances and the action(s) it is performing.[3] It will be recalled that in both its stages the patient's gesture consists of an open hand which is waved successively over the chest, the object of the doctor's attention. In both stages the gesture criss-crosses the line of regard of the doctor and in consequence intermittently conceals the chest from his view. Thus by gesturing over the chest the patient hides her chest if only partially from the doctor's view. As he withdraws his gaze she abandons the gesture. On finding the doctor once more looking at her chest, the patient reproduces the initial gesture and once more intermittently conceals her chest from his wandering eye. The gesture therefore serves to interrupt the other's looking and perhaps encourages him to abandon his interest in her partially naked body.

If the sole concern of the gestures were to conceal the chest from the gaze of the doctor then one might expect the patient to simply place her hand on its surface or in some other way conceal the source of her embarrassment. The patient's gestures, however, may not be solely concerned with concealing the object from the doctor's view, but also to manage other demands and constraints within the local interactional environment. The moment of embarrassment occurs as the doctor finishes a telephone conversation and is about to begin the examination of the patient. Consequently, as the doctor finishes the call the patient reorientates towards the doctor and presents her chest for inspection. It is at this moment that the patient finds the doctor looking at the chest rather than moving forward to the patient to examine it. Simultaneously the patient is placed under two competing interactional demands; on the one hand, presenting the chest for examination, on the other, concealing it from the gaze of the doctor. The flustered gesture, the open hand successively passing to and fro over the surface of the chest, embodies these simultaneous constraints on her behaviour; she attempts to present the chest and remain available for the examination whilst concealing the focus of her embarrassment from the unwanted attention of the doctor. In consequence, it is hardly suprising that the patient's actions appear flustered and disorganized as she attempts to settle the sequential constraints of the appropriate next activity with the implications of the doctor's gaze.

The shape of the gestures and the patient's apparent lack of commitment to fully concealing the chest may also be related to the potential consequences of such action. However strong the patient's inclination to conceal the chest from the gaze of the doctor, such an action would have significant retrospective implications and might lead to further embarrassment and difficulties. Were the patient to fully conceal her chest, it would cast aspersion on the actions of the doctor, suggesting that his glance was untoward and problematic. It would imply that the doctor's looking lay outside any warranted medical practice and suggest that less professional motives underlay the actions of the doctor. Fully concealing the chest would be tantamount to refusing to be examined for reasons which arose in the course of the doctor's behaviour and both patient and doctor might be called to account. In such circumstances we can understand why the patient might avoid wholesale commitment to a course of action which would generate a definition of the other and their actions which could well undermine the very foundation of the consultation.

A characteristic of shame and embarrassment described in both literature and the sciences is of the sufferer 'not knowing where to look' and shielding the eyes from the gaze of the onlooker(s). Darwin captures a flavour of these difficulties in his classic treatise on the expressions of emotion in man and animals.

> The habit, so general with everyone who feels ashamed, of turning away, or lowering the eyes, or restlessly moving them from side to side, probably follows from each glance directed towards those present, bringing home the conviction that he is intently regarded; and he endeavours, by not looking at those present, and especially not at their eyes, momentarily to escape from this painful conviction.
>
> (Darwin 1979: 330)

In fragment 1, as with many instances of embarrassment, the patient is overcome with difficulties as to where to look. She begins by turning from the doctor to her chest, quickly returning her gaze to the doctor and then once again glancing at her chest. Finally she turns to one side and lowers her eyelids as if in shame. Coupled with rapid changes in the direction of her gaze the patient successively blinks and very slightly shakes her head. As Darwin suggests, the individual who suffers embarrassment and shame becomes restless, looking hither and thither or lowering the eyes. The patient during this brief episode appears quite simply not to know where to look or rest her eye. She appears to be simultaneously drawn and repelled by the gaze of the doctor.

The behaviour of the patient arises in part through the power of a look to affect another. A number of studies of gaze in face-to-face communication – for example Kendon (1967), Goodwin (1981) and Heath (1986) – show how looking at another serves to elicit particular actions, not infrequently a return of gaze by the person who is being looked at. A look is sequentially implicative, encouraging the other to respond and, in cases where the invitation is declined, we typically find the recipient of the gaze progressively turning further away from the other, often touching their face and shielding their eyes from the onlooker.[4] In the case at hand, at least two interactional aspects of looking at another come into play. The patient is drawn by the gaze of the doctor to return his look, if only to check whether he is continuing to stare at the chest. Yet, were the patient to return the gaze, then the doctor might well be encouraged to look the patient in the eye; the moment of mutual gaze giving rise to a shared recognition of the doctor's preceding behaviour and an intimacy between the participants which might well generate further difficulty. Embarrassment thrives on one person seeing another see them, and so on; the reflexive recognition kindling further the fires of discomfort.

Yet if the patient is reluctant to face the doctor she is also troubled by looking at the object of her embarrassment. No sooner does she turn from the doctor to the chest than she looks up, then turning once again to her chest, she rapidly looks away. Looking at her chest provides little relief from her embarrassment. It is of course first noticing the object of the doctor's attention which gives rise to the initial gesture, and finding the doctor 'continuing' to look, which leads to further activity across the chest. It is as if looking at the chest and sharing the focus of the doctor's curiosity generates the embarrassment and encourages it to continue; the patient's difficulty arising as she sees herself and her body in the light of another seeing her. Again, there is something in the mutual recognition of the body which fires the embarrassment. The interactional constraints which give rise to the embarrassment and feature in its organization derive from the power of the look, in particular the sequential significance of a person's gaze in environments in which persons are co-present yet not fully engaged in the mutual production of an activity.

The organization of the behaviour of the patient in fragment 1 is not dissimilar to other cases of extreme embarrassment found within the data corpus. In each instance one finds that the gaze, or potential gaze, of another, to part of the patient's body fires a range of apparently haphazard behaviour; behaviour described in detail by Goffman and the sources from which he draws. Typically we find the patient turning rapidly to and from the embarrassable and the co-participant, often accompanied by a flustered gesture and not infrequently by a self preen or some other bodily focused activity. And in each instance, whereas the behaviour at first appears idiosyncratic, confused and irrational, it becomes apparent on closer inspection to be systematically organized with respect to the local environment of action; the situation itself. In each instance the individual who suffers embarrassment does not so much 'flood out' but becomes over-immersed in the sequential constraints at hand; attempting too much rather than too little self-control.

Thus the individual in each case of embarrassment reveals an excessive commitment and attention to the interaction; attempting as in fragment 1, to deal with simultaneous but contradictory demands on their behaviour. The patient tries to both present herself for examination and conceal her body from the doctor's gaze; she tries to turn away but is drawn by his gaze, she attempts to look at the object but is at the same time repelled by its vision. And embedded within these demands and commitments is the patient's recognition of the retrospective and prospective implications of particular forms of action and her grounds for seeing the doctor. The difficulty for the patient does not simply arise from a problem of self and identity, though that is not to suggest that disjunctures in role presentation and requirements may not be involved in generating embarrassment. Rather, the patient is attempting to reconcile the sequential implicativeness of different actions within the local configuration of activity, and through her commitment to the situation finds herself overcome by these contradictory constraints. And in the course of attempting to deal with these demands the sufferer becomes momentarily aware, self conscious, of her own behaviour. It is at that moment we find the individual taking grip and backing out of the situation.

THE AVOIDANCE OF EMBARRASSMENT

A well-bred person should always avoid exposing without necessity the parts to which nature has attached modesty. If necessity compels this, it should be done with decency and reserve, even if no witness is present. For angels are always present, and nothing is more welcome to them in a boy than modesty, the companion and guardian of decency. If it arouses shame to show them to the eyes of others, still less should they be exposed to their touch.

(Erasmus 1530 quoted in Elias 1978: 128)

It was mentioned earlier that actual outbursts of embarrassment during the medical examination are relatively rare, though it would be wrong to conclude that this particular area of social life is not permeated with the potential of embarrassment. With the advance of the threshold of embarrassment from the sixteenth century onwards, especially in relation to the presentation of the naked body and the corresponding expectation of modesty, it might well be assumed that exposing oneself to another even in the apparent security of the doctor's surgery is not without difficulty. Following

Goffman's (1956) recommendations, in this section I wish to briefly suggest a couple of ways in which embarrassment is typically kept at bay during the medical examination.[5]

The episode of embarrassment in fragment 1, like many which occur during medical consultation, occurs in the juncture between the request to examine the patient and the actual investigation of the chest. As suggested, the source of the difficulty lies in the state of involvement in this phase of the consultation and, in particular, the absence of a jointly sustained activity whilst the participants remain together in close co-presence. In such circumstances, which are also found elsewhere in social life, a glance at another can be (mis)construed as a look, giving a significance it would not have if contained within some business at hand. Yet, despite its potential for embarrassment, it is relatively unusual to find the participants in difficulty during this juncture of the consultation. The actions of both patient and doctor, following the request to conduct an examination and its acceptance, serve to avoid any potential problems until the examination begins. Often before the completion of the request, the patient and the doctor turn away from each other and become engrossed in distinct but related concerns. The patient removes the necessary clothing and the doctor prepares the equipment, reads the medical records or in other ways becomes occupied. Temporarily the participants disengage and involvement in the consultation is fragmented, allowing both doctor and patient to conduct activities which neither require nor demand the concern of the other. And, as the patient removes the final relevant article of clothing and turns to present the body, the doctor reorientates, and the participants become once more orientated towards and involved in a common activity.[6]

By the time, therefore, that the doctor turns his gaze towards the disrobed patient, his looking is part of beginning the medical examination. The looking is embedded in the activity and warranted in terms of the medical investigation of the patient's complaint. By becoming engrossed in their individual concerns as they prepare for the examination, both doctor and patient are able to display an apparent lack of interest in the activities of the other and avoid taking notice of or be seen to notice their co-participant. The doctor provides the patient with a little privacy to prepare for the examination and the patient is able to disattend the doctor's presence by turning away and concentrating on their particular responsibility. None of this is to suggest that either participant is unaware of the actions of the other; rather whilst remaining co-present they collaborate in displaying, as Goffman (1963) might suggest, a 'civil inattention' to each other by becoming engrossed in independant activities. Both doctor and patient protect themselves and each other by temporarily disengaging prior to the actual beginning of the examination.

There comes a time when the doctor begins the physical examination and however warranted the activity, in accord with medically relevant procedure, it may not be devoid of the possibility of embarrassment. The avoidance of emotion during the examination is accomplished in part through an action undertaken by the patient. The action is captured in drawings 6.2 and 6.3 and with the medical examination is discussed in detail in Heath (1986).

DRAWING 6.2   DRAWING 6.3

During the examination patients adopt a characteristic pose. This pose occurs in most types of examinations and is maintained throughout the course of the activity. In each case the patient at the moment the examination begins, turns to one side and slightly lowers the eyelids, as if looking into the middle distance, away from the doctor yet at no particular object within the local environment. Whether the doctor is listening to the patient's chest, testing his blood pressure, tapping the body or simply inspecting a difficulty, the patient looks neither at the doctor nor the areas of examination and seemingly becomes inattentive to the proceedings. As the examination is brought to completion, the middle-distance look is abandoned, and the patient once again orientates towards the co-participant, taking note and attending his action and activity.

The middle-distance orientation allows patients to cope with the contradictory demands of the physical examination. In turning away patients can render their body for inspection and become insensitive to the operations performed by the doctor; temporarily transforming themselves from a fully fledged participant into an object of test and inspection. However, in turning to one side, rather than right away, the patient is able to retain some sensitivity to the proceedings, monitoring the doctor's actions on the periphery, out of the corner of his or her eye and in this way is able to co-ordinate the presentation of the body with the in-course demands of the examination. The middle-distance orientation also keeps self-consciousness and embarrassment at bay.[7] In turning away both from the other and the area of the examination, the patient is able to 'ignore' the doctor and his inspection of the body. It allows the patient to avoid noticing the other's looking and reduces the intimacy which might arise from closely monitoring the others' work or glances. By not watching the other looking at their body, and by not having the other see you watching them, self-consciousness and the more social, even sexual overtones of the examination are avoided and dispelled. By adopting the middle-distance orientation and 'apparently' disengaging, the patient is able to distance herself from the examination, to seemingly ignore the attention of the doctor, whilst continuing to co-operate with the moment-by-moment responsibilities inherent in the production of medical examination.[8]

However, this precarious balance in the way in which the participants attend to each other during the physical examination can easily be upset.

Fragment 2 Transcript 1

```
Dr    now:::: just:t(t): (1.2) put your arms::
      (.5)
      < there you are:
P     whe::re:     [quaver]
Dr    jus::t: (.2) rela:x::
      (.7)
Dr    he ⌈h(°hh) alrigh:t:?
P        ⌊(I'm) n:ot very good at that:h(t) hhh he ⌈he he heh hhhh
Dr                                                 ⌊h heh heh hh hhh
      (1.2)
Dr    eh::(.) the pain: was there(.) wasn't it
```

In this instance the patient is about to undergo a thorough breast and chest examination and is sitting naked from the waist up in front of the doctor. As the doctor utters 'just::t: (.2) rela:x::' he holds the patient's wrists and positions her hands just above her knees.

Fragment 2 Transcript 2

holds patient's wrists

```
┌─────────────────────────────────────────────────────────────┐
```

at breasts
V

— — — — — .... ─────────────────────────────

jus::t:--rela:x::   ------- he ⌈h(°hh) alrigh:t:?
                               ⌊(I'm) n:ot very good at that:h(t)

                  ··,, ‾ ,,,,,,,,,,,,,,

                      ^   ^
                    turns to   turns away, rolls eyes
                    ceiling and
                    rolls eyes

During his utterance the doctor is looking at the breasts and the patient is looking down towards her knees. At the completion of the word 'rela:x::' the doctor turns from the breasts to the patient's face; an action which encourages the patient to respond. The moment his gaze arrives the patient turns from her knees upwards towards the ceiling, grips her mouth and rolls her eyes. And in turning to the ceiling she specifically avoids meeting the doctor's gaze by swerving to one side as her own face passes his. Yet he maintains his gaze on her, and after her glimpse at the ceiling the patient glances at the doctor. Momentarily meeting his eye, she swerves off to one side rolling her eyes and gritting her teeth. It is as their eyes meet for that brief moment that the doctor, continuing to clasp her wrists, produces the laugh token 'heh' to which the patient responds, producing an account of why she is unable to 'jus::t: (.2) rela:x::'. The patient's actions, both visual and vocal, embody many of the characteristics commonly thought of as embarrassment.

In fragment 2 (depicted in drawing 6.4), rather than disengaging prior to examination or allowing the patient to distance herself from the inspection of the body, the doctor attempts to retain the patient's

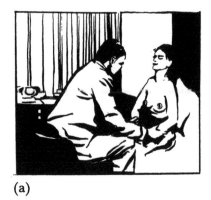 

(a)   (b)

DRAWING 6.4a and b (FRAGMENT 2)

involvement as a fully fledged participant. He not only talks and physically adjusts her position but turns his gaze upon her, encouraging a response. In so doing, the doctor throws the patient into confusion and the sorts of fluster we have observed earlier. Yet even within her outburst of self-consciousness and embarrassment, the patient specifically avoids meeting the doctor's eye; and when the inevitable happens she looks quickly away. It is pushing the patient into mutual involvement and in particular mutual gaze that gives rise to the patient's embarrassment; an episode in which she is simultaneously drawn and repulsed by his gaze. By being more familiar, perhaps more relaxed, certainly more involved, the doctor forces the patient into a state of mutual attention which much of her behaviour until this point is designed to avoid. By pushing the patient to respond and thereby re-engage, the doctor instigates a moment of mutual awareness of the patient's body and inadvertently generates embarrassment. It is moments such as these and the mutual awareness on which they rest, that the middle-distance orientation and the fragmentation of involvement during preparation for the medical examination, serve to avoid and dispel.

DISCUSSION

In forming a picture of the embarrassed individual, one relies on imagery from mechanics: equilibrium or self-control can be lost, balance can be overthrown. No doubt the physical character of flustering in part evokes this imagery. In any case, a completely flustered individual is one who cannot for the time being mobilize his muscular and intellectual resources for the task at hand, although he would like to; he cannot volunteer a response to those around him that will allow them to sustain the conversation smoothly. He and his flustered actions block the line of activity the others have been pursuing. He is present with them, but he is not 'in play'.

(Goffman 1956: 265–6)

In all these settings the same fundamental thing occurs: the expressive facts at hand threaten or discredit the assumptions a participant finds he has projected about his identity. Thereafter those present find they can neither do without the assumptions nor base their own responses upon them. The inhabitable reality shrinks until everyone feels 'small' or out of place.

(Goffman 1956: 269)

As Goffman suggests, the popular idea of embarrassment both in the sciences and literature is of an individual whose balance is temporarily lost, who momentarily loses control, until he or she regains composure. The objective and subjective symptoms of embarrassment whether culled from actual instances of the phenomenon or secondary sources support this popular impression – the darting and uncertain eyes, the apparent tenseness of the muscles especially around the mouth, the haphazard gesture and the uncertain hand movements. It is not surprising therefore that embarrassment is understood both by Goffman and a number of other scholars as an outburst of disorganized and irrational behaviour; behaviour in which the individual loses self-control and falls out of play, unable to participate in the stream of activity. As Goffman points out, face-to-face interaction requires those capacities that flustering is guaranteed to destroy, embarrassment undermining the foundations of mutually co-ordinated activity. And in accord with the analytic considerations found elsewhere in Goffman's studies, embarrassment is treated as the product of contradictions and conflicts in the presentation and perception of self and identity in encounters.

Whatever else, embarrassment has to do with the figure the individual cuts before others felt to be there at the time. The crucial concern is the impression one makes on others in the present – whatever the long-range or unconscious basis of this concern may be. This fluctuating configuration of those present is a most important reference group.

(Goffman 1956: 264–5)

Encouraged by Goffman's initiatives we can begin to examine actual fragments drawn from recordings of face-to-face interaction as a way of developing our understanding of phenomena such as embarrassment. Video-recordings of naturally occurring interaction provide the behavioural scientist with unprecedented access to the fine details of human conduct as it occurs within its natural environment.[9] If we take a brief look at an episode of embarrassment we are faced with the participants engaged in a series of actions and activities, visual, vocal or a combination of both. Various aspects of these actions and activities reflect characteristics of the phenomenon described by Goffman and others; yet initial observations of embarrassment do not evoke wholesale commitment to these previous analyses. For example it becomes difficult to conceive of the phenomenon in terms of issues of self and identity or to relate ideas concerning impression management to the conduct found within an episode of embarrassment. More importantly perhaps, if we bring to bear a model of the situation which conceptualizes the conduct in terms of self and impression management to the actual data, then we are faced with having to ignore the complex of action and activity which occurs within the local environment of embarrassment. The analysis remains on the boundaries of the phenomenon and leaves unexplicated the actual conduct of human beings during such moments of social life.

Embarrassment, like other phenomena which emerge in and through social interaction, is sequentially organized. It consists of actions and activities, systematically co-ordinated by the participants, at some here and now within the interaction itself. Embarrassment emerges in relation to a specific action produced by a co-participant. The specific movement, for example which embodies the individual's fluster, is designed in part with respect to the immediately preceding action, the offence, whilst simultaneously attempting to deal with related sequential constraints on their behaviour at that moment in time. In fragment 1 the patient's flustered gesture embodies two contradictory readings of the immediately preceding action; on the one hand peering at the patient's chest, on the other a medically warranted glance. Similarly, the gaze of the embarrassed individual is flustered as it attempts to reconcile competing local constraints and implications. The behaviour of the embarrassed individual is organized sequentially, both retro- and pro-actively with respect to the local configuration of action and the implication of possible future courses of conduct.

None of this is to suggest that embarrassment is unrelated to the problems of self and identity and impression management; in fact in both our instances, there is a sense that the offence emerges in relation to an action which renders the other, rather than their action, momentarily relevant. Rather, having drawn our attention to particular phenomena, the analytic model conceals the actual conduct of the participants, it is placed to one side as their behaviour is conceptualized in terms of issues of self and identity. The actual interaction itself is lost, and with it our ability to explicate the social organization which underlies the production and recognition of the participants' conduct in its natural settings. Nor does an exploration of information exchange and the production of definitions of the situation, solve this problem; again we are left with analysis devoid of the actual action. This only matters of course, if we are concerned to explicate the 'interaction order' and if we are committed to a analytic framework which treats the 'perspective of the actor' seriously.

Despite these misgivings, Goffman's analysis of embarrassment and other phenomena can be extremely useful in explicating and conceptualizing aspects of interactional organization. For example, in the collection Interactional *Ritual* (1967) Goffman discusses the problem of maintaining attention in face-to-face inter-action – a discussion which casts some light on the organization of conduct during episodes of embarrassment and the difficulties embarrassment generates for interaction in general. Social inter-action relies upon the participants maintaining their own and each other's attention in the business or topic at hand; yet as Goffman points out, the individual 'cannot act in order to satisfy these obli-gations, for such an effort would require him to shift his attention from the topic of conversation to the problem of being spontaneously involved in it' (1967: 155). These remarks direct our attention towards a whole realm of social organization, unexplicated by Goffman,[10] in and through which interactants maintain each other's attention; a social organization upon which they rely whilst necessarily disregarding its operation. One aspect of the threat posed by embarrassment is that it renders the individual conscious of his or her own actions and his or her involvement in interaction with others.

Fragment 1 provides various insights into the relationship between embarrassment and the participants' involvement in the interaction. For example, the actual episode of embarrassment, like others in the data corpus, entail, as Gross and Stone (1964) have suggested, a career. The career begins with the actions of the doctor, the offence, and concludes with the episode subsiding, as patient and doctor once again disengage. Yet even within the embarrassment itself there are distinct but related stages. It begins with the patient becoming apparently flustered as she attempts to reconcile competing interactional demands; it moves towards completion as the patient grits her teeth and begins to turn from the doctor. In the initial phase it as if the patient is immersed in the complex of action and constraint, and then becoming progressively aware of her own participation she passes into the next phase as 'she takes control' of herself and selects a particular course of action, backing out of the situation. Thus self-consciousness may emerge within the course of embarrassment as the individual attempts to reconcile incompatible sequential constraints and obligations within the interaction.

The relationship between embarrassment and the involvement of the individual may then lead to one of the central debates amongst scholars concerned with the study of the emotions. It was James and Lange (1922) who sparked the debate, by suggesting that the experience of emotion derived from the individual's perception of their own physiological changes, rather than the more common idea that physiological changes derived from the experience of an emotion by the individual. The behaviour of the patient in fragment 1, as in a number of other instances in the data corpus, suggests that in a certain sense the ideas of James and Lange are reflected in the interactional structure of embarrassment. Individuals become increasingly aware of their own actions during the episode of embarrassment; the self attention emerging as they attempt to deal with the local configuration of action. The emotion, the experience of the situation and its heightened sensitivity, emerging as the individuals progressively attend to the production of their own actions; the emotional experience deriving from their perception of and involvement in the action in which they are engaged.

More generally, embarrassment is embedded in the form of the individual's involvement in the interaction in a whole variety of ways. For example, in fragment 1 as in many of the instances in the data corpus, embarrassment, especially the more complex episodes of difficulty, emerge in circumstances in which the nature of the individual's involvement in interaction is at issue or ambiguous. As suggested the juncture between the request to examine the patient and the actual inspection of the body is a particular locale for embarrassment; as are other areas of social life where persons are found in each other's immediate co-presence whilst lacking a mutually co-ordinated activity to which they are committed. It is in this way that doctor and patient during this stage of the consultation share difficulties which arise in very different situations in social life, the bus, the tube, the waiting room, and the like, where a momentary glance can generate difficulty for another and give rise to a variety of 'bodily focused activities' – scratching the head, straightening the clothes and not infrequently concealing the face or eyes. The difficulties which emerge during the preparatory phase of the consultation and these related occasions derive from the absence of a common framework of involvement; the actions of the individual lie unembedded within some business or topic at hand, and are thereby subject to less charitable interpretation. It is of course the gaze of the individual which, freed from the constraint of mutually co-ordinated activity, can lead to difficulties, as it is rendered 'looking at' the other rather than simply attending to the activity in which they are engaged.

Yet, the conduct of the doctor and patient in setting the scene for the examination and during the inspection itself, frequently allows the interaction to proceed with little difficulty. The formal request to inspect the patient's body, followed by the acceptance or declination, the fragmentation of involvement and individual's pre-occupations until the actual beginning of the examination, provide a step-by-step progression to the activity which avoids the potential ambiguities of attention which can give rise to embarrassment. The formality of the procedure, reflected in the marked shifts in engagement, allow the doctor and patient to temporarily distance themselves from each other and their actions and thereby remain on a secure footing. And during the examination, patient and doctor manage the potential difficulties by the one adopting the characteristic middle-distance orientation and the other focusing his attention solely on the domain of the medical activity. Whilst apparently disengaging from each other, yet retaining some semblance of attention to their mutual concerns, by delicately balancing the state of mutual involvement, the participants are able to minimize embarrassment during the medical examination.

Ridding the medical examination of this formality and the forms of engagement and disengagement it entails, can generate severe difficulties for the participants – difficulties which can undermine the very accomplishment of the activity. In recent years there has been a growing interest in training general practitioners in communication skills and, in particular, in encouraging doctors to develop rapport with their patients and adopt a more informal approach during the consultation. These initiatives are to be welcomed but needed to be handled with care by individual practitioners especially when conducting the examination of the patient. As we saw in fragment 2, taking a more informal approach to the examination, retaining mutual involvement if only to put the patient at ease, forces the patient into an intimacy with the doctor and the activity which can give rise to a flood of emotion; emotion which the patient's behaviour is designed to avoid. In the collection of video-recordings of medical consultations, it is a small number of practitioners who over and over again cause distress for their patients by encouraging mutual involvement during the medical examination. Inadvertently, from consultation to consultation, they generate severe embarrassment, both for their patients and themselves.

Throughout his brilliant essays, Goffman drives our attention towards the situational character of ordinary conduct and reveals a whole realm of social organization for analytic inspection. His work places hitherto unnoticed phenomena on the sociological agenda and renders them relevant to detailed inquiry. His contribution should not rest with the complex substantive insights he provides concerning the nature of social life, however powerful they intuitively feel; rather his studies serve as a background of initiatives for the detailed, empirical analysis of situational conduct. It is likely that though Goffman's essays direct our attention towards particular phenomena, on closer inspection they do not necessarily provide a clear understanding of the interactional structure of the participants' conduct. We may well find it difficult, in some cases even unhelpful, to labour under Goffman's analytic frameworks. Yet this does not deny his substantial contribution to sociology nor the relevance of his work to the progress of the discipline. Most importantly, it is crucial, at least for the development of sociology, that we follow Goffman's example and treat the 'interaction order' seriously, as a topic in its own right, worthy of close analytic attention, and in particular explore the situational and sequential organization of ordinary conduct, social action and activity.

NOTES

I should like to thank Paul Drew and Tony Wootton for their very helpful comments on an earlier draft of this paper and Katherine Nicholls for her illustrations based on stills from the original data. I would also like to thank

Cambridge University Press for their permission to reprint the drawings of the middle-distance orientation from Heath (1986). This paper is drawn from a larger study concerned with interaction during the medical examination and the organization of embarrassment. The discussion is formed around an analysis of one instance of embarrassment which is presented through transcripts and drawings; sadly there are no substitutes for the actual data, the video-recording. Due to the relative lack of space it was impossible to organize the paper through a discussion of a series of examples of embarrassment; a way I would have preferred. In consequence the discussion of embarrassment and the medical examination is in various ways truncated.

1 In this paper I have deliberately avoided a discussion of the central theoretical debates on the expression of emotion and its relationship to behaviour and physiological states; debates kindled by Darwin, transformed by James and Lange, continued by Russell's observations and the subsequent studies on the physiological and behavioural manifestations of the emotions. For a detailed discussion from a sociological standpoint, see Hochschild (1979). I am keen to sidestep these issues in order to throw a little light on the interactional organization of actions we might characteristically, or better conventionally, consider to embody embarrassment. I assume that in a different way that is precisely what Goffman is doing in his essay. It is likely that the detailed empirical study of the phenomenon in interaction may cast a little light on some of the issues central to these debates, for example the relationship between the 'stimulus' and its experience; see James and Lange (1922). It is interesting to note that in fragment 1 we find a temporal organization in the characteristics of embarrassment; self-consciousness and self-interest emerging as the fluster subsides.

2 The role of gaze and other forms of visual behaviour and their relationship to the production and receipt of talk are discussed in detail in, for example, Kendon (1967), Goodwin (1981) and Heath (1986). Of particular relevance here is the way in which gaze has been repeatedly found to feature in the mutual production of the activity. Goffman captures a flavour of the issue when he suggests: 'It is as if they [listeners] were to look into the speaker's words which, after all, cannot be seen. It is as if they must look at the speaker, but not see him' (1981b: 141).

3 The interactional design of body movements such as gestures is described in detail in Heath (1986), in particular chapters 3 and 4.

4 The ability of a look to affect another is described widely in sciences and literature. In ethology for example, Wada (1961) points out how certain species of primate undergo a marked increase in electrical activity when looked at, and a number of related studies have demonstrated how threat displays are initiated by looking. In a rather different vein, Gilbert Austin in his classic treatise on oratory suggests: 'The whole person seems to be in some measure affected by this influence of another's eyes,

but the eyes themselves feel it with the most lively sensibility' (1966: 101). Elsewhere, Heath (1986: chapter 2) discusses in detail the way in which gaze at another during a period of mutual disengagement can be seen to initiate actions such as talk, or if the opportunity articulated through a look is declined, various forms of 'bodily focused activity'.

5 Addressing an issue such as the 'avoidance' of embarrassment generates severe methodological problems; problems which haunt sociology and which have been widely discussed at least since Weber's important contribution. The issue is characterized by Sacks (1963) as the 'problem of relevance' and turns on whether the analyst can warrant an account of some phenomenon unless the participants themselves can be shown to be orientated to the proposed description, categorization, rule, procedure, course of action, etc. In describing the ways in which certain actions seem to avoid embarrassment, I can offer little firm evidence for the characterization. Hence, the paper has largely focused on actual instances of the phenomenon.

6 This process of disengagement prior to the actual examination occurs independently of the sex, class or ethnicity of either doctor or patient.

7 Three current postgraduates at the University of Surrey – Jane Batchelor, Kay Ching and Gill Davies – have collected and are analysing video-recordings of veterinary consultations. They have found that the owner of the animal routinely adopts a middle-distance orientation during the more 'embarrassing' moments of the physical examination, in particular as the vet measures the animal's temperature by placing the thermometer in its behind. Otherwise, the owner remains fully engaged throughout the vet's examination of the animal.

8 See Frankel (1984) for a detailed analysis of the way in which a doctor can, by talking during an examination, encourage the patient, a child, to disattend the activity at hand.

9 As discussed elsewhere (Heath 1986: chapter 1) video-recordings of naturally occurring interaction allow us to capture the fine details of human conduct and subject them to detailed scrutiny using action-replay and slow-motion facilities. Video-recordings provide a raw data base to which the analyst and academic community can have access, thereby providing at least in public presentations the opportunity for others to evaluate and comment on analysis in relation to the raw data.

10 For a detailed discussion of vocal and visual actions and their organization used by individuals to maintain attention 'without addressing the problems of involvement in its own right', see Goodwin (1981) and Heath (1986).

7

Putting Linguistics on a Proper Footing: Explorations in Goffman's Concepts of Participation

STEPHEN C. LEVINSON

GOFFMAN AND LINGUISTICS

In this paper I want to offer an appreciation of Erving Goffman from a linguistic perspective. Although Goffman published a number of papers in linguistics journals (1976, 1978), his contributions to linguistic thinking are perhaps much less obvious than his contributions to other social sciences. That is partly because linguists are the snobs of social science: you don't get into the club unless you are willing to don the most outlandish presuppositions (like a psychological reductionism hardly consonant with Goffman's position). But it is also because Goffman's ideas have been filtered through intermediaries who may not always have succeeded in passing the credit back to its source. For example, the 'face-work' ideas have been recycled as a theory of linguistic politeness by Lakoff (1973), Brown and Levinson (1978), Leech (1983) and others, spawning a really substantial literature (see Brown and Levinson 1987) much of which makes little or no reference to Goffman (see, for example Leech 1983). That is but one example: another would be Goffman's emphasis on situation and the role that this has played (again partly filtered through, partly augmented by, Hymes, Gumperz, Labov and others) in sociolinguistics and the ethnography of speaking.

However, another reason for the apparent lack of impact on linguistics is simply that the full force of his ideas has yet to make itself properly felt. This force will in fact be relayed and amplified by the many disciplines and specialisms that nowadays contribute to the study of social interaction – and it is as one of the principal founding fathers of *that* (rather perhaps than as the author of ideas about face-work, response cries, footing or other specific contributions) that he will in time come to be seen to have had a lasting effect on linguistic theorizing.[1]

In order to illustrate these points, as well as to underline Goffman's particular contributions to linguistics, I shall take up some suggestions that he made under the rubric of *footing*. It is a frequent complaint about his work in general that not only is it not empirical, but that it is not clear how it might be so. Here I shall attempt to answer this criticism by showing how a number of quite different kinds of evidence can be brought to bear on his ideas about 'footing'.

FOOTING OR PARTICIPATION STRUCTURE

Goffman was concerned from his very earliest work (1953) with the nature of participation in social encounters, the special nature of participation in 'focused' encounters *versus* the studied inattention in unfocused encounters, the ratification of participation, and the different kinds of participation that interactants recognize (for references and discussion see Williams 1980; Goodwin 1981: ch. 1). Talk is properly analysed, he argued, only in the context of the participation status of each person present in an encounter: 'the study of behaviour while speaking and the study of the behaviour of those who are present to each other but not engaged in talk cannot be analytically separated' (1964b: 62; quoted in Williams 1980: 216). He criticized the preponderance of the dyadic model of verbal interchange and suggested that re-analysis of the underlying forms of participation should 'be approached by re-examining the primitive notions of speaker and hearer' (1981b: 128–9), and in effect decomposing them into their underlying constituent concepts.

He went on to develop in several papers a number of analytical distinctions (most of which can be found in fact in incipient form in his dissertation), for example that between addressees and mere overhearers, but the mature statement to which almost all my remarks will be addressed is the short paper called 'Footing' (Goffman 1979), republished in the book *Forms of Talk* (Goffman 1981b).[2]

Goffman has often been accused, with some justice I think, of substituting arrays of categories for both proper theory and proper observation (see e.g. Lofland 1980). Although his remarks on footing have the same character, there are two extenuating circumstances: first, in such uncharted territory there really seems to be a need for some sort of preliminary Linnean operation; secondly, although he didn't feel it necessary to emphasize this, there are important connections both to his concept of the social self and, more obviously, to the other substantive focus of his work, the social encounter. Here however I shall largely ignore these theoretical connections, which provide the theory breathing life into the categories, seeking only to assess and improve the analytical categories he offered.

'Footing' as the Heart of Deixis

Before proceeding headlong into details, let me briefly sketch why issues of footing, or (as I shall prefer) *participant role*, might be of central interest to linguistics and other disciplines concerned with communication. The central question raised, from a linguistic point of view, is: What are the essential concepts that underlie the phenomenon of *deixis* (or indexicality, as the philosophers prefer)? Deixis concerns, of course, the way in which utterances are semantically or pragmatically anchored to their situation of utterance, by virtue of the fact that certain key words and morphemes have their reference fixed by various (temporal, spatial, participant role and social) parameters of the speech event. Now the importance of the phenomenon to linguistic theory is fundamental and multi-stranded: (a) it introduces an irreducible context-dependence into the nature of meaning; (b) in so doing, it also introduces an irreducible element of subjectivity (Lyons 1982); (c) it may been seen ontogenetically to be the source of reference in general (Lyons 1975); and (d) it has a pervasive influence on many aspects of language structure and meaning (Fillmore 1975). At the heart of deixis are the concepts of participant role – *here* means close to speaker, Latin *iste* means close to addressee, and so on. Yet linguists (and philosophers) have operated with unanalysed concepts of first and second person. If these can be shown to be decomposable, that is a fundamental contribution to our understanding of the whole phenomenon.

For philosophers, many of these same concerns recommend an interest in deixis, and they have also emphasized the interconnection of indexicality, reference, truth-conditions and assertion. But in all this there are signs of serious mistakes, or at least oversimplifications, arising from the assumption of dyadic verbal interchanges as the basic (or sole) form of human communication – thus the infelicitous term 'hearer' is used with vague application by philosophers both formal (e.g. Montague 1974, Stalnaker 1978) and informal (e.g. Searle 1969). For example, the failure to make the elementary distinction between addressee and hearer seems to be at the heart of some of the prolonged debate over the Gricean analysis of communication (see Schiffer 1972). The failures of speech-act theory consequent on this under-analysis of the concept of 'hearer' are nicely brought out by Clark and Carlson (1982). Thus many issues in philosophy of language turn on a proper analysis of the categories of participant role that underlie the phenomena of deixis.

Of course there is a sociological and psychological interest also. Ancient grammarians like Apollonius insisted that the concepts of grammatical person were roles like dramatic characters – on this view the pronoun *I* labels a transient role and is not a name for a denotatum (Buhler 1982: 19). It is clear that these are the first such roles learnt by the child and it may be essential to the acquisition of the concept of social role to see the distinction between role and incumbent made at the rapid rate at which the roles of speaker and addressee alternate. It is of considerable interest that children pass (somewhere between the ages of two and three) through a specific phase during which the first and second person pronouns are incorrectly thought to be names and not alternating roles (Clark 1978; see too Bellugi and Klima 1982: 309ff.). Curiously, the nature of participant roles as the prototype social roles *par excellence* is something presupposed rather than stressed by Goffman.

Criteria for Setting Up Categories of Participant Role

We need, it will be argued (following Goffman 1981b), more categories of participant role than are provided by traditional descriptions of the communication situation. In effect, this amounts to the decomposition of the concepts of *speaker* and *addressee* (or 'hearer') into their underlying component concepts – allowing them to be recombined into other, related but more specialized participant roles. But how are we to decide how many such categories we need, and exactly which? (Goffman was not explicit here.) I am going to suggest that two rather different kinds of evidence should be brought to bear on these decisions: (a) the examination of grammatical distinctions made in the languages of the world, and (b) the analysis of actual language use. The underlying rationale is this: there is an interplay between language structure and language use such that usage properties often have effects or correlates in linguistic structure. Thus, by looking at both the more *recherché* aspects of deictic systems of natural languages and at aspects of verbal inter-action, we may hope to obtain the best heuristics for putting together a set of potentially universal distinctions – distinctions that may show up in the *use* of one language, but in the *structure* of another (see Levinson 1983: 42ff., for general discussion of this strategy for pragmatic analysis).

In what follows, we shall pursue this strategy. First, we shall develop an elaborate set of categories for possible participant roles. Then we shall review some of the lesser, and underexplored, categories of deixis in a range of languages, attempting to show that at least some of these distinctions in participant role are well-motivated by the grammatical facts. We turn then to matters of language use, distinguishing the study of speech events from the study of the concurrent assignment of participant role during the production of single utterances, and show that, again, good motivation can be had from the study of language use for the finer distinctions in participant role that Goffman and others have recom-mended.

CATEGORIES FOR THE ANALYSIS OF PARTICIPANT ROLE

Long traditional in our culture is the threefold division between speaker, hearer, and something spoken about. It has been elaborated in information theory, linguistics, semiotics, literary criticism, and sociology in various ways . . . All such schemes appear to agree either in taking the standpoint of an individual speaker or in postulating a dyad, speaker–hearer (or source–destination, sender–receiver, addressor–addressee). Even if such a scheme is intended to be a model, for descriptive work it cannot be.

(Hymes 1972: 58)

Unfortunately, beyond one or two suggestions, Hymes does not offer us any better scheme. How then to proceed? Let us review some earlier suggestions.

Some Earlier Schemes

One way is to take the grammatical distinctions of first, second and third person, and then distinguish special cases: e.g. we could divide each such category according to presence/absence from the speech event, and this is perhaps part of the traditional wisdom on the subject.[3] Thus we would have speakers who speak for themselves *versus* those that speak for absent others (spokesmen), addressees who are intended recipients, *versus* those that are vehicles for a message to absent others (messengers), and third parties who are present (audience) *versus* third parties who are absent (non-participants), as in figure 7.1.

FIGURE 7.1 'Traditional' scheme

(present) *speaker*   (present) *addressee*
(absent) *source*   (absent) *target*
                        3rd parties
                        (present) *audience*
                        (absent) (not part of speech event)

Or, alternatively, we might adopt and refine the communication theoretic treatment developed by Shannon and Weaver (1949) and now part of the 'commonsense' about communication (see Lyons 1977: 36ff.). This distinguishes *sender* (source of message) from *transmitter*, and *destination* (goal of message) from *receiver*, as in figure 7.2.

FIGURE 7.2   Communication theory model

sender → *transmitter* → (via channel) → *receiver* → *destination*

However, simple schemes of either of these sorts will not capture the kinds of participant roles actually employed in speech events. For example, consider < 1 > :

< 1 >   (from Sacks, Schegloff and Jefferson 1974: 717)
  Sharon You didn' come tuh talk tuh Karen?
  Mark No, Karen- Karen 'n I're having a fight,
     (0.4)
     after she went out with Keith an' not with (me)
  Ruthie Hah hah hah hah
  Karen Wul Mark, you never asked me out.

Intuitively, Mark's utterance has as *addressee* Sharon, but as *target* Karen, inasmuch as (a) Sharon asked a question, and we expect a reply to her from Mark – making Sharon the natural addressee, and

(b) Karen is referred to in the third person, ruling her out as an addressee. Nevertheless, the remark is delivered in Karen's presence, and being a report of a 'fight' and an imputation of blame clearly picks out Karen as a recipient – who may be expected to respond with a defence or counter-complaint (which is in turn forthcoming).

This sort of example is problematic for both the simple schemes above. In the case of the 'traditional' scheme, we have an indirect target who is nevertheless present and attending to the utterance in question; and in the case of the communication-theory scheme we have a receiver (Sharon) and also a destination (Karen), but the message is not transmitted by virtue of a physical link between Sharon and Karen. And whereas the traditional scheme at least has something to say about Ruthie's appreciative laughter (she's in *audience* role), the communication-theory scheme seems quite unhelpful here.

So we need at least more terms, like some term for the source of the spokesman's message, and some term for third parties who are neither audience nor absent. Further, we need a compositional analysis that breaks these categories down into minimal constituents and then shows how they are re-assembled into apparently simple concepts like (present) *speaker* in the traditional scheme. In short we need some finer-grained conceptual analysis, and a bundle of terms to label the constituent and compound concepts.

Before proceeding, it is essential to note a systematic ambiguity in the use of terms like *speaker*, *addressee* and *audience*, namely a *speech-event/speech-act* ambiguity. Thus one can identify the speakers, addressees, and members of the audience during an entire *speech event* (e.g. a conference), but also during a single speech act, or as we shall prefer *utterance-event* (in order to avoid some of the baggage of speech-act theory). This leads to a systematic ambiguity in the use of terms like *speaker* and *audience*: for example, a guest speaker at an interactive seminar may be the designated speaker in the speech-event sense even when someone else is doing the talking (a speaker in the utterance-event sense). The ambiguity arises, of course, because particular participant roles may be systematically and unevenly distributed over the personnel present, throughout a speech event. Here, however, we are specifically concerned with the *utterance-event* use of terms like *speaker* and *addressee*; for the speech-event usage is parasitic on this primary usage, in ways I hope to show. In due course, we shall see that the notion of an *utterance-event* is itself problematic, but for the moment let us say that an utterance-event is that stretch of a turn at talk over which there is a constant set of participant roles mapped into the same set of individuals – i.e. that unit within which the function from the set of participant roles to the set of individuals is held constant. Think of the categories to be proposed below, then, as a blow-by-blow analysis of the proceedings during some speech event, *not* an overall summation of roles held throughout such a speech event. (Those roles, and many other factors, may be involved in the recognition of which participant roles are activated in a single utterance event; but I am here distinguishing questions of *process of category assignment* from questions about the primordial set of categories themselves.)

Goffman's Categories of Participation in Talk

Goffman begins with a notion of *footing* that is not entirely clear; indeed it seems intended to have some pretty global and correspondingly vague application. Issues of footing occur where 'participant's alignment, or set, or stance, or projected self is somehow at issue' (1981b: 128); examples range from a President's switch of frame from press conference to remarks to a journalist on her dress, to a lecturer's switch from text to self-commentary or aside (ibid.: 174ff.), to a radio announcer's change in voice consequent on change of subject matter (ibid.: 237).

However, changes of footings are communicated especially through changes in *participation*, these expressed linguistically: 'linguistics provides us with the cues and markers through which such footings become manifest' (ibid.: 157). Indeed, Goffman sometimes speaks as if footing reduced to matters of participation status: 'the alignment of an individual to a particular utterance whether involving a production format, as in the case of a speaker, or solely a participation status, as in the case of a hearer, can be referred to as his *footing*' (ibid.: 227). Thus questions of participation status at least partially exhaust the notion of footing, and I shall not be over-cautious in my use of the two terms.

Goffman (like his colleague at Pennsylvania, Hymes, quoted above) emphasized the inadequacy of the terms 'speaker' and 'hearer', as incautiously used by linguists and philosophers, and the dyadic model of communication that those terms seem to presuppose.[4] He suggests the need for 'decomposing them into smaller, analytically coherent elements' (ibid.: 129). The notion of hearer should be decomposed into a set of categories for different kinds of recipient, collectively termed *participation framework* in a later essay (ibid.: 226); while the notion of speaker should be decomposed in a similar way into a set of categories he termed the *production format* (ibid.: 226). Table 7.1 outlines the kind of categories he had in mind (note my suggested reformulation of his terminology). Goffman notes (ibid.: 136) that the inclusion of bystanders in this set of categories implies application not just to the focused social encounter but also to the wider *social situation*, 'the full physical arena in which persons present are in sight and sound of one another'. Thus those studiously 'disattending' a conversation come within our orbit too; as do those *response cries* produced outside a ratified circle of reception solely for the benefit of bystanders.

Unfortunately, although Goffman's categories are a notable advance on earlier schemes, they do not seem sufficient. First, they appear empirically inadequate, simply not providing sufficient distinctions: thus Karen's role in <1> remains undesignated, as it did in the earlier schemes (here, she'd have to be in the same role as Ruthie as 'unaddressed ratified participant'). Secondly, they remain essentially unexplicated – we are not given sufficient characterization to make the application of the terms at all clear. Thirdly, he fails to consistently make the crucial distinction between *utterance-event* and

TABLE 7.1 Goffman's participation roles (1981b page references)

Production format (henceforth *production roles*):
1   *animator* 'the sounding box' (p. 226)
2   *author*   'the agent who scripts the lines' (p. 226)
3   *principal* 'the party to whose position the words attest' (p. 226)

Participation framework (henceforth *reception roles*)
A: *ratified* (p. 226)
   1   *addressed recipient* 'the one to whom the speaker addresses his visual attention and to whom, incidentally, he expects to turn over his speaking role' (p. 133; cf. 1976)
   2   *unaddressed recipient* (p. 133) the rest of the 'official hearers', who may or may not be listening
B: *unratified*
   1   *over-hearers* 'inadvertent', 'non-official' listeners (p. 132) or *bystanders*
   2   *eavesdroppers* 'engineered', 'non-official' followers of talk (p. 132)

Note that Goffman's misleading term 'participation framework' will henceforth be replaced by 'reception roles', retaining 'participation' – as Goffman sometimes used it (ibid.: 137) – to cover both the production and reception role sets.

speech-event applications of these terms (although he indicated his awareness of the ambiguity (ibid.: 137)). This leads him to suggest that his categories are only applicable to one kind of activity, namely conversation, and that in others, such as 'podium talk', other sets of categories like 'actor' *versus* 'audience' will be required (ibid.: 140). In that case, all such sets of categories would be activity-specific, and of course culturally relative, playing no possible part in a comparative ethnography of speaking. All three failings are, I believe, important analytical errors, which I shall try to correct.

Some Further Systematization

There are at least two ways of developing a systematic set of relevant categories. We could take some participant roles as basic or primitive, and then define derivative participant roles in terms of the basic ones.

For example, we could set up a simple scheme, as in table 7.2, in which we make a distinction between *source* and *speaker* (or utterer), noting that sources may or may not be participants in an utterance event; and a similar distinction between *addressee* and *target* at the receiving end (targets being not necessarily, but possibly, participants). Employing the same notion of *participant*, we could say that an *audience* is constituted of those participants who are not *producers* (= sources or speakers) and not *recipients* (= addressees or targets). (Note that this is an utterance-event definition of the

TABLE 7.2 A system of basic and derived categories

Basic categories
    source = informational/illocutionary origin of message
    target = informational/illocutionary destination of message
    speaker = utterer
    addressee = proximate destination
    participant = a party with a ratified channel-link to other parties

Derived categories (formed from Boolean operations on basic categories)
    producers = sources or speakers
    recipients = addressees or targets
    author = source and speaker
    relayer = speaker who is not the source
    goal = an addressee who is the target
    intermediary = an addressee who is not the target
    etc.

---

concept of audience, and that we would naturally use the speech-event definition rather differently – there, the audience may be the target, etc.) Then, with a basic set of categories like that, we could go on to define derivative categories of some utility – e.g. we could say an *author* is someone in the role of both *source* and *speaker*, a *goal* someone who is both *addressee* and *target*, etc.

Such a scheme is quite adequate for most purposes, but it would be more satisfactory if we could break down the basic concepts into defining features and re-assemble them to make the more complex categories we need. This requires an understanding of the underlying categorial dimensions, which are by no means easy to discern. But as a first approximation, we might offer the feature analyses in tables 7.4 and 7.5 (table 7.3 introduces the method through a simplifed version). These employ the rich classificatory potential of matrices of polythetic defining characteristics – I borrow the 'technology' unadulterated from phonology.[5]

The terms suggested are, I am aware, far from felicitous; but natural English metalanguage (although helpful up to a point with terms like 'spokesman') could hardly be expected to run to this level of discrimination, which is hopefully of some universal application. But the terms themselves are of no analytical importance. What is essential, though, is the set of underlying discriminations – the labels utilized here are I hope more or less transparent, although the underlying concepts may be anything but that, as we shall see in the next section. However, let me indicate roughly what I have in mind: *TRANSMISSION* is the property that utterers or actual transmitters have, *MESSAGE ORIGIN* the property of originating the message, which in the more complex scheme (table 7.4) I have split into having the *MOTIVE* or desire to communicate some particular message, and devising the *FORM* or format of the message. On the receiving end (table 7.5), we have the feature of *ADDRESS*, i.e.

TABLE 7.3 Production roles (simple version)

	MESSAGE ORIGIN	*TRANSMISSION*
author	+	+
indirect source	+	−
relayer	−	+

Super-ordinate ('natural') classes:
speaker = + *TRANSMISSION*
source = + *ORIGIN*

TABLE 7.4 Production roles (complex version)

Term	PARTIC	TRANS	MOTIVE	FORM	Examples
(a) Participant producer roles					
author	+	+	+	+	ordinary speaker
'ghostee'	+	+	+	−	ghosted speaker
spokesman	+	+	−	+	barrister
relayer	+	+	−	−	reader of statement
deviser	+	−	+	+	statement maker
sponsor	+	−	+	−	defendant in court
'ghostor'	+	−	−	+	copresent ghost writer
(b) Non-participant producer roles					
ultimate source	−	−	+	+	source of military command
principal	−	−	+	−	delegate's constituents
formulator	−	−	−	+	absent ghost writer

Redundancy rule:

+ *TRANSMITTER* → (implies) + *PARTIC*

        corollary: − *PARTIC* → − *TRANSMITTER*

Useful superordinate categories (unspecified for other features):

speaker = + *TRANS* (Goffman's animator)
composer = + *FORM* (Goffman's author)
motivator = + *MOTIVE* (Goffman's principal)
source = (+ *MOTIVE*, + *FORM*)

TABLE 7.5 Reception roles

	ADDRESS	RECIPIENT	PARTICIPANT	CHANNEL-LINK	Examples
(a) Participant reception roles					
interlocutor	+	+	+	+	ordinary addressee
indirect target	−	+	+	+	see Karen in <1>
intermediary	+	−	+	+	committee chairman
audience	−	−	+	+	see Ruthie in <1>
(b) Non-participant reception roles					
overhearer	−	−	−	+	bystanders
targetted overhearer	−	+	−	+	Barbadian 'butt'
ultimate destination	−	+	−	−	

Redundancy rules:[6]

+ *PARTICIPANT* → + *CHANNEL-LINK*
  (Corollary: − *CHANNEL-LINK* → − *PARTICIPANT*)
+ *ADDRESS* → + *PARTICIPANT*

Useful superordinate classes:
recipient = + *RECIPIENT*
addressee = + *ADDRESS*
participant = + *PARTIC*
hearers = + *CHANNEL-LINK*
  etc.

whether the message picks out a recipient by means of a feature of address, including second-person forms, vocatives, gesture, gaze or a combination thereof, or even just sheer singularity of possible recipients. *RECIPIENTSHIP* may be indicated by linguistic form, e.g. by formulation of information, but is hard to define – informally it is about who a message is *for*. Being a *PARTICIPANT* has something to do with what Goffman calls a 'ratified role' in the proceedings, and presupposes *CHANNEL-LINKAGE* or ability to receive the message. As we shall see, these concepts are none too clear, but at least using them we can define a provisional vocabulary with discriminations sufficient for what follows.

Finally, I should note that one area that I'm glossing over at present is exactly how to think about utterance events that imply prior to following utterance events; e.g. 'Tell Charles to empty the garbage' projects a succeeding utterance event, and 'Harry said to tell you to empty the garbage' implies a preceding utterance event. By invoking the distinction $+/-$ *PARTICIPANT* we may distinguish between sources and recipients linked to this utterance event by other ones – thus in these cases we may talk of the ultimate source or *origin* (Harry) and (ultimate) *destination* (Charles). Again, I am not sure that this is a useful conceptualization, but it will be sufficient for current purposes.

Underlying Dimensions

Our ready ability to construct schemes of this sort should not distract us from analysis of the underlying dimensions on which they are constructed. However, this analysis proves quite difficult and is probably best done by examining the empirical materials that motivate these distinctions in the first place. It will be useful, though, to consider in advance some of the problems that arise.

First, consider the implications of the idea that these are social roles. On the dyadic analysis of a social status (as in Warner 1937, or Goodenough 1967), a single status (like 'father', 'doctor') implies a 'grammatical' pairing of social identities ('father/son'; 'doctor/patient'), to which the rights of one identity constitute the duties of the other. In a dyadic conversation, the assignment of speaking role to A will thus imply addressee/recipient role to B. (The same may hold of two-party speech-exchange systems, where each party may consist of more than one individual, as in press conferences (q.v. Schegloff 1987(b), in press) – reminding us once again that issues of role are to be distinguished from issues of incumbency.) However, we are especially interested in just those cases where this dyadic mode of analysis seems inadequate – where more parties are presupposed than just speaker and addressee.

But this does raise the important question of the connection of concepts of participant role to the essentially dyadic system of turn-taking in conversation. From the perspective of such two-party arrangements, issues of participant role might be held (I believe erroneously) to more or less reduce to the study of the turn-taking system, and its associated back-up systems. The turn-taking procedures are a set of mechanisms that provide participants with a reasonably clear procedure for deciding *whose* turn to speak it currently is, and consequently who is thus in the complementary set of (non-speaking) roles – audience/recipient/addressee. The back-up systems provide, *inter alia*, for ways of resolving whose turn it is when simultaneous speech has started. These systems have been deeply explored by Schegloff and associates and I shall not attempt to summarize their findings here (see Sacks, Schegloff and Jefferson 1974; Levinson 1983: ch. 6; Goodwin 1981 specifically addresses the relation of the turn-taking system to Goffman's categories of participant role). Suffice it to say that the turn-taking system in conversation 'organizes but two speakers at a time, "current and next", and is not overtly directed to the size of the pool from which current and next are selected' (Sacks, Schegloff and Jefferson 1974: 712), hence its elasticity in handling from two speakers up to indefinitely many. Further, many kinds of non-conversational turn-taking systems likewise assume just two parties, where one (or more) of the parties may have multiple incumbents (Schegloff 1987(b); cf. the press conferences mentioned immediately above).[7] Thus, it seems that we cannot look to the turn-taking system for any direct analysis of participant role. This is despite the fact that the turn-taking system is clearly deeply related to issues of participant role. Consider, for example, that the so-called 'back-channel' markers like *mhmm, uhuh*, etc., are transmissions effectively renouncing speaker role (see Schegloff 1982); that they typically violate the phonotactic rules of the language is perhaps an iconic indication that they are not a speaker's speech. Consider too that from a turn-taking point of view 'a party may be a speaker even though he is not saying anything at the moment' (Goodwin 1981: 3).

In any case, what we are concerned with here is what happens when this dyadic pattern of analysis appears to be inadequate, for example when the speaker with the current turn is not to be thought of as the source of the message, or when there is no other party being addressed, or where who is addressed is not the intended destination or target, and so on. Thus, the turn-taking system, while certainly germane to many of these issues, appears to operate at a higher level of abstraction as it were: it assumes two parties, without distinguishing the different possible compositions of each of those categories. Quite probably, the universal tendency in languages to distinguish, in pronominal categories or elsewhere, primarily and prototypically the two deictic categories of first and second person, is related closely to the superordinate categories of speaker and addressee/recipient that are the basis of the turn-taking system.

Another initial problem is to clarify the distinction between role and the two aspects of incumbency: self-presentation as an incumbent of the role *versus* other-assignment of self as incumbent of a role. Consider, for example, that a speaker may seek a particular individual (e.g. by gaze) as an addressee, but that party may choose not to attend in that capacity; meanwhile another party may attempt to usurp the role of addressee by displays of recipiency (see Goodwin 1979, 1981: ch. 1; and discussion in 203–5 below). Clearly a participant role is, from the point of view of participants, not something that is unilaterally assigned, but rather jointly negotiated.

Let us turn now to the set of roles themselves and indicate some of the problems that assail any such mode of analysis. The concepts involved in the production set of roles are, compared to the reception end, relatively unproblematic. Of these, message transmission, or emission, is the most straightforward; but even here there are kinds of language use where the application of the property is not so clear. We have noted already that if 'speakership' is a role assigned by the turn-taking system, then an individual can be the incumbent of that role when he is silent and someone else is transmitting (back-channel cues, laughter or other signs of recipient role) – thus the relationship between speakership and transmission is not straightforward. Consider too, for example, simultaneous translation: A transmits a message in code L to B, who transmits the 'same' message in code M to C – is there one speaker but two transmitters? Or consider cases where the natives hold that something or someone is transmitting a message, but an observer may be in doubt, as in cases of divination (cf. Evans-Pritchard 1937: part III) or when the Ojibwa claim that the thunder says determinate things (Hallowell, cited in Hymes 1974: 13). Or, to bring the problem home, when the mother interprets the child's one 'word' utterance as the determinate proposition P (see 208–9 below), has the child actually transmitted P? (For the Wishram, children's pre-speech babblings were considered sensible transmissions in a language known only to babies, dogs and coyotes – Sapir, cited in Hymes 1974: 74). The point is that the concept of transmitting ('speaker') role is not at heart so straight-forward. However, if we keep in mind that participant roles are interactively assigned, then we can see that the fact that the 'natives' might assign transmission-based roles where the analyst might not is hardly a serious conceptual problem.

Leaving transmission aside, we turn to the characterization of the *source* of the message. The distinction between *source* and *transmission* may be clear enough in the case of the newscaster reading from a script – although even here prosodic 'colouring' can play an important role in the perception of the message (Goffman 1981b: 227ff.). But it becomes much more difficult where the individual doing the transmitting has some partial role in the origin of the message. (Consider, for example, the distinction between directly quoted and indirectly quoted speech.) One underlying problem here is to distinguish the source of the information from the source of the illocution – the proposition P may derive from some other party, but the commitment with which it is relayed may vary, and the very indication of a source other than the transmitter may weaken or strengthen that commitment (see discussion of evidentials in 184–6 below). Or consider a military order issued through a chain of command: it presumably has the illocutionary force derived from both the original source and the most proximate source or transmitter; in contrast, it seems unlikely that an actor could be sued if the TV advertisement he enacted made false claims – the transmitter there carries no illocutionary commitment. Thus, it may be argued, it is not sufficient to distinguish just two elements of the *Source* (namely, *Motive* and *Form*) – we may also need a distinction between different kinds of *Content* (namely *Force* and *Proposition* or the like).

However, it is the reception-role set that is especially resistant to analysis. First there is the issue of what constitutes *channel-linkage*. In the case of verbal communication, being within audible range of the transmitter is clearly a precondition. For some cultures, that will not be sufficient, as when in Guugu Yimidhirr much essential referential information is indicated gesturally (Haviland 1986b). But in any case more is presupposed; specifically, it may be claimed, a shared code – unless that should properly require an additional feature (or features).[8] Yet the basic message of sociolinguistics is that concepts like 'shared code' are highly problematic. Glossing over these difficulties, let us say that being able to 'tune-in', then, to both channel and message code, will constitute the essence of channel-linkage – but an essence not easily explicated.

· The notion of *participant* is problematic in part because it is hard to escape the speech-event level of analysis; in speech events, the processes by which 'ratification' in that role is achieved are potentially perhaps as diverse as the varieties of speech events themselves. In the speech-event sense, it is possible to be a participant that is non-attentive, even temporarily not in channel-linkage (as when the international delegate takes off his headset through which simultaneous translations are delivered). However, in the utterance-event sense central here, a participant is such just by virtue of actual or presumed attentiveness, and it is here that studies of displays of participancy have been most instructive. Heath (1982, 1984), for example, argues that kinesic and postural displays of 'availability' for participation are systematically distinguishable from displays of 'recipiency': whereas the former indicates readiness for interaction should it occur, the latter may actually invite another to speak (1982: 154ff.). Goodwin (1984) shows that while a speaker A tells a dinner-table story to addressee B, the members of the audience C and D so time their non-verbal activities that they properly coincide with the pivotal points in the story (so that, for example, they are not involved in other activities when the punch line is reached). Further, where C is the butt (indirect target) of the story, he will so organize his movements that his facial display is appropriate precisely at the moment (at the end of the punch line) when all gaze is turned to him. Thus the roles of C and D are also systematically distinguished posturally and kinesically. Thus, participation is a demonstrative social role,[9] where each kind of participant role requires a particular kind of appropriate display by its incumbent (we return to these issues in 204–5 below).

Recipientship and *address* are best discussed together. A recipient is someone whom a message is *for*; it is thus perhaps essentially a role defined by the pertinence of the *informational (or attitudinal) content.* The roles of recipient and addressee come apart in our culturally favoured genre of speech event, the formal chaired meeting, where the addressee is always properly the chair, and the recipient often some other individual. Because recipientship is essentially informational, the means whereby it is recognized are perhaps primarily matters of content and sequencing: in a chaired meeting, a question about books may be clearly aimed at the librarian present, while a retort to a challenge may have its target made clear by its sequential location immediately after the challenge. The sequential aspects of talk designed for overhearers have been subject to preliminary investigation by Heritage (1985). He finds, for example, that in courtroom and news-interview talk there is an almost complete absence of the news receipt tokens (like 'Oh, really') typical after reports in conversations (1985: 98). This he suggests is primarily because such tokens presuppose that their speakers are the 'primary addressees' of the prior utterance, while in courtrooms and news interviews the elicited reports are in fact primarily for others (1985: 100). Instead of 'Oh, really' and the like, reports are often received in these settings with 'formulations' that further direct the talk in specific channels useful to the overhearers. However, there are also subtle linguistic and kinesic indicators of intended recipiency, about which more later (203–21). In short, recipients are designated destinations for messages, but the ways in which these destinations are distinguished from other participants (or non-participants) are both subtle and hardly understood.

Address is, in the last resort, quite puzzling. It is often suggested that the addressee is that participant with the right to reply (Lyons 1977: 34; Goffman 1981b: 133), but it is clear that this is not definitional (as when the judge sentences the defendant, or the priest blesses the congregation; see also conversational counter-evidence in 209–20 below). Although there are formal linguistic features of address in second-person pronouns and other grammatical features encoding second person, these do not generally in and of themselves serve to pick out one addressee from other participants. (Exceptions are forms reserved for particular dignatories, etc.; in languages with rich honorifics, these too may serve to unambiguously single out addressees; and as Goffman notes (1981b: 126), citing Gumperz, the choice of a minority language in code-switching situations may convert all non-addressees into non-participants.) Vocatives (names, titles, etc., often with special inflections) may serve to exactly identify an addressee, as may an ostensive gesture (making clear the envisioned division of labour in an utterance like 'You do the dishes and you clean the floor'). But only some small proportion of utterances are so directly addressed, making gaze and body posture, in English anyway, central (Beattie 1983; Goodwin 1981).

Why do languages, and users of them, not make more verbally explicit the feature of address? It seems that the deep analytical difficulties that attend analysis of the recipient-role set in fact follow naturally from the intrinsic nature of the vocal-auditory channel that has been selected in evolution to carry the bulk of human communication. That channel is, as Hockett (1960) put it, the natural choice for 'broadcast transmission' – sign language will fare ill in the jungle or in the dark. For generalized warning signals, that broadcast nature will hardly be a limitation; but for human social organization it is deeply problematic. Consider, for example, the operation of a rule of the sort 'don't tell people what they already know' (for which there is ample evidence (Levinson 1986)); how can such a rule operate in a broadcast system of communication? Or how can one ensure that insults go to one's inferiors but not to those who rule the roost? Skilful use of amplitude is one natural (and much used) solution (see 205–8 below and Goldberg 1978), but more is required. The solutions, I suggest, are attempts to create, via the features of address, a directed focal channel of communication in a medium that is essentially resistant to it. It is this perhaps that explains the special role of gaze in conversational activity, specifically the finding that speakers' gaze at addressees to check whether reciprocal gaze is forthcoming (Goodwin 1981: 74ff., and references therein) – the visual medium of gaze providing a precise alignment of channel (Beattie 1983: 23) necessarily absent from the aural medium. But given the recalcitrant medium, we cannot expect address to be always unequivocal – indeed we can see that achieving successful address without the use of unambiguous vocatives is indeed an achievement.

Finally, we should note that issues of informational *versus* illocutionary nature emerge at the receiving end of communication, just as they do at the production end. Consider an utterance of the sort 'The last one to leave the room turn off the light': none of the addressees may, in the event, be the last one to leave the room – others may come; the instruction is for the last one to leave the room, whomsoever he or she is (for the theoretical consequences of this sort of example, see Clark and Carlson 1982). Is this person the intended recipient (if so we shall have to alter our scheme so that + *RECIPIENT* does not imply + *PARTICIPANT*)? I think not: it is one of those (problematic) cases where what is said projects a future utterance event.

Some Consideration of the Minimal Components in an Utterance Event

It is tempting to say that for an utterance event to occur we need *minimally* a *speaker* and a *recipient*. To clarify the discussion, we should, following Goodwin (1981), distinguish the participant *roles* from the *incumbents* of those roles. Doing that, we can see that 'talking to oneself' is not a counter-example to the hypothetical necessity for at least a speaker and a recipient, but rather just the limiting case where the incumbent of both roles is the same person. But what is a counter-example, perhaps, is the phenomenon of *out-louds* (Goffman's (1981) term is *response cries*). A Goffmanesque example might be: I am standing in a bus queue and finally the bus is seen rounding the corner – I say 'Phew, at last!'. One analysis here would be that there is a recipient, namely myself and any others that care to elect themselves. Another analysis would be: there is no recipient, unless someone elects himself, such utterances being designed to make possible, but not to presuppose, the existence of a possible set of addressees or audience. Whatever the status of these English *out-louds*, there seem to be certain speech acts in many languages that do not presuppose an audience; certain expressives like *ouch!*, *damn!* etc., do not seem to be addressed to self or others (they may well of course have *indirect targets*); or consider *imprecatives*, conventional curses or blessings, that do not seem to require a co-present addressee or audience (though they may presuppose an omnipresent spiritual bystander). There will be further discussion of this below, but the relevant upshot here is that for a verbal expression to constitute an utterance event which invokes the categories of participant role, all that seems to be necessary is that there is a transmitter or speaker. [10]

One important point raised by the distinction between role and incumbency is that any role may be occupied by any number of incumbents simultaneously (in the case of speakers, of course, this implies a chorus). Alternatively, one individual can stand duty for a joint incumbency (as when the chairman of the jury announces 'guilty'). This makes possible some further potentially distinctive participant roles, e.g. we could define a *representative* as a speaker (transmitter) who is one of a set of persons in the source, or *goal-member* as an addressee who is one of the intended recipients, etc. But as long as the distinction between incumbency and role is not forgotten, we can handle such cases with analytical clarity when they occur.

GRAMMATICAL MOTIVATION FOR CATEGORIES OF PARTICIPANT ROLE

Grammatical Category of Person versus *Participant Role*

Let us turn now to examine evidence from language structure for the finely discriminated kinds of participant role we have considered.

We shall here be concerned with the ways in which the concepts underlying *first* and *second* person must (arguably) be broken down into their component concepts, at least for the description of some languages. However, it is important to bear in mind that there is a distinction between the *grammatical categories* of person, and the *interactional* and indexical notions of participant role (Lyons 1977: 636ff.).[11] It seems reasonable to suppose that the set of potential participant roles are universally relevant (which is not to say that some may or may not be in much greater use in some societies) and the present paper is based on this assumption.[12] But it is very much an empirical question as to how, and to what extent, the set of participant roles are *grammaticalized* in specific languages.[13] Thus I shall try to argue that participant roles more specialized than simple speaker (first person) and addressee (second person) are sometimes encoded in the structure of languages, although my data here is still rather sparse. The necessity and utility of making the distinction between the grammatical categories of person and the interactional categories of participant role is demonstrated by the *slippage* that can occur between the two sets of categories. For example we are all familiar with cases where grammatical second-person forms are used for referents that are not in specific participant roles at all ('You can never tell nowadays'), or third-person forms used for persons in addressee participant role (as in 'Your Honour is ruling on a point of law?'), or first-person forms used for persons in addressee role (the condescending *we*). Nevertheless, despite the sometimes indirect relation between the two sets of categories, there may be much to be learnt from grammatical distinctions about the kinds of participant role we need to distinguish between.

First and Second Person as Prototype Categories?

It is only comparatively recently (starting with Bühler [1934] 1982) that serious linguistic attention has been paid to deixis (see Levinson 1983: ch. 2 for a review). The three 'persons' of the classical linguistic tradition are of course central here, and the dramaturgical analogy (*persona*, player's mask, character in a play) employed in classical thought was, insists Bühler (1982: 19), entirely appropriate: 'the words *I* and *you* refer to the role holders in the on-going speech drama'. (Part of Goffman's interest in participant roles must indeed have been in their nature as ontogenetic prototypes for social roles in general.)

The classical analysis has held up remarkably well in the face of recent comparative analysis.[14] The great majority of languages exhibit the three persons in a paradigm of pronouns, verb agreements or elsewhere (Forchheimer 1953; Ingram 1978; Anderson and Keenan 1985). It's important of course to see that 'third person' is a residual category – neither speaker nor addressee – and for that reason there are languages without third-person pronouns (as in the Ngaanyatjara dialect of the Western Desert of Australia, Dixon 1980: 357; Australian languages seem therefore to invalidate Ingram's (1978) putative universals). Some languages appear to lack proper pronouns, using third-person titles for reference to speaker and hearer; this seems to be an areal feature in SE Asia, where it is linked to elaborate honorific systems (see Sansom 1928; Emeneau 1951: ch. 4; Cooke 1968). But Lyons (1977: 641ff.) argues that such systems presuppose the concepts of first and second person that they seem to do without.

However, with these exceptions in mind, it does seem that there is something natural enough about the grouping of concepts into 'speaker', 'addressee' and 'other' to make the classical three-person system recur in most natural languages. Given the kinds of possible distinction explored in tables 7.4 and 7.5 above, this calls for explanation: why should most languages utilize first- and second-person grammatical categories that are indifferent to all the finer distinctions that are possible? One answer may be that pronouns universally exhibit a 'prototype' semantics (Fillmore 1982) based on a canonical situation of utterance where there are only two participants, so that the composite notions 'speaker' and 'addressee' exhaust the relevant participant roles, and third persons are non-participants. Another possible kind of explanation for the omnipresent dyadic categories of first and second person is to be found in the two-party nature of the turn-taking system, which appears to be (in this respect at least) universal for informal talk; the two-party system being indifferent to the number of possible participants and to the exact participant role in which they stand.

Despite this indubitable tendency for first- and second-person grammatical categories to be realized in such a way that they conflate the finer distinctions we have explored, these finer discriminations are often grammaticalized in less salient ways in (perhaps) most languages.

In searching for grammatical realizations of participant role, it is important to remember that person deixis – that is, participant role – can be grammatically encoded *directly* in many ways other than by pronouns, e.g. quite typically in verb morphology and perhaps always in vocative forms. Thus in many languages one can say 'The

woman am complaining' meaning ['I (female) am complaining']*
where the category of first person is carried only by the verb
agreement (e.g. Spanish, Warlpiri, Tamil; see Anderson and
Keenan 1985: 264). Secondly, participant role is *indirectly* encoded,
or presupposed, in many other aspects of deixis: in time deixis,
tenses and time adverbs are normally interpreted relative to the time
the message is encoded by speaker or writer; in place deixis,
locations are typically expressed relative to the location of speaker or
addressee or both; in social deixis, the social relationship of the
speaker to the addressee or to a third-person referent is what is
typically encoded (for a review of each of these areas, see Levinson
1983: ch. 2). Person deixis has an importance in linguistic theory not
only because it guarantees an irreducible subjectivity in language
(Lyons 1982), but also simply because it is pervasive.

Grammaticalization of Non-prototypical Participant Roles

I wish now to show that unanalysed notions like 'speaker' and
'addressee' are inadequate to handle the grammatical distinctions
made in the deictic (and other) systems of various languages.
Instead, just in order to describe these facts properly, we shall need
to use the decomposed concepts coalesced in those putatively prototype categories.

Let us start at the production end. The prototype notion
'speaker', we've suggested, subsumes the concepts of transmitter
(Goffman's 'animator'), motivator (Goffman's 'principal') and
composer (Goffman's 'author'). One clear area of grammar where
these decompose is in what Jakobson called *evidentials* (Jakobson
1971: 135). Many languages require that one specify the personal
commitment with which an assertion is produced, the epistemic
basis for assertions being intrinsically linked to degrees of commitment beyond mere transmission. Consider Hidatsa: there are six
sentence-final affixes that signal six 'moods' (Matthews 1965:
99ff.):[15]

1   'period' mood (-*c*): this 'indicates that the speaker believes the
    sentence to be true; if it should turn out otherwise, it would
    mean that he was mistaken, but by no means a liar' – the most
    used form;

* Editors' note: in this chapter glosses of expressions or statements in the text are
notated through the form ['. . . . . .']; actual, or purportedly actual, utterances are
notated, as in other chapters, with single quotation marks alone.

2   'emphatic' mood (*-ski*): indicates certainty and commitment and can be used to signal a promise;

3   'quotative' mood (*-wareae*): glossed as 'they say', indicating a second-hand but indefinite source, used, for example, to retell stories and myths;

4   'report' mood (*-rahe*): 'indicates that the speaker was told the information given in the sentence by someone else, but has no other evidence of its truth value';

5   'indefinite' (*-toak*); and

6   'question' moods: 'the question and indefinite mood are alike in that they both indicate that the speaker does not know whether or not the sentence is true. The indefinite also means that the speaker thinks the listener (sic) does not know; whereas the question means that the speaker thinks the listener does know.'

Matthews (1965: 101) also notes that there are systematic patterns in the relation of first tellings to second tellings, such that if A tells P to B, and B relays this to C, the relayed message has a largely predictable mood:

Original Mood A → B	Mood on Retelling retold by B → C
Emphatic	Period
Period	Period/report
Quotative/report	Quotative/report
Indefinite/question	Indefinite/question

One would like to know a lot more about how such a system is actually used, but it is clear that the epistemic basis for a statement, and thus its authorial status, is here distinguished in various ways from its mere transmission. (Incidentally, Tagalog appears to have a similar distinction between quotative and reportative sentences – see Sadock and Zwicky 1985: 168, citing Schachter and Otanes 1972: 414.)

Systems of evidentials are apparently common, especially in Amerindian languages. Thus Boas (1911, vol. 1: 496) lists four contrastive suffixes for Kwakiutl:

1   - 2 *la* = 'it is said/hearsay';

2   *-emsku* = 'as I told you before';

3   *-xent* = 'evidently, as shown by evidence';
4   *-eng.a* = 'from a dream'.

Similarly in Tzeltal (Brown & Levinson 1978: 152ff.) and Lahu
(Matisoff 1973: 331ff.) there are numerous evidential particles. In
Guugu Yimidhirr (Haviland 1979a; supplemented by author's
fieldwork), myths and well-known historical tales are properly told
using a special aspect marker (similar to the use of quotative in
Hidatsa) on all appropriate verbs, so that the communal status of the
subject matter is clearly distinguished from the transmitter's role (a
fact which fits together in a complex way with 'ownership' of stories
by birthright; see also Dixon 1980: 49). Or in Turkish, the
'inferential mood' 'conveys that the information it gives is based
either on hearsay or on inference from observed facts, but not on the
speaker's having seen the action take place' (Lewis 1967: 122, cited
in Sadock and Zwicky 1985: 169). But, Lyons (1982: 111) reminds
us, we do not need to go so far afield: French has a verbal form
known as the 'quotative conditional' (*le conditionel de citation*) which
implies an indirect source:

Le premier ministre serait (cf. *est*) *malade*
['The prime minister is, reportedly, ill']

He points out that the gloss is misleading in that it erroneously
suggests that such a sentence can be adequately paraphrased by
another that makes the 'quotative' nature explicit – a point that
holds for all the evidential forms we have reviewed.

Clearly, what most of these evidentials do is distinguish between
(in the terms of tables 7.3 and 7.4) the relayer or transmitter and the
informational source. Now there may be some doubt that such
distinctions in *informational* source are closely related to distinctions
in what one might wish to see as *illocutionary* source: it may be rather
different to say something on one's own behalf that one has heard
from another than to be paid to say something devised by another
for that other's purposes (as in a TV commercial). But there is
clearly a close and intrinsic connection: indeed on a Searlian
analysis of assertion, I cannot sincerely assert P just because you told
me to assert P, unless I have reason to firmly believe P. Thus differing
strengths and grounds for belief imply differing illocutionary forces,
a point made well by those languages that signal a gradation of
forces from assertion to question, usually by particles. Tamil is one
such language (Brown and Levinson 1978: 164ff.), Japanese
another (Tsuchihashi 1983).

Related to the phenomena of evidentials is the set of grammatical distinctions between different kinds of reported speech. In moving from 'John said "I'm coming"' to 'John said that he would come' it is often said that we move from a 'verbatim' to a 'gist' report and thus from relayer role to formulator or spokesman role (see Banfield 1973; Lyons 1968: 174). Indirectly, authorial or non-authorial status can also be indicated by the fact that a number of languages have forms only used by *authorized speakers* (much like *gringo* can hardly be used by a white North American). What is interesting then is what happens when the speaker is not fully the source. Thus Haas (1964: 230) records that in Koasati, female speakers used different verbal suffixes from male speakers; but a female speaker reporting what a male speaker said would use the appropriate male suffix – thus indicating that she did not author the utterance.

Turning now to the reception set of categories of differential participation status, let us start by noting that languages often provide special forms where the speaker indicates that no-one, or no-one present, or no-one other than himself, is addressed. Thus in Japanese there are two particles that contrast in the following way: *kana* is 'used when talking to oneself with others invited to listen' as in:

soo   kana
that speculative ['I wonder about that']

kashira is contrastive: 'unlike *kana*, which invites others to listen in on one's musings, one is really talking just to oneself' (Tsuchihashi 1983: 365). The Tamil particle *-oo* serves both these functions (Brown and Levinson 1978: 164), while the Lahu particle *na* (with low tone) seems especially to perform the second function: thus it can be used to indicate that the speaker is calculating a response as in 'In this village there are – *how many-na* – 270 people' (as in English 'let's see now'; see Matisoff 1973: 375). (It is noted of a similar particle in Dyirbal (Dixon 1972: 49) that although it accompanies hesitation or a word-search it is specifically not used to invite an addressee's guess.) Thus these particles serve to indicate that although words were spoken, they were not addressed to anyone other than the speaker, and although they may have been heard by others, the particles may (as with Japanese *kashira*) or may not (as with *kana*) exclude a ratified audience role to those listeners.

Many languages have minor sentence types (additional to the major and almost universal imperative, declarative and inter-rogative types), some of which presuppose a special reception setting. Consider for example *imprecatives*, or special formats for cursing. Curses do not seem to require the presence of any listeners, and the target of the curse is perhaps often not addressed (but cf. English 'Damn you!'). Thus in Turkish there is a special future suffix *-esi* which 'occurs only in: *gor-mi-y-esi* ([´May he not see!´])' (Lewis 1967: 115; cited in Sadock and Zwicky 1985: 164). In a similar way, blessings may occur in a special sentence type, as in English 'May the blessings of the Lord be with you!'; the same function is performed by the Lahu particle *pi-o* 2 (with two high falling tones; Matisoff 1973: 354). In the case of blessings, although the target (or beneficiary) of the blessing may occur in the second person, it would not seem to be essential that the beneficiary has channel-linkage to (or is co-present with) the speaker at all!

Clearly, other minor sentence types like exclamations may presuppose a special reception organization. Exclamations might be taken to be prototypically 'out-louds' or 'response cries' in Goffman's (1981b) terminology, requiring no addressee. On that analysis, English sentence types of the sort 'How amazing!', 'Wow, can he ever run!' would be syntactic forms specialized to indicate that no addressee is necessarily presupposed (Goffman 1981b: 90). Perhaps most languages have specialized exclamatives, often further divided according to degree of surprise, positive or negative attitude, etc. (see Sadock and Zwicky 1985: 163 for some examples; Brown and Levinson 1978: 156 for Tzeltal). Related in that they again presuppose no addressee are the minor sentence types called *optatives*, which express a wish, as in the archaic English 'Would that I might marry Celeste', or the more current 'If only Celeste would come'. Languages with true optatives (false descriptions abound; see Lyons 1977: 815) include, for example, Greenlandic Eskimo (Sadock and Zwicky 1985: 164). In any case, optatives normally seem to occur with first- or third-person subjects, as we might expect from their non-addressed character.

Of special interest, though, is the kind of minor sentence type often called *hortative* (or sometimes, *desiderative*) or non-second-person imperatives (Sadock and Zwicky 1985: 177). These are the forms often glossed with semi-archaic English *let*, as in 'Let him be welcome'. Some languages use the identical verbal inflection for 'imperatives' in all persons, as in Guugu Yimidhirr (Haviland 1979a: 92), Onandaga (Chafe 1970: 20) and Hidatsa (Matthews 1965: 107ff.): thus compare the following Hidatsa sentences, where the first is in the 'period (declarative subtype) mood', the second in the (third-person) imperative:

1   *wio a ate awahu kuo axuo-c*
    The woman hid in the house – *Period*
2   *wio ate awahu kuo axuo-ka*
    The woman hide in the house – *Imperative*
    ['I demand that the woman hide in the house']

Some languages have specialized forms, like current English 'Let's go' restricted to the first-person-plural inclusive, or Tamil verbal suffix -*TTum* restricted to third-person hortatives.[16]

The interest of these forms is this: a third-person imperative is a request to an addressee to get some third party to do something. It thus presupposes two speech acts: the current one, and the one projected between the current addressee, then speaker, and his addressee, the third party mentioned. Thus the illocutionary target, the person to do the thing requested, is distinct from the addressee, and this is encoded in these forms. Curiously, there is a construction in English which, unnoticed I think, performs exactly this special function. Consider where A says to B:

<2>   Johnny is to come in now

and then B says to C (Johnny):

<3>   You are to come in now

As far as I can see, this infinitive construction in English is usable just in case *either* the addressee is not the target (as in <2>), *or* the speaker is not the source as in <3>. More exactly, <2> is appropriately used to direct a message to an indirect target or destination via an intermediary, and <3> to indicate that the message comes from an indirect or ultimate source via a relayer (where such an indirect target and such an ultimate source are normally non-participants). This example is of interest because it suggests that many minor sentence types of this sort have escaped the grammarians' notice, and not only in unfamiliar languages.

We turn now to another area of grammar where one might expect to find some of these underlying kinds of participant role invoked, namely spatial deixis. Demonstrative pronouns do not always have the prototype semantics that English *this* (['close to speaker']) and *that* (['far from speaker']) exhibit; they are often so organized that while the demonstrative glossed 'this' prototypically indicates an object close to the speaker, the pronoun glossed 'that' in fact indicates an object close to the addressee (Fillmore 1982; Anderson and Keenan

1985: 284ff.). Thus in Kwakiutl, a language 'characterized primarily by an exuberant development of location' (Boas 1911: Pt I 446), one is forced to specify location by one of six demonstrative suffixes, which gloss (1911: Pt I, 527ff.):

1	near to S (speaker)	+ visible
2	near to S	− visible
3	near to A (addressee)	+ visible
4	near to A	− visible
5	near to third party	+ visible
6	near third party	− visible

We shall return to the visibility criterion in a moment, but note that so far we have no need to invoke other than the three traditional grammatical persons. However, an extension of such a system seems to exist in Samal (a language in the Philippines), where the distinctions are (W. Geoghegan, (personal communication)):

1 near to S
2 near to A
3 near to ratified participant other than S or A
4 near a non-participant

Such a system permits a speaker to cut a person, demonstratively, out of the conversation by referring to an object close to that person using the fourth form![17]

The visibility condition on the use of demonstratives is found not only in the NW Coast Amerindian languages (Boas 1911), but also in Australia (Dixon 1972: 45; 1977: 180ff.). An interesting question is: visible *to whom*? Anderson and Keenan (1985: 290ff.) interpret this dimension as invariably visibility to the *speaker*, but Boas's descriptions do not make this self-evident. Dixon's descriptions are also not clear, but are interpreted by Fillmore (1982: 45) as visibility to both speaker and addressee. It is entirely consistent with the descriptions that the condition is in fact 'in the visual field of the ratified participants', and I hazard the hypothesis that this is in fact the correct interpretation.

Another grammatical area where we might expect to find the finer shades of participant role reflected in grammar is social deixis, where the social relationships of participants to the current speech event are encoded in linguistic forms (Levinson 1983: 89ff.). Most typically what is encoded is the relative social rank of speaker to addressee, or speaker to third-person referent – where the canonical three persons are descriptively sufficient. However, there are also honorifics (and other kinds of encoded relationship) which make necessary reference to other kinds of participant role, especially to bystanders or overhearers or audiences. Consider for example the Australian so-called 'mother-in-law (or brother-in-law) languages'. According to Haviland (1979a), Guugu Yimidhirr 'brother-in-law' language was canonically used in the *presence of* but not *to*, tabooed relatives: 'A husband speaking with BIL [brother-in-law language] words, directed messages to his father-in-law via his wife. And a father, speaking either in BIL or EV [everyday language] words, gave his daughter messages for his son-in-law' (1979a: 376). On this account Guugu-Yimidhirr BIL language systematically lexicalizes the role of *indirect target*. However, further material from this and other Australian languages seems to indicate that what is really lexicalized or indexed by these lexical alternates is probably the set of non-producing roles that exclude addressees – i.e. the set {indirect targets, audiences, overhearers}. (See too Dixon 1972: 32, and analysis in Comrie 1976.) This set of participant roles is grammaticalized in languages in other parts of the world too. For example, some Ponapean royal honorifics encode that addressee is a royal, *or* that addressee is not a royal, but a member of audience *or* a bystander is a royal (Garvin & Reisenberg 1952: 203). Similarly, the Abipon of Argentina suffix every word with *-in* if any person present (or participating?) is a member of the warrior class (Hymes 1972: 61). Unfortunately, the lack of a proper analytical vocabulary makes such descriptions often unclear – is what is encoded that a member of the Ponapean royalty, or an Abipon warrior, is merely in channel-linkage, or must they be in more specific roles?

As a postscript it is worth mentioning that the folk *metalanguages* of some languages divide speech events and kinds of speaking along the lines of our more complex analysis of participant role (note the English terms *chorus, audience, spokesman*, etc.). Tojolabal is especially interesting in this respect, with terminological distinctions made between, for example, different kinds of prayers where God is the addressee or where God is the target but a human the addressee, or different kinds of dispute where a speaker speaks for himself *versus* one where someone else speaks on his behalf (Furbee-Losee 1976: 34f.).

We may conclude this brief account with the observation that writers of descriptive grammars have clearly not been looking for the finer discriminations in participant role that we are interested in, so what information we can glean from published sources is surely only the tip of a probable iceberg. Nevertheless, what is evident is that there is considerable support from comparative grammar for the psychological reality and grammatical pertinence of at least some of those fine distinctions.

INTERACTIONAL MOTIVATIONS FOR THE CATEGORIES

That finely discriminated categories of participant role are not merely handy but necessary for the proper description of interaction has been illustrated by Goffman (1981b), Hymes (1972: 61, 1974) and recently demonstrated in more detail by, for example, Goodwin (1977, 1979, 1981, 1984) and Heath (1982, 1984). I cannot here compete with the exemplary detail of description and analysis in some of this more recent work. Instead I shall attempt to illustrate the general scope and importance of participant role assignment to the analysis of verbal interaction, first to some problems in the ethnography of speaking, then to some details of category assignment in some more familiar kinds of interaction. In considering the ethnographic remarks, though, a basic limitation of the present enterprise should be borne in mind: we are not here primarily concerned with the *processes* through which particular participant roles are assigned or claimed, except in the most sketchy way. Rather, we are concerned with *what kinds* of categories we need to capture the assignment that we intuitively perform. There is little doubt that what is really interesting is precisely how such categories are invoked and manipulated, and what background expectations and linguistic and conversational devices play a role in these assignments.[18] But to study *that*, we need to have in advance some provisional idea of what kinds of categories we may encounter – although in the final analysis any such system of categories should include just those that emerge from the careful analysis of interactional data.

A second issue that immediately arises with interactional materials is the discourse unit over which participant roles are to be assigned. Recollect our distinction between *utterance event* and *speech event*, and our decision to restrict ourselves in the first instance to the level of utterance events, which are primary, and allow a secondary definition of participant roles in speech events. We might then want to say that an *utterance event* corresponds to a turn at talk: however, although there is perhaps a tendency to such a correspondence, it will certainly not be sufficient in all cases. Sometimes during the production of a single structural (utterance or turn) unit, not only the incumbents but also the participant roles change. This will make the notion of utterance event problematic and *post hoc*: I shall stipulate that *an utterance event is the maximal unit within a turn in which the participant roles are held constant*, and it may or may not correspond to structural units like turn segments or sentence tokens – more of which later.

Some Applications to the Ethnography of Speaking

The ethnography of speaking is especially concerned with the description of two kinds of recurrent and patterned speech activity: short verbal routines of a culturally salient kind on the one hand, and 'speech events' or cultural activities in which speech plays a crucial role on the other (see Hymes 1972, 1974; Bauman & Sherzer 1974). Let us take these in turn, illustrating the application of participant role categories primarily to data from non-Western societies, where concepts other than 'speaker' and 'addressee' are clearly required.

First, an Australian example. We have already mentioned the specialized vocabularies of Australian languages that, in some cases at least, lexicalize the category of indirect target. But considerable interest attends their use. For example, Thomson (1935; quoted in Haviland 1979a: 376) notes that among Umpila speakers:

> A father-in-law . . . may speak to his daughter's husband . . . but the latter may not reply directly. The son-in-law may talk 'one side', that is, while he may not address his elder in ordinary speech (*koko*) he may speak in the language known as *ngornki*. Even in this language, however, he may not address his remarks in the first person directly to his . . . [father-in-law], but to his child, or even to his dog, to which he speaks as to a son, and not directly to the person for whom the remark is intended.
>
> (Thomson 1935: 480–1)

An interpretation of this is: since the taboo language encodes indirect target role, the son-in-law A talks to the dog B with the father-in-law C in hearing; hence A is *speaker* and *source*, B (the dog!) is *addressee* and *intermediary*, and C is *indirect target*. Unfortunately, these systems no longer seem to operate, or at least not as they once did; but examining the accounts carefully, it seems that the usage of these avoidance languages varied with the degree to which the taboo relative was respected or avoided. Thus mothers-in-law do not seem to have been even indirectly targettable, so that use in their presence indicated that they were mere overhearers, fathers-in-law could be indirect targets but could never be addressed, and in some cases brothers-in-law may have actually been addressed in the avoidance language (see Haviland 1979a: 369, 379). But the generalization seems to be: when channel-linked to a taboo relative, one had to use the avoidance language, and in most cases, could not address in it. (A stronger interpretation would be that such systems basically encoded the channel-linkage of a taboo relative exclusively in overhearer role – i.e. that they specifically excluded the possibility of participation by the taboo relative. On this interpretation C in the example above would be *targetted overhearer* rather than *indirect target* of A's remark. There is evidence for the cultural importance of participation withdrawal from, for example, Warlpiri sign language, currently under investigation by Adam Kendon (1989), where signs are used by widows as a marker of partial withdrawal from participation status.)

A second example, from New Guinea, illustrates a different kind of phenomenon where we are in need of refined categories for participant roles. Schieffelin (1979: 87ff.) details a certain kind of routinized 'triadic' interaction pattern in Kaluli. In these routines A says to B 'X-elema', which glosses as ['Say to C (the pragmatically indicated party) X right now'].[19]

So we have interactions like the following, where A is a mother, and B and C two children (Schieffelin 1979: 96), omitting for a moment B's responses, and representing the triadic relation (A tells B to tell C) as (A to B(>C)):

<4>   Kaluli triadic interactions (Schieffelin 1979)
      A to B (>C)   Eat! *elema*
      A to B (>C)   Binaria (= C's name)! *elema*
      A to B (>C)   Pandanus. Eat pandanus *elema*

What we have here is a conventionalized routine for a three-party transfer, from A to B to C, which would make A a source, C a target or destination, and B an intermediary, in terms of the categories we have proposed. Things are not quite so simple though: A may be proposing that B do the suggested speech act as if B is *author* – i.e. A may be suggesting that B take it upon himself to author the utterance (or at least act as 'ghostee'). (Indeed it is possible that this is the real (illocutionary) force of *elema*). Here a distinction between proximate sources (in this utterance event) and ultimate sources (in a prior utterance event) may help: even if B delivers the suggested speech act as *author*, A may be an ultimate source. These routines are quite generally done when all three parties are present, so both source and speaker of B's forthcoming utterance is clear enough. However, that co-presence makes problematic the proper analysis of the receiving end. At the very least while A is addressing B, C is A's indirect target. In actual fact, in this particular episode, this was especially clear: just prior to it, C had been begging mother A for pandanus, of which she has already had her share; the mother (A) then angrily picks up an inedible leaf and offers it to C. Thus when A is telling B to tell C to eat pandanus, A is mocking C: C is *indirect target* for A's remarks, which are addressed to B. If we now consider B's responses, where B is only two years old, again our categories become relevant:

<5>   (Schieffelin 1979: 96)

A to B(>C)	Eat! *elema*
B to C	Eat!
A to B(>C)	Binaria. *elema*
B to C	Binaria
A to B(>C)	Pandanus
B to C	Don't eat!
A to B(>C)	Eat pandanus! *elema*
C to A	He (B) says don't eat pandanus [*whining*]

One analysis might be as follows: B happily follows the *elema* instructions until mention of pandanus, whereupon he *authors* the negative imperative 'Don't eat' addressed to C. Just because this particular utterance does not have A as source, C can then complain to A about it, ignoring the irony of A's instruction to B to tell C to eat pandanus. The point is that interactionally these 'triadic' utterances have different consequences from 'dyadic' ones. Schieffelin's claim is that they play a very special role in Kaluli language acquisition, which consequently follows a very different path from Western acquisition patterns: instead of the use of 'motherese' in dyadic interaction, for example, one finds direct demonstration of proper, adult-like interaction by an adult intervening in a child's play with another child (Schieffelin, in press).

Barbadians provide us with another kind of interactional routine, especially distinctive of language usage in the island (Fisher 1976) and possibly the Caribbean in general. They call the routine *dropping remarks*, and an example is as follows:

<6> Barbadian 'dropped remarks' (Fisher 1976)
A to B in the hearing of C I hear you got a new boyfriend

Although clearly addressed to B, the remark is not for B, and if the 'dropped remark' is to come off, B had better not have just acquired a new boyfriend, while the overhearer C should indeed have done so. Only if these conditions are met has A 'dropped a remark' to C (Fisher 1976: 231), and such remarks are always insults or digs. Note that C has to be a non-participant in channel-linkage. Two subtypes of dropped remarks need to be distinguished: in the one case, illustrated immediately above (<6>), C may perhaps not know that the properties attributed by A to B can really only apply to C – i.e. the overhearer may not know that he or she is targetted. In the kind of case illustrated in <7> below, the properties may clearly only apply to the overhearer, leaving C in no doubt about the 'dig', and placing him or her in the role of *targetted overhearer*.

<7> Another Barbadian 'dropped remark'
A to B in the hearing of C Oh, I thought your mouth was burst
(Where C is a woman wearing gaudy lipstick, and B is a man whose lips are perfectly in order.)

(Note that the butt of these remarks is not an *indirect target* of the sort familiar from English interactions (as in <1> above), as he/she is *not a participant* – but a channel-linked non-participating recipient. What is also unfamiliar, from an English point of view, is the technique of 'misaddress' by gaze and posture.)

Fisher's analysis of these and different kinds of exploitations of overhearer role makes use of a small set of categories of the sort employed by Goffman and developed here, and we have both benefited from his observations. Incidentally, Fisher goes on to show that there are important connections to these indirect insults and many details of West Indian culture.

The examples so far are verbal routines drawn largely from those informal, ordinary kinds of talk we call 'conversations'. As Haviland (1986a) points out, however, much insight into the nature of participant roles may accrue from consideration of talk in specialized 'institutional' settings – law courts, seances, religious services, committee meetings and the like – where the gross roles of producer and receiver may be surgically dissected for institutional purposes, testing any analytical set of categories severely. Thus for example, when a counsel interrogates a witness in court, that interrogation is conducted in order to be assessed by (and partly on behalf of) channel-linked adjudicators, namely judge and jury. Hence in cross-examination in a crown court, say, there is an assignment of *participant roles* to *institutional roles* roughly along the following lines (Carr 1983):

<8>   Cross-examination in an English court of law
    Counsel   (1)   speaker (of questions), but not fully source.
                        Since counsel speaks on behalf of client, we perhaps need here to split source into *sponsor* (client) and *spokesman* (counsel). So counsel is speaker and spokesman;
            (2)   addressee (of witnesses' answers; and of judge's rulings on objections, etc.);
    Witness   (1)   speaker (of answers), here more wholly source – however, note that *sponsor* is prosecution or defence, who may also be *ghostor*;
            (2)   addressee (of counsel's questions);
    Jury   (1)   audience;
            (2)   indirect targets;
    Judge   (1)   speaker (and source) of rulings;
            (2)   addressee of objections;
             (3)   indirect target;
            (4)   audience;
    Public gallery   audience or ratified overhearers.

There are many details of interrogation format that display a sensitivity to the fact that the crucial participants (judge and jury) are in audience role (see Levinson 1979; Atkinson & Drew 1979; Drew 1985: 136f.). Clearly, the proper description of such a complex speech event involves the complete specification of such assignments for each and every stage of the proceedings. Although it would be foolish to pretend that such analyses take us far in the understanding of such complex events, they must surely be preliminary to any proper speech-event analysis.

In many cultures, there are professionals who specialize in some of our participant roles: marriage brokers who act as spokesmen and intermediaries (in the speech-event sense), mouthpieces for princes, or orators, poets or advocates who plead for a fee. The Wolof of Senegal are interesting here, with a Bardic caste (Griots) to relieve the great of the need to speak (nobles affect a disdain for both speech and grammar, adopting a lofty ungrammaticality; see Irvine 1974). Members of the caste are useful too in the expression of ritual jealousy (Irvine 1981). For example, during weddings, when the bride is brought to the groom's house for the first time, she is met by a Griot woman who addresses the bride with an elaborate chanted set of slanders and insults aimed at the bride or her kin. This is performed on behalf of the women (including co-wives) of the groom's household. Here the Griot woman is the *spokesman*, the co-wives who bought her services the *sponsors*, the bride the *addressee* and her kin the *indirect targets* (if they are present) and *ultimate destinations* (if they are not).

Finally, one should note that in many cultures the dyadic pattern of the speaker/single-addressee pair dominates in cases where a speaker addresses a group: the storyteller or speech-maker requires a designated responder, who will provide the customary 'back channel', without whom the performance cannot proceed (especially clear, for example, in Mayan languages, see Haviland 1986a; Brown, n.d.). (This is presumably the origin of the sung responses in the English liturgy, to be found in improvised form in Pentacostal services where the preacher's sermon will be punctuated by 'hallelujah' and the like.)

Problematic Aspects: Process and the Attribution of Categories

We have now seen that having some well-developed set of categories for participant roles may be of some utility both to the correct description of deictic categories and to the ethnography of speaking. However, so far we have ignored processual aspects, and in particular how participants, and analysts, might actually assign such categories to other parties during the course of an utterance event. One way of exploring these issues is to examine cases where the attribution of participant role seems to be a problem for participants. We will take up some cases, focusing first on the production then on the reception end, where attribution is a problem for analysts, participants or both; or where the attribution of participant role is demonstrably equivocal.

Source Problems

Clearly, the attributions of the roles of speakers and sources are less likely to be interactional problems than those of non-producers – speakers, after all, are usually visibly, or at least audibly locatable as current transmitters. Of course one can know that a particular someone is speaking without knowing *who* they are – but this is a question of relating participant role to incumbent identity; such problems of identification are of great interest in their own right (see Schegloff 1979), but we merely note here the very important role that voice quality plays in this.

Nevertheless, problems of producer-category assignment do arise, even in face-to-face interaction, and we shall consider some which are problems for analysis and sometimes for participants too. Let us start with another ethnographic example, a case of spirit possession in Tamilnadu. The ethnographic details do not concern us here – we merely note that a woman who has been possessed comes to a NaTTarayan temple, well known for that God's ability to banish spirits. The priest addresses the woman. His problem is: who is he talking to, and who is responding? Ghost or woman? Consider extract <9>:

<9>   Tamil Film 18: Ghost Possession
      P   . . . *onkaarattai solli nii enka uur enkeyeerntu inke vaantaay*
          Say the chant, which place, from where have you
             come?
          iitooTene enne viTTu viTTu inta poNNu naan ille nnu
          Go away at once! 'I am not with this girl'
          oru onkaarattai pooTu
          Chant that!
      W   [*silence*]
      P   *naaTTaya saami peeril pooTu*
          Sing in the God NaaTTarayan's name
      W   *Goovintaa:::::   inta:::::::*
          Govintaar! [God's name]
      P   *sattam* [*momentary recording break*] *yaaru*
          Who is yelling?
      W   *onkaarattai pooTTatu koLLimalai karuppu*
          The one who is yelling is the Kollimalai Ghost

P *koLLimale karupp enke pooce-nnu poNNu enk iruntaay*
   Where did the ghost go? Where did you possess the
   girl? Say!

W *poNN ooTa kaaTTle koNToontu poNN-ooTa piTikka*
   solli veccaankoo
   They said that having taken the girl into the jungle
   (I) was to 'catch' her
   [*W sways violently for a number of seconds*]

P *kaTTuviTTU poNN ellaam*
   Everything has left the girl?
   naaTTa saami peeril nnu kaTTuviTTu kiTTu ellaam
   In the name of NaaTarayan God has it all gone?

W *naaTTaaya saami peeril kaTTuviTTu pooTTeen*
   In the name of NaaTarayan the God I am leaving

P *inta poNNaam kiTTee irukka paTaatu*
   You shouldn't stay with this woman

W *irukka maaTTeen*
   I won't stay

P *seeri muunu onkaaratte pooTu*
   Okay, shout three times

The priest starts off assuming he's talking to the ghost, and tells it
to chant the promise ['I'm going'] in front of the God NaTTarayan
who can enforce it. The woman, swaying violently, chants another
name of the god. The priest then asks ['Who is yelling?']: in context,
this would appear to be ambiguous between a question about
incumbency (is the source a woman or a demon?) and a question
about identity (is the source demon A or demon B?). The demon
takes it the latter way, identifying himself as the Kollimalai ghost
– and the priest asks how he came to possess the woman. Later, after
a period of violent swaying, the priest checks whether the source of
speech is still the ghost or not (*In the name of NaTTarayan, has it all
gone?*) – for the proximate potency of the god may banish the demon
at any moment. The ghost is still the source, but he announces he's
on his way. (It later transpires that there are six more to get rid of!)

The example makes the point that in certain circumstances one
can be clear about who the speaker is without being clear about
whether the speaker is acting as *relayer* or *author*. It also reminds us
that when we have relayers who are not formulating or motivating
the message in any way, we cannot assume that there was some
prior separate speech or utterance event in which the relayer was
informed by the source of what he was to say. Incidentally, note that

the disassociation of source and speaker is marked here by chanting register and dissociated behaviour; in some cultures (e.g. Bali) the possessed speak in an accurate representation of the voice qualities of the dead possessors (see the film *Balinese Trance* by Patsy and Tim Asch).

There are more plodding cases where the *source* can be in doubt. One is a standard kind of interviewer response in news interviews, namely the reformulation, of the sort 'So, you're really accusing them of profiteering' (Heritage 1985: 109), where the reformulation may just be a summing up of what the other said for the benefit of overhearers (the radio listeners), but may be an aggressive probe that will be resisted. Another kind of common case is a certain kind of sarcasm, as in <10>, where towards the end, in response to constant goading by F and after a series of escalating 'out-loud' protests, C says softly 'Imperial mission, example to the world'. Clearly, C is not *author*; rather he is attributing the utterance to F as *motivator* (or *sponsor*), although, given the extreme formulation, F is likely to resist the imputation (see <22> below).

<10>   Stop the Week (8/5/82: Aiwa 191)
          C = Bernard Crick, F = Anthony Flew
          F   . . . now if um these trip-wire forces many of
               which are all around the world and by *far* the
               most important is in West Berlin if these if one of
               these is allowed to be over-run with no response
               and people all say 'Oh well it's ridiculous to fight
               a war over this' [as many
          C   ➝   [*sigh*]
          F   people said it was ridiculous to fight a war over
               Danzig .hh someone else will try it. The
               Venezuelans are already looking to knock out a
               bit of Guyana, which might be ⌈(a very good thing)
          C   ➝   ⌊(Good God)
          F   ⌈There are half a dozen other places in– in Africa
           | where
          C   ⌊[*softly*] Imperial mission, example to the world! ◄
          F   people are eager to – but above all there's West
               Berlin

To see that people can take it upon themselves to speak for others, consider sentence-completions by others. In <11> we have a jokey completion, accepted by the first speaker. Note that the first speaker was evidently having a 'word-search' problem – presumably for the item 'flowers'. Had B supplied that item, we might say that he had merely transmitted (*relayed*) what A had *devised* – it being clear exactly what item A had in mind. But B supplies what is, as it were, an improvement, a jokey substitute ('shrimps' for 'flowers of shrimp plant'). Besides, he offers it not in the way that other-repair is normally done (with a tentative offer, like 'you mean flowers?' – q.v. Schegloff, Jefferson & Sacks 1977), but rather in the way that self-repair is normally done, that is immediately, after a 'cut-off'. Thus the sentence completion has a deeply equivocal status – built like a speaker's self-repair, it incorporates the other's inventiveness. The first speaker accepts the offering with an appreciative laugh, in laughing acknowledging the other's contribution. More straightforwardly, in <12> we have a neutral chairman completing, for the sake of brevity, BK's statement of his position.

<11>　Gardening Questions (Partic Tape B: Aiwa 45)
　　　　A　　. . . and it's the most descriptive name ever,
　　　　　　the shrimp plant because it looks like a –
　　　　　　what eighteen inch high bush covered with little
　　　　　　shrimps . . .
　　　　　　[*some mins later*]
　　　　　　And then wait until it starts just into growth
　　　　　　again and then knock it out and repot it ur (.)
　　　　　　if possible into only one pot bigger, don't give
　　　　　　it too much to work on or it runs to leaf instead
　　　　　　of er –
　　　　B　　→ Shrimps!
　　　　A　　instead of shrimps heh

<12>　(continuation of <23>)
　　　　BK　There's a resolution-
　　　　　　[*some turns later*]
　　　　CH　I think you are referring to the calling of a
　　　　　　ceasefire
　　　　BK　Certainly, resolution 502 =
　　　　CH　= it calls for a cease-fire ←

Sentence completions by others are used interactionally for various purposes (see Sacks 1965–72 for many observations), but one reason of course is precisely to display collaboration, or joint telling (Sacks 1971: Lecture on 19 October) – in short to display joint authorship through doing it together! (The alternative, joint simultaneous production or chorus, being harder to achieve on a sustained improvisational basis.) It is arguable (and surely Goffman would have so argued) that it is the peculiar production status of jointly authored sentences that accounts for their interactional uses. On the other hand, these sorts of examples raise the fundamental question whether the collaborative nature of verbal interaction does not make inherently problematic the attribution of participant role. The linguistic, philosophical and psychological traditions treat the utterance as 'the product of a single speaker and a single mind', whereas 'the conversation-analytic angle of inquiry does not let go of the fact that . . . more than one participant is present and relevant to the talk, even when only one does any talking' (Schegloff 1982: 72), non-verbal feedback often serving to guide the production of an utterance (Goodwin 1979, 1981 and see below). The issue cannot be pursued here, but it is of course of considerable importance to the present enterprise.

Other cases where producing roles can get complex are of course when individuals speak in the institutional role of spokesman (using the term in the speech-event sense) – they may at times speak for themselves as well as for others (acting in *author* role but as representatives of other like-minded *principals*), while at other times they may act as mere *relayers* (for some *indirect source*) or *spokesman* (for some *principal*) in our restricted participant role sense (see table 7.4). The potential vagueness of the participant role associated with the institutional role is of course an exploitable resource – the utterances of official spokesmen can be repudiated if expedient. One sometimes wonders just what role institutional spokesmen, or persons other than the official source, have in the formulation of the message, and the White House transcripts provide some interesting glimpses here. In <13> Nixon and Ehrlichman prepare (or *ghost*) a presidential statement: in throwing out ideas they are not producing statements for this series of utterance events, but for some future series in which the President will be source (*ghostee* in my awkward terminology) and Ehrlichman *ghostor* or *formulator*.[20]

<13> White House Transcripts (*New York Times* edition, p. 702)
E = Ehrlichman, P = President Nixon
(Preparing a Presidential statement)
E . . . how about going on with the next sentence?

> P 'The judicial process is moving to get all the facts.' Or, 'Moving –'
> E 'moving ahead as it should'
> P 'Moving ahead as it should. As I have said before all government employees, especially members of the White House staff, are to fully cooperate with the Grand Jury.' Or do we want to say 'Grand Jury'?
> E How about 'fully cooperate' period
> P 'Fully cooperate in this investigation', 'to fully cooperate with law enforcement authorities'. How's that?

Problematics of the Reception End

Given the 'broadcast quality' of the vocal-auditory channel, it will come as no surprise that there are often interactional difficulties in assigning addressees, recipients and other non-producing roles; but it is also noteworthy that these very difficulties are often exploited for interactional purposes (as in the Barbadian 'dropped remarks', that make for unaccountable and deniable insults). But let us begin by seeing that speakers often have to work hard to gain satisfactory addressees. Consider <14>:

	<14>	(from Goodwin 1979, with simplifications)
1	*J*	I gave, I gave up smoking cigarette::s =
2	(*J to D*)	_____ _____
3	(*D to J*)	_____
4	*D*	= yeah
5	*J*	I – uh one – *one* week ago t'da:y. acshilly
6	(*J to B*)	_____
7	(*J to A*)	_____
8	(*B to J*)	((no gaze))
9	(*A to B*)	____
10	(*A to J*)	___

Goodwin gives a complex micro-analysis of this one sentence of J's (*viz.*: 'I gave up smoking cigarettes, one week ago today, actually'), which relies upon an analysis of gaze as a device for selecting an addressee. He argues that during the course of the production of this single sentence, J shifts addressee three times, to D, from D to B, and from B to A. He argues that there is a rule, crudely, that speakers should gaze at addressees, and addressees should recognize this by making eye-contact (see also later formulation in Goodwin 1981: 74–5). In the transcript, simplified from Goodwin's, gaze is indicated on the lines below the utterance in question, by a line, with gazer and gazee in the margin.

The argument then proceeds roughly as follows. J starts off talking, fails to get gaze, re-starts (this being a conventional 'request' for an addressee), looks at D (line 2), who finally looks at him (line 3), and slips in the response *yeah* (line 4). Now it turns out that J thinks D doesn't know this piece of news (that J gave up smoking), and that D's response (*yeah*) is hardly of an appropriate sort (cf. 'Fantastic!', 'Oh good for you', etc.); J therefore shifts gaze in search of some more sympathetic addressee, settling on B (line 6). B however is a co-habitant with J, and therefore J's giving up smoking is hardly news for B; thus in switching addressees from D to B, J switches from a telling of news (the giving up smoking) to the announcement of an 'anniversary' (a week without the weed – line 5). Yet B's gaze does not move to engage J's (line 8); and having failed to elicit B as addressee, J seeks out A (line 7), who has displayed attendance by looking at B (line 9) for the non-forthcoming response. J's switch to A (not a knower of the news) requires once again a switch from the announcement of an anniversary of some old news, to an announcement of some new news, a switch partly achieved by the insertion of *actually*. And towards the end of *actually*, J finally gains an addressee, namely A (line 10). (But see Goodwin for detailed justification.)

Some important points that emerge from Godwin's argument are these: (a) a single unit, whether sentence token or turn, can have different persons in the same participant roles throughout the course of its production. Hence the importance of the *incumbency/role* distinction. This is in part detectable by the study of gaze (although this will certainly not work in gaze-avoidance cultures like the Highland Mayan Indians of Chiapas; cf. Goodwin 1981: 57n.); in part by the study of ongoing reformulation of an utterance, so that parts can be seen to be directed at some addressees, other parts at other addressees (here, the *news/anniversary of the news* distinction); (b) a speaker may be assured of an *audience* and yet lack satisfactory *addressees* (a point also made by the widespread cultural practice, noted above (see also Haviland 1986a), of requiring a single designated responder when telling a story to a group); and (c) persons can control, at least to some extent, whether or not they will be incumbents of participant roles for which they are selected by speaker (or, in ethnomethodological terms, incumbency is *negotiable*).

Notice the implications of Goodwin's analysis for my concept of *utterance event*: if this is a unit defined by constancy of the mapping of participant roles onto individuals, then this single sentence and short turn is constituted of no less than three utterance events. Now I want to pick on two particular reception problems, those associated with *out-louds* and *indirectly targetted utterances*.

Out-louds[21]

We have already mentioned out-louds as interesting in that, on one analysis, they do not seem to presume any roles other than speaker (on another, they presume but one incumbent of both speaker and addressee roles). Given this, out-louds have their uses when used in channel-linkage to other parties, e.g. in beginning a conversation with a stranger without unequivocally taking a first conversational step (Goffman 1981b: 100). So we find utterances produced as out-louds that actually have recipients and targets in mind. A relatively simple case is <15> from a radio 'phone-out': the compere is dialling up a member of the public, who will then be on the air, to wish whichever member of the couple answers the phone a happy wedding anniversary. While we radio listeners, the overhearers, are waiting through the ringing of the telephone, the compere is producing the sort of now-hopeless, now-hopeful out-louds one might produce, or think, to oneself when no-one answers at the other end. They are responses to the situation, tucked neatly between and responsive to the ringings of the phone – in Goffman's (1981b) terminology *response cries* – and are not addressed or directed to anyone. Yet, in an obvious way, they are essentially for the radio audience; not only do they fill an awkward gap created by this broadcast format, they also serve to keep us posted about how long the compere is likely to hang on:

<15>   Radio Phone-out (Partic: Aiwa 336)
        (A is telephoning B: the radio audience can hear both
        ends) [*telephone rings*]
    A   Hopefully it's Penny and Steve Davis [*ring-ring*]
        They're celebrating their wedding anniversary
        today [*ring-ring*]
        They won't want to get out of bed too early will
        they [*ring-ring*]
     ➤ huh huh huh huh (.) [*gloomily*] huh huh [*ring-
        ring*]

➤ huh huh huh [*resignedly*]
➤ hmm [*ring-ring; sound of receiver being picked up*]
➤ Oh hang on!
B　Hello?
A　Is that Steve?
B　Yeah
A　Hello mate Pete Wagstaff calling from Chiltern
　　Radio

More complicated, but perhaps clearer, is the 'Oh God' in
<16>, which is of a recurrent type. Here we have a well-known
broadcaster on astronomy groaning at the use of the phrase 'moon-
shuttle'. Note that the groan occurs *sotto voce* and in overlap right
after the offending term. The groan could be a sheer reflex (like
'ouch'), but a version of it is repeated a shade louder at the end of
the offending turn. Note the switch from 'Oh God' to 'Oh dear!',
which seems to be a reformulation of the out-loud for overhearers.
As Goffman (1981b: 97) puts it, 'A man who utters 'fuck' when he
stumbles in the foundry is quite likely to avoid that particular
expletive should be trip in a day nursery'. (Goffman also notes that
having once embarked on talking to oneself, one is under obligation
to explain it – motivating the repetition, which seems to be a
common feature). Again, like the preceding 'Oh God', we can't say
that this 'Oh dear' is addressed to anyone. But the second
occurrence at least is fairly clearly *for* the studio audience (in *audience*
role) and radio listeners (in *overhearer* role), by virtue of three features
(a) it is said louder, (b) it occurs clear of overlap, (c) it is
reformulated for public consumption. The audience promptly
laughs, and the chairman then treats it as a turn out of turn.

<16>　'Patrick Moore' (Partic: 1982: IA: Aiwa 464)
　　　　CH　Let's move on now please to another question
　　　　M　　Marie Higgins (.)
　　　　　　　Would the team agree (.) that the millions of
　　　　　　　dollars now spent on a moon-shuttle (.) ⌈could
　　　　PM　　　　　　　　　　　　　　　　　　　　　　　⌊Oh God
　　　　M　　be better utilized to solve the problems of this
　　　　　　　planet =
　　　　PM　　= Oh dear!
　　　　　　　(.)
　　　　CH　huh⌈-huh-huh
　　　　AUD　　⌊[*crescendoing laughter*]

     CH   Well you just wait a moment Patrick – you just
           hold on. We'll have your professional expertise
           a little later

In panel sessions, where turns are strictly allocated, such devices
for getting a turn out of turn are quite frequently used: there's
another case in <17>, and it shows the same repetition of the out-
loud, with greater amplitude, the escalation eliciting an audience
response that makes it impossible to ignore what serves to disrupt
the proceedings but (being unaddressed and officially not part of the
proceedings) cannot be viewed as an interruption (see also
<21> below).

   <17>   Question Time (I, Ulster: VHS1: JVC 382)
           (*CH* = chairman, *AM* = Agnes McCormack, Socialist,
           JP = Jim Prior; *A* = Audience)
           CH   I'd like a brief reply on that from Mr Prior and
                then we'll move on
           JP   [*gazing at A*] Well I agree with that
                and I think that ⌈the-
           AM [*softly*]   ⌊ Good God! ←
           JP ⌈the more-
           AM ⌊Good God!   [*louder*] ←
               [*JP glances at AM, and grimaces*]
               [*Laughter*]
           JP   I don't know whether that'll get me into trouble
                or not but er (.) I think we do tend to put
                labels on people . . .

Now while on the first occurrence such out-louds might be held to
presuppose no other participant role than speaker, on the second or
later escalation they might arguably be held to presuppose not only
an appreciative audience role but also, perhaps, an indirect target
role for the individual whose utterance they respond to. But perhaps
they achieve what they achieve just by being precisely equivocal over
what participant roles they project: for if a second occurrence is
recognizably the 'same thing' as an earlier occurrence, but the
earlier occurrence has the low-profile characteristics (low amplitude,
eclipsed by overlap) of a guarded response cry produced in polite
company, then the second occurrence cannot be unequivocally an
addressed or targetted turn even though it occurs loud and clear of
any other turn! Again, the Goffmanian analysis would be, I take it,

that it is the peculiar reception status of 'out-louds' that accounts for their sequential properties (e.g. escalations with audience appreciations) and their interactional uses (like getting a turn when turns have been allocated to other parties).

One very important reason for being interested in out-louds is that they seem to play a special role in language acquisition. Child-language researchers have elaborate categories to call such things (e.g. Dore's *labellings, practicings*, etc. – see Atkinson 1982: 148ff.), but they do not seem to have closely attended to the special participant role configurations of children's utterances. In <18> for example, the child's utterances are perhaps without exception out-louds which are responses to either the cars passing outside, or the toy car within. The adult's attempts to engage the child in conversation, and to interpret the utterances as directed at him or her, may then be based on a strategy of wilfully interpreting these out-louds as actually addressed or at least indirectly targetted utterances. But it would be a mistake to make the same wilful interpretation as an analyst (note how the transcriber in noting 'whining' seems to be making just such an attribution).

<18>   (simplified from Greenfield 1979: 161)
     Ch   [*car going by outside*] car
     Ad   What's the car doing? Where's it going?
     Ch   Byebye, byebye
           [*pointing to his toy car, 'whining'*] car, car
     Ad   You want your car?
     Ch   [*pushing car*] byebye, byebye, rr-hh-mm
           [*patting car*] beep-beep
           [*hears car going by outside*] car! car! car!
           [*looking for toy car which has fallen*] car
     Ad   Whatcha doing?
     Ch   [*throwing toy car down*] down, down, car
           [*car going by outside*] car
           [*looks for toy car*] car

It is interesting to speculate on the reasons for the prevalence of 'out-louds' in children's speech: they might be attributed, of course, to some Piagetian tendency to egocentric thought; or they could be attributed to the same factors accounting for their frequency in chaired discussions as in the earlier examples – namely as devices for evading restricted rights to speak. Alternatively, they might be interpreted as devices addressed to a more fundamental issue – namely limited participation rights; if children are often treated as channel-linked overhearers, then an 'out-loud' recommends itself for just the same reasons as 'Phew, at last' does in a bus-queue – it invites participation without demanding it, and if ignored (as childrens' utterances no doubt largely are) implies no snub and thus no loss of face. Viewed from this perspective, the verbal ecology of the child perhaps looks rather bleak, seeking momentary participation rights by virtue of attention-inducing out-louds. In any case, the fact that out-louds appear to be characteristic of childrens' speech certainly recommends their serious study.

Indirect targets

Let us turn now to another class of utterance which pose specific problems for the analysis of reception roles, namely indirectly targetted utterances. We may begin by returning to example <1>:

> <1   (from Sacks, Schegloff and Jefferson 1974: 717)
>   *Sharon* You didn' come tuh talk tuh Karen?
>   *Mark*   No, Karen- Karen 'n I're having a fight,
>   (0.4)
>   *Mark*   after she went out with Keith an' not with
>   (me)
>   *Ruthie* Hah hah hah hah
>   *Karen*   Wul Mark, you never asked me out.

Applying our categories to describe the participant roles involved in Mark's utterance(s), he is presumably *author*; but who is/are *recipients*? We have already pointed out that while Sharon is the apparent *addressee*, Karen is the *indirect target*, and that we know this in part because of linguistic features of person (*she* for Karen), and in part because of interactional expectations to do with responses to questions normally being directed at the questioner (making Sharon addressee), and to do with blamings eliciting justifications or excuses (hence Karen's response). To take another similar case:

> <19>   (from Sacks 1974: 338)
>   *K* You wanna hear muh - eh my sister told me a
>   story last night
>   *R* I don't want to hear it. But if you must.
>   (1.0)
>   *A* What's purple an' an island. Grape-Britain.
>   ➤ That's what iz sis//ter -

K   No. To stun me she says uh there was these three ,
        girls
        [*dirty story follows*]

A's utterance here is in various ways *disaffiliated* from K's offer to tell a story: he's suggesting, for one thing, that the kind of story will be the 'kiddy humour' illustrated by 'Grape-Britain'. But another way A's remark is disaffiliated is that it treats K as (at most) *audience*, (and, at least, possibly as mere *overhearer*), by virtue of the indicated participant role: for A uses third-person *his sister* to refer to the person K referred to with *my sister*. Thus the *author* of A's utterance (or turn) is A; the *addressee* is R (and perhaps others present); the *indirect target* is K. (Note the possibility that the first part of the utterance was in fact addressed to K – just as R's response is; while A might have then turned to others seeking appreciation for his put-down – but we have no video record.)

One circumstance in which utterances are often indirectly targetted are media political discussions, with a panel and studio audience. (And perhaps the occurrence of such utterances is in general typical of chaired meetings, where the chairman may be formally addressed but others intended – as in the parliamentary manner of 'Now, Mr Speaker, the Right Honourable Member for Tewkesbury North seems to be quite unaware of the 1957 Act'.) In any case, in such political panels, simply by an identification of participants with political parties, accusations of political incompetence (etc.) can readily pick out a representative of a political party as a non-addressed recipient, or *indirect target*. Typically, the non-addressed target immediately responds, as in <20> (and in <1> and <19> of course):

<20>   Question Time (I/I: VHS 1: JVC 662)
        BB = Betty Boothroyd, Labour MP
        WC = Winston Churchill, Conservative
        A = Audience
        LM = Lord Mayhew
        BB   [*gazing at A*] . . . my government left Sea-Wolf
        ➡ as a missile to be developed by the Conservative
        ➡ government. I hate to make this political
              but that's what it's all about isn't it, and it has
              not been yet fully developed so that – for use in
              that area =
        WC   = Hold on hold on Betty, you can't get away
              with that [*BB gazing at WC*] ⬅

LM (Huh)
BB Okay [*BB turns away to A and gestures*]
      Over to you! huh huh huh huh
      [*Laughter*]
WC [*gazing at BB*] The – the ships that are down
      there are ships that have been by and large
      developed and deployed over the last 15 years
      . . .

This has some theoretical interest because it throws light on the concept of an *addressee*. For example, it is tempting to claim that an addressee is in part identifiable as someone with a priority right of response; thus Lyons (1977: 34) writes 'The sender may then include as part of the signal some feature which identifies the intended receiver or *addressee*, and invites him to pay attention to, or respond to, the signal'; and Goffman (1981b: 133) identifies the 'addressed recipient' as 'the one to whom the speaker addresses his visual attention and to whom, incidentally, he expects to turn over his speaking role'. But indirect targets seem in the majority of cases to be the immediate responders, in contrast to the overt addressees (as in <1>, <19>, <20>) (and even where they desist from verbal response, they may be expected to produce visual displays – cf. <21> below and Goodwin 1984). A related issue is whether there is some close connection between the concept of *addressee* and what one may call the *illocutionary goal*. Clark and Carlson (1982) discussing examples like 'The last one of you to leave the room, turn off the light', claim that all present are the recipients of an *informative* illocutionary act, but only one, namely the last one to leave, is the recipient of the request. But a simpler analysis would be that the addressees are all those denoted by *you*, while the illocutionary goal is that addressee who is last to leave. But in any case, what the immediate responses by indirect targets show is that there is no close relation between illocutionary goal and conversational responder, which would seem to make the whole concept of illocution not a possible basis for a theory of discourse structure.

A central question about such indirectly targetted utterances is this: given that features of address in such utterances are not indications of the intended recipients, how does the recipient know that he is being targetted, and how do we as observers and analysts make such judgements? Recognition seems to be based on regular features of such utterances. Firstly, they occur in certain specific sequential environments; for example, in the political panel sessions investigated a typical pattern was as follows:

T1 A [*says something employing the description D*]
T2 B [*while addressing C but* not *A,
       challenges the description D*]
T3 A [*addressing B, defends the description D*]

Turn 2 is thus typically tied back to T1 by a repetition of some key lexical item or phrase (as will be illustrated in <21> below).

In addition to such sequential clues, recipients of indirectly targetted utterances may recognize that they are recipients by features of the turn (or turn part) – although addressed to others. It will concern them (typically, as above, by being an attack on what they have previously said); though lacking address, there may be third-person reference to themselves, or else they may find a description that includes themselves (e.g. 'anybody who talks about [keyword] . . .'). Finally, immediately at the end of the indirectly targetted turn, the recipient will note that he is being monitored by speaker and audience to see just how he is taking it. Thus we get momentary glances, or even full gaze, at just that point. If there were no such systematic clues, such indirect targettings would of course be indiscernible, and miss their targets.

The example in <21> is perhaps unusually explicit and transparent, but will thus serve well to illustrate the phenomenon. Here PJ (Peter Jenkins, well-known journalist) addresses a participating studio audience in a BBC panel-discussion series called *Question Time* – on this occasion the discussion takes place in Ulster (N Ireland) with a local audience. PJ tells the audience that they are not like the English (which becomes the keyword), gesticulating to himself and thus disaffiliating himself from the Northern Irish audience. His opponent, MR (Mervyn Rees, ex-Northern Ireland Secretary) then utilizes the sequence of upgraded out-louds that we have discussed in order to obtain an allocation of turn from the chairman: in that turn he purposely turns towards the audience, and while gazing at them gestures at PJ – however he is drowned by continuing audience applause and laughter and turns back to the table; on its subsiding, he turns again to the audience and delivers the indirectly targetted utterance 'There you heard the complete English view of Northern Ireland!', complete with keyword. The TV editor instinctively and immediately selects a picture of PJ (just as any interactant would naturally look to him at this point to see how he was taking the indirect attack) – but he fails to produce a quick retort and instead produces a facial display of discomfiture or embarrassment. Meanwhile there's audience applause at the jab.

<21>   Question Time: (Ulster VHS 1 JVC 310)
         PJ = Peter Jenkins; *MR* = Mervyn Rees
         PJ   [*gazing at audience throughout*] . . . it's no good
                     complaining to Westminster and saying why
             → don't – complaining to the English [*indicates
                     self*]
                     and saying 'Why don't you treat us like
                     everybody else?' You're not like everybody
                     else!
         MR   Nonsense [*sotto voce outloud*]
                     [*audience laughter and applause*]
                     [*PJ glances round table to find source of out-loud*]
         MR   Nonsense [*louder out-loud*]
         CH   Mervyn? [*pointing to MR*]
                     [*MR turns to Audience and gestures to PJ*]
         MR   Well the ⌐ (2.0) [*MR turns away as if to blow
                                                               nose*]
                           ⌊ [*drowning audience laughter*]
             →   [*gazing at audience*] there you heard the
                     complete
             →   English view of Northern Ireland!
             →   of Northern Ireland [*gaze to Audience*]
         PJ   ⌐ [*Visual display of embarrassment*]
                     ⌊ [*Audience crescendoing applause*]
         MR   [*gazing at PJ*] because Peter as much as er
                     (.) it used to strike me sometimes
                     that a large number of people didn't like me
                     very much and maybe not Jim and maybe
                     others I tell you that people of Northern
                     Ireland are the same sort of people Catholic
                     or Protestant as the other side of the [*turns to
                     Aud*] water
         Audience   [*Applause*]
         MR   [*gaze to PJ*] I really feel that
         MR   [*turning to Aud*] Except in one respect
                     [*Laughter*]
                     [*MR talks on, gazing at Audience*]
                     . . . I want nobody to be in the United
                     Kingdom to be there by force they must be

> there because they want to be there and that
> is not something that I could support, I am
> fervently against integration [*turns towards
> PJ*] but Peter for heaven's sake they may
> have different sorts of politics but this
> English view that you put forward is one
> reason why the English will never ever solve
> it [*turns to Audience*]
> ⌈A Welshman by birth [*points to self*]

Audience   ⌊[*Applause*]

The recurrent features of indirectly targetted utterances (as they occur in such panel discussions) are here instantiated:

1 the target-to-be produces the offending description, with the keyword 'English';
2 the indirectly targetted utterance appears in second position, although not strictly in second turn given the constraints of the allocated turn-taking system in such panel discussions, which require the prior negotiation of the right to reply;
3 the indirectly targetted utterance contains the offending keyword, and although it lacks any features of address to PJ (gaze being directed at the audience) there was an abortive gesture towards him; further, the implied description ['the articulator of the English view of Northern Ireland'] clearly applies to PJ;
4 immediately at the end of the indirectly targetted turn, the two normal events occur: (a) the target is monitored for signs of discomfort, brave comportment or retaliation; and (b) audience appreciation is expressed; and
5 although the target fails to retaliate, that response may be held to have been 'conditionally relevant' in the sense that a slot is provided for it (MR stops after the indirectly targetted utterance), and its absence constitutes an acknowledgement of 'defeat'.

The rest of the extract is provided here partly because it contains further evidence for the underlying mechanisms involved in recognizing an indirectly targetted utterance. As noted, the original offending turn by PJ affiliated PJ with 'the English' and disaffiliated him from the 'Irish' audience. MR's attack then made use of this affiliation, by including PJ amongst those with the English view of

N Ireland – and thus by implication excluding MR from the affiliation. Note then that MR ends the extract with a gesture to himself,
accompanying the utterance 'A Welshman by birth', which precisely
mirrors PJ's gesture to himself accompanying 'the English'.

The remainder of the extract also makes the point that a skilled
orator can make considerable use of rapid switches of participant
role assignments. As MR continues after the indirectly targetted
utterance, there are a series of switches of reception roles, six in all,
so that at one moment the audience is being addressed with PJ as
indirect target, the next PJ is being addressed with the audience as
indirect target, with these switches being indicated both by
swivelling of the body and determinate gaze movements. Once
again it is clear that the notion of an utterance event as that unit of
speech with a constant constellation of participant roles (and
incumbents of them) has the consequence that a single turn may
consist of multiple utterance events. Note incidentally that applause
is appropriate from the audience (in the speech-event sense) when in
either addressee role (as after the utterance 'the complete English
view . . .') or in indirect target role (as after the utterance beginning
'Because Peter . . .') – the right to applaud being apparently indifferent to various kinds of reception role.

The example in <21> serves to indicate, I hope, that an
utterance can have a recipient clearly distinct from the addressee,
and we – whether as analysts or participants – can be left in no doubt
about who is indirectly targetted. Sometimes, though, the
participants themselves can indeed be in doubt. For example,
<22> illustrates that the misattribution of *indirect target* role can
sometimes be suspected by participants. Thus P's 'anyone who has
genuine compassion' (arrowed) is a response to T, but also a
possible follow up of earlier attacks on C (see <10>, which comes
some eight minutes earlier in the same discussion; just prior to that
extract there is a characterization of C as ['hating Thatcher'] which
is part of what C is responding to in <22>). It may therefore be
interpreted as an indirectly targetted utterance. C jumps in with a
retort, but the chairman (CH) intervenes to question whether C was
really the indirect target rather than T ('I don't think he was aiming
his views at you Bernard . . . he had Laurie in his eye when he was
speaking').

<22>   Stop the Week (Aiwa 425: 8/5/82)
        CH = Chairman, Robert Robinson,
        C = Bernard Crick, socialist and philosopher

F = Antony Flew, conservative and philosopher
T = Laurie Taylor

T   . . . I suppose that there was an acknowledged
     war [in Vietnam] and America seemed involved
     in it and saw the issue of world communism as
     a threat .hh

F ➔ I think that anyone who has any genuine
     compassion for human beings as opposed to
     being a doctrinaire socialist and pro-Soviet
     figure .hh would have some sympathy
         ⌜for the victims of the::
C   ⌞Oh I very much resent these silly
     things like my hatred of Thatcher – I hate her
     policy towards unemployment I think her policy
     on Ireland is excellent so don't *im*pute
         ⌜the things – the stereotypes
CH   ⌞I don't think he was aiming (his views) at
     you Bernard =

C   = no I mean this is a stereotype of intellectual
     socialism and I'm speaking ⌜as a philosopher
CH ➔   ⌞He had Laurie in
     his eye ⌜when he was speaking
C   ⌞and you huhuh

C   and you are ranting as a-a:::: Tory

T   As Milton will tell you I'm a well known pro-
         ⌜Soviet advocate
F   ⌞Well

F   Look =

CH   = You must have a point to make
         ⌜I'm sure Anthony
F   ⌞We are threatened-
     we are threatened, you may not worry about it
     because you may be a CND supporter I am
     worried about it
         ⌜because I care for my country
C   ⌞Well no we've heard the (   ) of both
     parties

F   We are threatened by the ever-
         ⌜extending Soviet emp-
C   ⌞mocking stereotypes

F   empire(.) now people in the Kremlin are
     watching this as they are watching everything

else (.) if we do not back up the marines who
were overrun if we do not do that they will
think 'What about West Berlin?' and I'm sure
that Bernard Crick will be saying 'Why should
one have a conflict over West Berlin – just let
the Russians have it', then they'll make the
next move

CH Oh I don't think you can make up his
argument for him

    ⌈ he's perfectly competent at it ⌈
?   ⌊ huh huh

F   ⌊ Just-

CH Now Bernard

The fact that whom F was 'aiming at' can be explicitly a conversational issue suggests that participants are indeed monitoring utterances for more participant roles than just speaker and addressee.
This is of course a more direct line of argument that participant role
assignment is an ongoing task that preoccupies participants, and is
not just a problem of *post-hoc* analytical categorization. The other
line of argument that we have been developing is less direct, but
more powerful if it can be sustained: namely, we can attempt to
show that 'out-louds', 'indirectly targetted utterances', etc., are
utterances with particular interactional and sequential properties
which follow directly from their characteristic participant role
projections.[22]

I offer now a final example of the second kind of argument. Can
we show that participants are constantly alert to the possibility that
they will be cast by the speaker into one or another reception role,
where each such role has different consequences for action and
displays of participation? Consider the following conventional
peculiarity of English vocatives: normally, names can only figure in
vocative expressions if they occur as first names alone, or title-plus-
last name. (There are exceptions of course: those bred at English
private schools, or serving in the armed forces, may feel able to use
last names alone in vocative expressions – but the sociolinguistic
value of such usages would appear to be precisely in their contrastive
nature.) Thus in saying, for example, 'Bruce Kent' in the presence
of Bruce Kent, there will be a point during the production of the
phrase where what is coming might be a vocative of direct address
(namely 'Bruce'), that possibility evaporating with the appearance
of the initial consonant of 'Kent' ('Bruce Kent' not being, outside

roll-calls and the like, a possible English vocative[23]). A second relevant point is that although vocatives have remarkably free syntactic placement, as a major indicator of address they perhaps normally occur in utterance-initial position. Now consider the following extract:

<23>   Question Time (II: VHS 1: JVC 595)
       BB = Betty Boothroyd, Labour MP
       LM = Lord Mayhew, *BK* = Bruce Kent, CND
       WC = Winston Churchill, *CH* = Chairman
       A = Audience
       BB   [*gaze at A*] . . . this is where the United Nations
            has an enormous role to play in monitoring that
            withdrawal in seeing to it that we also withdraw
            our forces from around that area and for them to
            move in and I believe very sincerely that this is
            our only salvation
       CH   [*gaze at BK*] Bruce Kent?
       BK   [*gaze at A*] Well of course one has to move if – if
            you get into intransigent positions, you have to
            shift because life goes on and there will be a
            solution. In ten years time we'll look back and
            say 'I wonder how did we get into this jam?'.
            Everybody has to move. General de Gaulle er
            was the saviour of Algiers for the French er
            colonists but in a few years he'd worked around
            and he left and all was done. Of course we have
            to compromise [*slight head nod to BB*]
       → I'm just amazed to hear Betty talking about
            this upholding of the United Nations [*turns back
            to A*] but precisely what we're doing is in
            violation of the United Nations =
       BB   [*gaze at A*] = No
       BK   That is the critical ⌈point
       BB   [*at A*]   ⌊No no [*out-loud*]
       WC   [*gazing at BK*] [*shakes head*]
       LM   [*gazing at BK*] No
       BK   [*gazing at A*] That is to be got over very
            strongly =
       BB   = No [*upgraded out-loud*]
       BK   We asked for a resolution we got a resolution
            and now we are on this madcap course which

puts our fleet at grave peril. One doesn't – you
don't have to be a pacifist or non-pacifist to
think that this operation has no intelligent end.
What can victory actually mean? We succeed in
killing another couple of thousand to put people
ashore on the Falkland Islands and then what?
What is that victory mean that is what I'm
asking

BB→[*gazing at BK*?] No Bruce K– [*BK looks at BB*]
[*BK takes a drink*]
You know Bruce Kent is quite wrong, we are
not in violation of the United Nations charter
[*BB moves gaze from BK round table and back*]
we must not allow ⌈them to get away with this
BK   [*to A*?]   ⌊(there's a) resolution
                                      resolution
BB   No you – you talk about the resolution. I have it
in front of me [*in breath*] Article – Article 51

Here BK attacks BB ('Betty') in the first arrowed utterance in the
third person, with body position and gaze firmly away from BB and
to the audience. In response BB produces *No's* that seem to be out-
louds (low amplitude, vague gaze) – finally getting in a proper
response at the second arrowed utterance. Here, though, she starts
off with a term of reference that could be a term of address ('Bruce')
– precisely at this point Bruce Kent rapidly glances up at BB,
presumably to check if she is gazing at (and thus addressing) him.
He starts to turn away again after the initial 'K–' that indicates that
'Bruce' was in fact the first part of a third-person reference form and
not a possible vocative. But simultaneously BB, presumably
monitoring that glance, does a self-repair and abandons that
utterance-initial placing of the name: 'No Bruce K– you know Bruce
Kent is quite wrong'. Now, Goodwin (1981: 60ff.) has shown that
such re-starts are closely involved in the search for addressees, and
even where addressees are attending may request the attention of
further addressees (1981: 61, n. 8). Thus it seems certain here that
BB is engaged in deft work to undo the apparent address of 'Bruce',
the re-start being reinforced by gaze movement around the panel.
Incidentally, a factor that predisposes BK to think he may be being
addressed is the tendency we have noted, and which is exemplified
at the end of this extract, for an indirect target to respond with direct

address to the targetter, and he (BK) had just previously indirectly targetted BB (first arrowed utterance).

In any case, it is through examples of this sort that one may hope to make the argument that utterances are constantly monitored by participants for the participant roles that they project, and that deft footwork may be required to make mid-stream adjustments consequent to signs that the projections have been misunderstood.

Turning away from indirect targets, let me just point out that further kinds of reception role are amenable to study. For example, there are many ways in which utterances can be designed for overhearers. (Good clues are provided by the use of sociolinguistic 'markers', e.g. address forms – thus academics may switch from a first name to a title plus last-name exchange in the presence of students.) Nowhere is this more obvious than on the radio, where interviews often have a curious quality in that the interviewer states what the interviewee clearly already knows well (for example an interviewer addresses a newly elected mayor of humble origin with 'You were a very good milkman, you did a double round'), and in so doing reveals a depth of knowledge about the subject matter that makes his questions clearly only for the purpose of obtaining answers of benefit to overhearers. This curious quality is best appreciated by contrasting it to the whole series of conversational devices that seem precisely designed to avoid the possibility of telling people what they already know – e.g. pre-announcements (like 'Did you hear the wonderful news?') that make a telling conditional on its newsworthiness (see Terasaki 1976; Levinson 1983: 349ff.; see also Sacks 1971: 19 October, p. 9; Levinson 1986). Thus, talk for overhearers is recognizable not only because of the subject matter (where e.g. A tells B about B-events, to use the terminology of Labov and Fanshel 1977), but also because it lacks many conversational devices that either seek to establish in advance what may be 'news' or serve to acknowledge the newsworthiness of an informing (see Heritage 1985).

My purpose in bringing up these rather *ad-hoc* and grossly under-analysed examples is simply to make the point that having a set of participant role categories is one thing – but working out *who* stands in *which when* can be quite another, on a vastly greater plane of complexity. But such problems of category assignment, I hope to have shown, are not only the self-imposed difficulties of analysts, but also occasionally problematic for participants, and there is at least *prima facie* evidence that advances in this area would significantly aid our understanding of interactional process.

CONCLUSIONS

In this paper, I have tried to show, following suggestions by
Goffman in particular, that 'Speaker' and 'Hearer' are not sufficient
categories for the analysis of participant role. Instead, both the
producing and the receiving end of an utterance can be broken down
into constituent categories of some complexity. It then becomes clear
that, in the dyadic dialogues we tend to think of as the canonical
situation of utterance, where S and H (and the corresponding
grammatical categories (first and second person) will almost do as
analytical notions, these complex categories are actually collapsed
onto just two incumbents: so sponsor = 'ghostor', source = speaker,
speaker = author, etc., while target = addressee, and addressee =
interlocutor, etc. [24] Thus the apparently simplest situation of
utterance may in this perspective actually hide an enormous
complexity more clearly revealed in situations where these roles are
distributed over more parties to an exchange of talk, as in specialized
institutional settings or the panel discussions that I have especially
drawn on.

Issues of participant role would seem to have a central importance
to many different branches of linguistics. In the first place, concepts
of participant roles underly the key grammatical distinctions of
person deixis. Since person deixis is at the heart of all the deictic
systems of natural languages the concepts of participant role are
fundamental to an understanding of the context dependence of
meaning, and constitute the very foundations of pragmatics. That
we might incidentally get better grammatical descriptions of deictic
categories in languages is of course an important payoff of
developing our understanding of this area. Secondly, in the study of
verbal interaction, there has been undoubtedly some bias towards
the study of dyadic interaction. But many of the world's social
settings do not afford the privacy that makes the dyad triumph in the
Western world. Further, in all societies there are institutionalized
multi-party gatherings for which at present we lack the proper
investigative techniques. Thus having the proper distinctions
between different kinds of participant role is essential to the ethnography of speaking and the comparative description of speech
events. Thirdly, it can be argued that the processual study of verbal
interaction in multi-party settings equally requires an understanding
of the underlying distinctions in participant role. For all these
reasons (and others, like the importance to the study of child
language), as I have tried to illustrate, the whole area is one that

demands further serious attention from linguists and discourse analysts.

For raising all these issues, and making concrete proposals for the analysis of participant role, we owe a special debt to Erving Goffman. Whether his own ideas on the subject will survive future intensive research it is surely too soon to know, but linguistics is certainly the beneficiary of his provocative suggestions. We have, after all, been within the straightjacket of first and second persons for a couple of millenia.

NOTES

This paper has been long in the gestation, and in various matters of conception and execution I am still unhappy with it; I publish it in the hope that further help may be elicited. It arises directly from some sessions of the Working Group on Language and Cultural Context, Australian National University, 1981, and in particular from a seminar on multi-party conversation led by John Haviland (see Haviland, 1986a); I am grateful to all the participants, especially Penelope Brown, Sandro Duranti, John Haviland, Judith Irvine, Elinor Ochs, Bambi Schieffelin and Michael Silverstein for the stimulus for, and some of the ideas in, this paper (I shall try to acknowledge specific contributions below). At the time I had no access to Goffman (1981b), and this explains to some extent the language of independent invention; but I drew heavily on Goffman (1976), Comrie (1976), Hymes (1974), Goodwin (1977), Fillmore (1975), Lyons (1977). Subsequent versions were given at the University of Sussex, and the Working Conference on the Sociology of Language, Plymouth Polytechnic, April 1983, each benefiting from comments and encouragement (I single out John Lyons, Anita Pomerantz and John Heritage for special thanks). My thanks also to Nigel Vincent for much needed help at a critical stage. This version has benefited from comments by participants at the conference from which this volume derives – especially those from Emanuel Schegloff, Paul Drew, Sue Ervin-Tripp, Adam Kendon, Christian Heath, Jurgen Streeck and others. Dick Hudson, Paul Drew, Peter Matthews and Emanuel Schegloff also supplied copious written comments which for reasons of space I have scarcely been able to take into account – I owe them all further elaboration at some point. Finally, the editors of this volume have helped greatly in the partial abbreviation of an overlong text; I have had to cut, amongst other things, some suggestions about the relation of stigma to limited participation rights, but I shall be happy to supply the longer version on demand.

1 Incidentally, his role in the founding of the systematic study of social interaction is curious, as other commentators have had reason to note: it

could hardly be said that he made the subject respectable (that was surely never his aim); nor that he made it systematic or scientific (from his writings one might get the impression that he lived before the days of recording equipment). What he did do was make the systematization conceivable by showing the kind of analytical distinctions that might be necessary; also, he released the study of interaction from the clutches of the back-room specialists, whether aberrant linguists, ethologists or kinesicists, by demonstrating its general sociological pertinence. Finally, by sketch treatments of so many ecological niches of everyday life, he inspired more detailed explorations of the collaborative effort beneath each smooth interactional surface.

2 In that paper (p. 128) Goffman draws attention to his earlier 'initial statement' in *Frame Analysis* (1974: 496–559). However, perhaps the most useful earlier reference is in fact the 1953 dissertation (especially part 4), where many of the ideas about participation are clearly laid out.

3 So suggests Silverstein; I have not actually been able to find anyone to attribute such traditional wisdom to, except for Jakobson's famous essay on shifters (1971; see especially 133–6). Similar in spirit is Hymes (1972: 58, 60–1).

4 In this emphasis there is an interesting convergence at about the same time between ethnographers of speaking (e.g. Fisher 1976; Hymes 1972, 1974; Silverstein 1976) and Goffman's own work. Those who have not seen Goffman's (1953) dissertation might be forgiven for thinking that Goffman borrowed this concern from the ethnographers; but perhaps the influence was the other way as Hymes' (1972: x) acknowledgement suggests; most likely though it was a happy confluence.

5 For those unfamiliar with this mode of categorization, borrowed from phonology, let me point out a few of its properties: (a) for n features you obtain up to 2^n categories; (b) one may specify redundancy rules, so that feature $F1$ implies $F2$, etc. (this will reduce the theoretical maximum); and (c) one may define superordinate categories, subsuming a number of basic ones, by leaving some features unspecified. (See e.g. Fischer-Jorgensen 1975: 150ff., and the following footnote.)

6 The effect of these two redundancy rules is to reduce the potential set of 2^4 (16) categories to six sensible reception roles, by (a) knocking out all eight possible non-channel-linked parties as non-participants (since the first redundancy rule has the de Morgan equivalent – *CHANNEL-LINK* →- *PARTIC*), (b) eliminating the possibility of (two kinds of) non-participants being addressed (remember that these are *utterance-event* categories: in contrast, in *speech-event* categories a heckler at a meeting being derided by a speaker might be thought of as an addressed non-participant; but at the utterance-event level, just by being addressed the heckler becomes a participant, as the second redundancy rule requires).

7 Emanuel Schegloff (personal communication) objects to the characterization of the turn-taking system as 'dyadic'; while it is true, he points

out, that it is organized in terms of an opposition between 'current speaker' and 'next', whether 'next speaker' is drawn from a pool restricted in kind or number makes all the difference between, say, a press conference (a two-party system) and talk at the dinner table (where there are as many parties as individuals). A lot hinges here on having a proper analysis of specialized turn-taking systems, which we still largely lack. Even if 'dyadicity' is not the relevant dimension of contrast between the turn-taking system and systems of participant role, yet it is clear (Schegloff would I think concede) that the systems are distinct but cross-cutting.

8 Otherwise, given a redundancy rule $+ PARTICIPANT \rightarrow + CHANNEL$-$LINK$, one could not be a participant to a conversation conducted in a language one does not understand. Perhaps, though, that is right: it may only be through a shared kinesic code (of nods, smiles, body position, etc.) that one can participate in such a conversation at all.

9 Although cultural relativists will take heart at finding that those troublesome Ojibwa treat stones (which are grammatically animate in Ojibwa) as participants (Hymes 1974: 14); and of course one of our cultural peculiarities is the treatment of pet animals as possible participants, indeed addressees. There are ethnographic reports of special registers and special pronouns of address for use to animals.

10 Note that there may not be any attributed source at all, as in the 'ravings' of a lunatic in our culture; such 'ravings' being attributed to spiritual sources in many other cultures.

11 I owe to Michael Silverstein some forceful reminders of the importance of this distinction.

12 But compare Hymes: 'serious ethnographic work shows that there is [only] one general, or universal, dimension to be postulated, that of participant' (1972: 58–9). If he's right then the present enterprise is of dubious validity; there is no way to construct a set of *a priori* categories. But this seems suspicious; for, at least prior to the technology of modern recording and communications, there did seem to be intrinsic constraints on the nature of participant roles to do with the underlying dimensions illustrated in tables 7.3 and 7.4. However, we can grant that in the long run any set of categories ought to be based on empirical work, whether on detailed work on the analysis of multi-party talk in our own society or comparative analysis of talk in 'exotic' societies. The issue then will be whether we can formulate an 'etic' level of description, of universal application, within which 'emic' descriptions of local practices can be properly captured.

13 The term grammaticalize is used throughout this paper in the broad (post-Chomskyan) sense inclusive of *lexicalize, phonologize*, etc., as well as *syntactize*. See e.g. Brown and Levinson 1978, section 8.0, for a clarification of what one might understand by functions performed by means of the structure of some languages, but by means of the use of utterances in others.

14 But not the analysis of number in pronouns, it should be added, which in many cases at least is best analysed in the minimal/augmented manner devised by Conklin and illustrated in Dixon (1980: 351ff).

15 Peter Matthews points out to me that the intimate interconnection between mood and participant role was noted early in the Greek tradition (see Appolonius' discussion of the verb in *Syntax*, book 3).

16 Tamil -*TTum* might be claimed not to mark a separate sentence type since it co-occurs with (unmarked) declarative and the polar question morpheme. However with the question particle -*aa* it has a specialized meaning, a request for permission, where it occurs with (predominantly?) the first person. A good case can therefore be made for considering the form to be homophonous, and in the third-person non-interrogative form to be a specialized hortative. See Andronov 1969: 175f. (who calls it the 'optative') and Asher 1985: 166, 170.

17 Mention should also be made here of systems like that in Sre (and a similar system in Quileute) with (a) a near-S form, (b) a near-A form, (c) a form indicating that S and A are close and the object referred to is distant, and (d) a form indicating that the object is remote or out of sight, presumably to all ratified participants (Anderson and Keenan 1985: 287f.). The third form is perhaps properly glossed as [not close to ratified participants'].

18 For example, even if utterance events are the units for which participant roles are assigned, such assignment is not necessarily based on units of that sort. Certainly, the process of assignment recognition and signalling inevitably requires, for its study, the analysis of sequential positioning of turns and many ethnographic considerations, e.g. about expectable role assignments in certain cultural events – see e.g. the suggestions about examination in a British court of law below, or Heritage's (1985: 113ff.) remarks about the institutional background to news interviews.

19 *elema* is formed from the present imperative *sama*, ['speak/say'] and the deictic element *ele*, ['like this']: thus *elema* glosses as ['Say like this'] (Feld and Schieffelin 1982). Since *elema* contrasts with *tolema*, ['speak words'], it is possible that (as Silverstein has suggested) *elema* is essentially performative in contrast to *tolema* which is essentially reportive. In that case *X elema* should gloss as ['Assert right now X']. However this is unclear from Feld and Schieffelin's description.

20 There are of course some general connections here, that need exploring, between questions of quotation and implied past and future utterance events.

21 I believe I take this term from Goffman, but have mislaid the reference. In the paper 'Response cries' (1981b: ch. 2 [1978], Goffman distinguishes true 'response cries' (non-lexemes but conventional vocalizations like 'Oops') from imprecations (taboo lexemes) and lexical talk, while showing how they have much in common. For these, I use the term 'out-louds' as a cover term.

22 Emanuel Schegloff (personal communication) notes that the sequential properties of 'indirectly targetted turns' might be accounted for not in terms of participant role but directly in terms of being utterances built to take a third-turn response, thus:

A: Turn 1: [*indirectly targetted utterance with C mentioned in third person*]
B: Turn 2: [*audience appreciation*]
C: Turn 3: [*target's response*]

He also points out that panel discussions might not be the best locus of research for this phenomenon, since political affiliations and the like so overdetermine 'targets' that we are not clearly enabled to see the methods more generally used for selecting a 'target' to respond.

23 In example <13> the chairman's use of the full name (at the top of p. 219) is precisely such an exception: Bruce Kent is called upon to speak – the call being an announcement, addressed to all participants as much as to Bruce Kent himself, of whose turn it is.

24 Emanuel Schegloff (in conference) made the point that talk of 'conflation' or 'mapping' of many participant roles onto only two interactants in dyadic dialogue would seem to presuppose the omni-relevance of the more finely discriminated set of roles. Can this, he asks, be shown? Or should we rather consider those discriminated roles as only pertinent to other kinds of setting, or multi-party talk? To demonstrate the omni-relevance we would need to show that, for example, a speaker in dyadic interaction needs always to be monitored for changes in 'footing'. Streek (n.d.) in effect attempts to argue this, suggesting that *relayed* utterances might not permit certain responses (e.g. other repair), but it is not clear that this is generally true. Another kind of possible evidence is provided by Schegloff's (1984) demonstration that some utterances in dyadic conversation are demonstrably treated as 'ambiguous' as to source (a point for which I am indebted to Gail Jefferson).

8

Minor Courtesies and Macro Structures

P. M. STRONG

INTRODUCTION: THE GOFFMANIAN LEGACY

> It seems to me that the dramaturgical approach may constitute a fifth
> perspective to be added to the technical, political, structural and
> cultural perspectives.
>
> (Goffman 1959: 240)

> My concern over the years has been to promote acceptance of this
> face-to-face domain as an analytically viable one.
>
> (Goffman 1983b: 2)

Goffman may have changed his terms but he rarely changed his
tune. What began as the 'dramaturgical approach' ended up, much
more broadly, as the 'interaction order', but the notion of a
distinctive micro-social world remained: a world with its own special
forms, rules, processes and problems. In his vision, this fifth
perspective was linked to, but analytically separable from, the
realms more traditionally studied by social science. To sketch its
nature and establish its viability, he devoted 30 years, a thesis, 10
books and collections of essays, and several important but so far
ungathered articles.

This legacy is vast, diverse and has much to offer on the key topics
with which this paper deals; power and, above all, ceremony. The
analysis of etiquette – of that ritual order which links the micro to the
macro world, lending weight and stability to each and every
encounter – is central to Goffman's writings. Yet most subsequent
commentators and researchers have had little to say on ceremony.
This paper tries to redress the balance. It contains four things: an

exposition of Goffman's view of the ritual order; a description of systematic ethnographic methods for its analysis; an illustration of the use of such methods (via research into a particular class of encounters); and, in the light of this research, an appraisal and critique of Goffman's position.

The absence of much sociological commentary or research on ceremony is not, in fact, unusual; much of his work has received relatively little development from others. Indeed, the great pomp of the funeral has not stilled the loud mutterings of a good many of the mourners. For all the fame that Goffman achieved in disciplines besides sociology, many in his own trade were reluctant to grant him much importance. As he remarked in his final essay on the interaction order, 'My colleagues have not been overwhelmed by the merits of the case' (1983b: 2) Part of this failure is due to the peculiar reluctance by many sociologists to concede any importance to the micro sphere. And some part, no doubt, to Goffman's particular theoretical and empirical frailties. But another part, perhaps the most important part, stems from his distinctive idiosyncracies, which were large, varied and, though attractive to some, offputting to many. Understanding any part of his work – and, more particularly, grasping the problems faced by all researchers in the fields that he mapped out – demands that these idiosyncracies be tackled head on. I shall begin, therefore, by citing a rare general statement of his aims and methods; things that Goffman never normally spelt out and which in consequence have been the cause of much confusion:

> I am impatient for a few conceptual distinctions (nothing so ambitious as a theory) that show we are getting some place in uncovering elementary variables that simplify and order, delineating generic classes whose members share lots of properties, not merely a qualifying similarity. To do this I think one has to start with ethnological or scholarly experience in a particular area of behaviour and then exercise the right to dip into any body of literature that helps, and move in any unanticipated but indicated direction. The aim is to follow where a concept (or small set of them) seems to lead. That development, not narrative or drama, is what dictates. Of course nothing gets proven, only delineated, but I believe that in many areas of social conduct that's just where we are right now. A simple classification pondered over, worked over to try to get it to fit, may be all that we can do right now. Casting one's endeavour in the more respectable forms of the mature sciences is often just a rhetoric. In the main I don't believe we're there yet. And I like to think that

accepting these limits and working like a one-armed botanist is what a
social naturalist unashamedly has to do.

(Goffman: personal communication)

So, contrary to common belief, Goffman viewed himself as a scientist, though one using naturalistic methods and working in an
adolescent (possibly neonatal) area. Moreover, as Robin Williams
(this volume) argues, he saw his scientific task as primarily conceptual, bringing some initial order to a morass of data through the
selection and preliminary testing of elementary variables.

In short, he was a theorist, though of a most unusual kind, for
data were central to his method of generating concepts (alas, a rarity
in the theoretically inclined). On the other hand, this close interest
in the empirical did not endear him to most conventional researchers. To them (and to some of his students) his methods seemed
wild. As for links to other theorists, these too were often strained;
though he discussed data endlessly, he rarely discussed other
writers, save only in footnotes. In addition to these sins, he invented
a cornucopia of theoretical terms – but changed them in almost
every book. Likewise, though he acknowledged the power and
priority of wider social realms, he himself worked solely in the
micro-social sphere and rarely bothered about making links. Finally,
in a solemn, committed and largely graceless profession (as the
public image has it), he was a cynic, a wit and a literary stylist; all
potent sources of misunderstanding.

What then did he leave us? The answer, obvious enough, is a
dazzling array of concepts and some major problems. Since he was
primarily a theorist he was not too fussy about the means by which
he derived his terms, or the manner in which others might opera-
tionalize them. And since he was driven on by his desire to map,
however provisionally, the many contours of his presumed new-
found domain, he tended to love the view he had just noticed and be
bored by autobiographical exegesis. Precisely how he had got there,
how one foray linked with another, were usually matters of little interest.[1] Thus the more systematic explorers who plod after him are
faced with both a vast terrain and, littered across the landscape, a
multitude of exploratory terminologies, most of them intriguing but
many apparently abandoned. Some perhaps wrecked, some only
partly built, some possibly in good repair, but none possessing any
clear set of maker's instructions. What this paper offers is, I hope,
an empirical way forward with one bunch of his ideas.

MINOR COURTESIES AND SIGNS OF DEFERENCE:
GOFFMAN'S THEORY OF CEREMONY

A lot of life is about things so trivial that we do not bother to record
them - only sometimes note their absence, as with manners.
(Oscar Wilde, cited in Shattuck 1986: 67)

A central argument in much of Goffman's work is that the ceremonial
order of the encounter, the etiquette that can be found on any social
occasion, is not some trivial matter, of interest solely to mothers,
pedants and social climbers, but has instead a profound importance
for the viability of the micro-social order. Later sections of this paper
attempt to test this argument, but I shall begin by spelling out
Goffman's own theory of these matters in some detail. Consider, for
instance, the main components of the ordinary service relationship:

> The interaction that occurs when client and server are together
> ideally takes a relatively structured form. The server can engage in
> mechanical handiwork operations . . . he can also engage in verbal
> exchanges with the client. The verbal part itself contains three
> components: a *technical* part . . . a *contractual* part and, finally, a
> *sociable* part, consisting of a few minor courtesies, civilities, and signs
> of deference.
>
> (Goffman 1961b: 328-9)

The first quote indicates that on particular occasions particular
events, roles and manners are in order. Such elements can be found
in any relationship whatsoever; they are not specific to service
relationships. Moreover, two of these, so Goffman argues, together
generate the distinctive reality of any one encounter. The specification of *this* set of events and *that* set of roles, constitute the *rules of
the game* which, when adhered to, produce a separate little world; be
it a medical consultation, a boxing-match or whatever:

> A matrix of possible events and a cast of roles through whose
> enactment the events occur constitute together a field of fateful
> dramatic action, a place of being, an engine of meaning, a world in
> itself, different from all other worlds, except the ones generated when
> the same game is played at other times.
>
> (Goffman 1961c: 26-7)

But there are lots of different games. How is the reality of any
particular game (or *play* or *frame* in other Goffmanian metaphors)

kept alive in the face of all our other involvements? It is here, so he asserts, that manners achieve their importance:

> The process of mutually sustaining a definition of the situation in face-to-face interaction is socially organized through rules of relevance and irrelevance. These rules for the management of engrossment appear to be an insubstantial element of social life, a matter of courtesy, manners, and etiquette. But it is to these flimsy rules, and not to the unshaking character of the external world, that we owe our unshaking sense of realities.
>
> (Goffman 1961c: 30–1)

Such principles for the management of engrossment, the *rules of relevance and irrelevance*, focus primarily on what should *not* be done. Their main concern is with indelicacy, with what must be avoided or ignored. And studying this is a useful heuristic device for understanding the entire encounter:

> It seems characteristic of encounters, as distinguished from other elements of social organization, that their order pertains largely to what shall be attended and disattended, and through this, to what shall be accepted as the definition of the situation. Instead of beginning by asking what happens when this definition of the situation breaks down, we can begin by asking what perspectives this definition of the situation excludes when it is being satisfactorily sustained.
>
> (Goffman 1961c: 19)

Here then, in the 'elegance and strength of the structure of inattention' (Goffman 1961c: 19) is the source of the sustained reality of the encounter. The powerful focus on just one set of meanings and the systematic exclusion of all others: this is the nub; not breakdown, nor the necessity of constant repair. The little world of the encounter is not a fragile thing.[2] Instead, it is an extraordinarily robust structure, capable of ignoring all kinds of routine trouble. Only in the most exceptional of circumstances is it seriously and overtly threatened. For present purposes in interaction, any features of the setting that do not fit, any alien qualities, emotions or involvements, all these, if they form no part of the current order, are treated, for the time being, as if they did not exist. Little children turn themselves into soldiers, old clothes into uniforms, chairs and tables into forts. So too, adults become lovers, parents, teachers, shoppers and politicians as the occasion fits.

But inattention is not quite everything. Two further quotations provide us with additional considerations. Both deal, according to Goffman, with other aspects of the ritual order which are equally fundamental:

> We have then a kind of interactional modus vivendi. Together the participants contribute to a single over-all definition of the situation which involves not so much a real agreement as to what exists but rather a real agreement as to whose claims concerning what issues will be temporarily honoured. Real agreeement will also exist concerning the desirability of avoiding an open conflict of definitions of the situation. I will refer to this level of agreement as a working consensus.
>
> (Goffman 1959: 9–10)

> To the degree that a performance highlights the common official values of the society in which it occurs, we may look upon it . . . as an expressive rejuvenation and reaffirmation of the moral values of the community . . . (as) a celebration . . . The world in truth is a wedding.
>
> (Goffman 1959: 35–6)

These quotations bring out the Janus-like nature of etiquette in Goffman's theory. One face is Machiavellian; it speaks of performances and actors, of merely overt ceremony, and of the delicate, covert assessment of power and place within the encounter. The other face is Durkheimian; it tells, instead, of the wider social values which ceremony necessarily celebrates – however murky the origins (or consequences) of these rituals may sometimes be.

Put another way, when we encounter others we are forced to put on public dress. That dress is determined by many different factors – power, status, role, the situation, our fellow-participants and even (partly) personal choice. But whatever we end up wearing, and whether we like it or not, our public garments invest that encounter with its own form and meaning, creating for the moment a distinct and palpable little world. Simultaneously (and equally for the moment) they reinforce and reaffirm some wider set of social values, however cynical or unwilling we may sometimes covertly feel: or so Goffman argues.[3]

So in our investigation of ceremony, we must look to both the *overt* and the *covert* sides of the interaction, to what people display publicly and what they say and do only in private. But we must also grasp the celebratory aspect. How may this be done? Several more hints are given by Goffman. *The Presentation of Self in Everyday Life* speaks of the *idealization* (1959: 34–51) that is essential to proper performances; it is in this sense that the world is a wedding. 'On face-work' then argues, first that *all* participants within the interaction are, typically, idealized – this is a *joint* venture: 'The person tends to conduct himself during the encounter so as to maintain both his own face and the face of the other participants' (Goffman 1967: 11). Second, that the *rules of relevance* and *irrelevance* are fundamentally moral rules; rules which have profound significance for the participants' identity and sense of self; rules which also, when taken together, form a coherent and (in part) self-equilibrating whole – we are dealing here with a kind of ritual micro-functionalism:

> These rules, when followed, determine the evaluation he (the actor) will make of himself and of his fellow-participants in the encounter, the distribution of his feelings and the kinds of practices he will employ to maintain a specified and obligatory kind of ritual equilibrium. The general capacity to be bound by moral rules may well belong to the individual, but the particular set of rules . . . (is) . . . established in the ritual organization of social encounters.
>
> (Goffman 1967: 45)

In short, in any type of encounter, so Goffman claims, there exists a distinctive and robust set of moral rules, rules which both knit together into a single, harmonious whole and which also present each participant in an idealized light, a light which in turn celebrates wider social values. That idealization and celebration is a joint task in which everyone has a part to play; but at the same time it is based on a purely temporary agreement. The ritual order is simply an overt display, a performance, which may well conceal great covert differences in opinion and power. Some people may be forced to celebrate against their will. Finally, the moral rules which compose any particular ritual order get their sustained reality from a further set of rules – rules of relevance and irrelevance – which govern precisely which matters the participants may focus on and those which they must gloss over and ignore. The joint idealization of this (often) purely working consensus depends on a shared and systematic inattention to anything that might disrupt the overt order of things.

But if that is the theory it was not one that Goffman himself ever tested. He never studied the minutiae of any particular ceremony, never systematically examined any specific rules of relevance or irrelevance, never rigorously probed the workings of this, or that, ritual equilibrium. For some this is a terrible fault but, as we saw earlier, Goffman was not a researcher in any conventional sense. He was a theorist working in an unexplored area, trying to make some initial sense, as best he could, of a huge and unfamiliar terrain. What he has to offer is, therefore, an array of (merely) plausible ideas – of possible forms, processes, rules, tasks and problems. Of course, Goffman's best may still turn out to be better than most others. But when we get right down and look in detail at a particular bunch of encounters, who knows what we will actually find?

FINDING RULES IN CEREMONY

Goffman's theory of the ceremonial order of encounters could be explored in many ways. The way I chose was to concentrate on just one type of encounter – paediatric consultation – and to explore this via intensive ethnographic methods. But if the focus was small, the instances were both large and varied. I gathered systematic data (via handwritten verbatim notes)[4] on the interaction in 1120 paediatric encounters. One hundred took place in an eastern city of the United States, some fee-paying ('private' in British terminology), some charity, the rest payed for by the Federal Government. The other 1000 consultations all occurred in a Scottish city of similar size and all took place within the National Health Service (NHS).

Aside from the differences in location and financing, these consultations occurred in many different types of clinic and with many different doctors – 40 in all (though focussing principally on just a handful). Such variety was more than matched in the types of case seen: from the rare to the routine, from the retarded to the insane, from the brief to the lengthy (some meetings lasted nearly an hour), from the one-off to the repeat (a few patients were observed up to 13 times in three years), from the chronic to the acute, from the rich to the poor, from the healthy to the doomed, from the hospital to the community clinic. Not all human life was there, but a lot was; enough perhaps for a beginning.

One central methodological problem was posed by the *rule of irrelevance*: how to notice significant absences, how to discover what might have been there but was instead systematically excluded? Consider the Scottish NHS clinics. A central part of their ceremonial order was the portrayal of the doctor as obviously and necessarily competent; a competence that could not be challenged by parents and did not stem from particular intelligence or training, but depended simply on being a doctor. Medical authority was (normally) anonymous, all-powerful and *ex officio*. It did not need to be proved; it was simply taken for granted. Parents, as non-members of the club, were portrayed, by contrast, as both passive and technically ignorant, whatever their other qualities. But getting to see these rules proved hard. Not only was my own medical experience solely within the NHS, but swimming inside the Scottish data (as I was for the first three years of the project) I was aware only of its variety; of how this parent, clinic or doctor differed, so markedly, from that. How then did I get to see the striking uniformities of the NHS clinic and the great diversity of action that was systematically excluded? How does the fish get to notice that it is surrounded by water (since it is there all the time)? Only when it is hooked out on to dry land, when it encounters the *deviant case*.

Here, the dry land came, above all, from the American data. Three thousand miles away in the United States one saw, at least in some clinics,[5] routine happenings that never or almost never occurred in any Scottish clinic; things that were (sometimes) unimaginable in Scotland; things which immediately revealed what was systematically absent from most NHS consultations. Consider, for example, the following Scottish extract. A young, middle-class child who had been seeing a psychiatrist has been referred to a paediatric neurology clinic for the first time. At the end of the half-hour consultation, the paediatrician asks:

Doctor	What was Dr Maxwell (the psychiatrist) planning for her?
Mother	Well, she said that someone would be seeing her. Someone interested in specific speech delay. Is that you?
Doctor	Well, I'm interested in it, but I don't think it could be me.
Mother	And the other person we'd be seeing is a paediatrician with an interest in coordination.
Doctor	That's me. The other one may be a psychologist.

                                                  (Strong 1979: 75)

How can we interpret this? Viewed from within the Scottish data, it was simply an oddity: an apparently competent woman sitting through a half-hour consultation without knowing who she was talking to. But, in the light cast by the data on American private consultations, it suddenly took on a new form. It could now be seen as merely an extreme instance of both a general patient passivity and a medical anonymity that were characteristic of almost all NHS consultations. Thus, routine occurrences in private practice revealed systematic absences in that of the NHS. Consider two private American extracts:

Intern	How did you get here?
Mother	Well, he's been seeing a psychiatrist and he diagnosed minimal brain dysfunction and prescribed X. But we also wanted to get Dr Stein's opinion as we felt we ought not just to have a psychiatric opinion.

(Strong 1979: 79–80)

Father	So it's a little too early to do this now?
Doctor	Right. We talk about this problem all the time at the moment and I've had discussions at the (New York) and (Boston) hospitals with the experts in the fields. I've spoken to Drs A, B, and C about it. We're all very interested in it but its early days yet . . . Remember, it's not just me who's telling you this, I've talked to lots of people who know more about this than I do. (He names them again plus some others). And they all agree that it's too risky at the moment.

(Strong 1979: 78)

In the first extract there is an important similarity to our previous Scottish case. Here too we are dealing with a child who has seen a psychiatrist and is now attending a paediatric neurology clinic for the first time. However, there are important differences. This is the beginning of the consultation (in fact the 'work-up' by an intern) and the American mother (slightly lower in social class) not only knows who she is going to see but has herself chosen this person. Moreover, she makes it plain from the beginning, though politely, that she has seen another specialist and is checking his opinion, just as she might, by implication, check that of Dr Stein.

By contrast, Scottish patients never displayed such open consumerism. Though they had nominal rights to seek a second opinion, in practice few patients dared. Moreover, whereas both private patients and doctors regularly commented on other doctors' views, this almost never happened in NHS clinics. Contrast, however, the second extract above. Here the doctor backs up his own opinion with a long list of other doctors' names and opinions. What is for sale here are highly specific skills and contacts. Private medicine is necessarily individualized; colleagues are also competitors; patients can and do go elsewhere. So doctors must display both their own skills and opinions and pass judgement on those of others. American doctors saw private patients not in the ordinary clinic but in their own room in the hospital, a room whose walls were covered with certificates from medical school. NHS patients were seen in anonymous public rooms; rooms which matched the impersonal, *ex officio* style of the expertise on offer.

Vivid deviant cases, like the data from American private practice, thus allowed the formulation of very general rules of relevance and irrelevance. Once my eyes were opened, I could then start looking much more systematically, both for fresh instances of the same phenomena and for other related kinds of activity and passivity. But this too requires a method. What kind of system can be used in this search? Ethnographic techniques have had a bad press from some students of the micro social; sloppy, subjective, impressionistic: these are common terms of abuse. Of course, some ethnographies do indeed have these characteristics, but such a description ignores the careful analytic techniques that have been developed. Two, in particular, stand out: the methods of, respectively, *constant comparison* (Glaser 1964) and *analytic induction* (Robinson 1951; Cressey 1971; Bloor 1978). I used both.

Constant comparison is a means for systematically elaborating detailed hypotheses about a complex, general phenomenon. It is also ideally suited to the analysis of very large bodies of data. For in this method, coding takes place only when one discovers variations from, exceptions to, or particularly dramatic instances of the rule in question. Each datum is used as a check on the validity of the hypotheses and classifications that have been developed up till that point. If the datum fits readily with what has gone before, no note is made; if it does not then either a new hypothesis is required, or else an old version will need some suitable amendment. Consider two further NHS extracts:

Doctor   We do like to see you just once in a while. I think I'm a charlatan really because there's nothing much we can do, but we just like to keep an eye on things to see if there is anything we can do.   (Strong 1979: 87)

Mother	Dr Brown (London) said that this hospital (Scotland) hadn't ruled out a hereditary cause.
Doctor	. . . I'm sure Dr McAllister (Scotland) couldn't have said that . . . Quite frankly the report from London is a puzzle to us. What they say under the heading 'diagnosis', where they say they don't know, differs from the bottom where they say its genetic . . .
Mother	. . . At the (London) hospital, Dr Brown seemed right out on a limb. He seemed definite, but no one else paid much attention to him.

(Strong 1979: 211)

Such instances illustrate the analytic power of the search for deviant cases; both turn out to be exceptions that help prove the rule. For example, behaviour of the first type was quite common with children suffering from severe, chronic conditions. But for a doctor to say such things was not to discount medical expertise, merely to describe its limitations from an expert point of view. It was medical staff, not parents who typically set bounds to medical competence. Likewise, the second extract (which breaks the rules of medical anonymity and consensus, and thus resembles a private rather than an NHS consultation) reveals the one chink in medical anonymity within the Scottish clinic. This particular mother was one of only two Scottish mothers in the study to request a second opinion from another hospital doctor. Getting that opinion (a difficult thing to do within the NHS)[6] transformed subsequent consultations at her local hospital; medical opinion was no longer collective but individual (and contradictory).

Constant comparison therefore broadens and deepens the initial set of hypotheses by its sharp focus on deviant cases. However, the method has a major flaw. While it is good at elaborating hypotheses, it is inappropriate to test them on the same body of data as that from which they have been generated. Enter analytic induction. Here the researcher is urged to collect only a small, initial body of data; to derive from it some initial hypotheses; to collect a further body of data; to test and modify the hypotheses on this fresh evidence; and to continue this sequence of data-gathering and hypothesis-testing until no further body of data produces any significant modification to the developed hypotheses. My data were collected all in one go.

So, instead, I simply divided them; the first half being used to generate detailed hypotheses (via constant comparison) about the ritual order of the paediatric clinics; the second half to test those same hypotheses. How, then, did Goffman's theory of encounter etiquette stand up?

A RE-ORDERED RITUAL

Further work may add detail to his analysis of ceremony,[7] but this initial examination strongly suggests that Goffman has got much of the broad outline right. Much, but not all: some qualifications must be made, two with important consequences for the links between the interaction order and those macro worlds which sociologists more conventionally treat. I shall begin, however, with the many key points on which he does seem to be correct. There was, indeed, a minute attention to a ritual etiquette in all these consultations. Each participant was offered a heavily idealized public character (whatever their private qualities) and the combined set of ceremonial identities formed a harmonious and smoothly interlocking whole. But to grasp this fully, it is important to complete my rough sketch of consultation etiquette. There were two equally central dimensions to this particular ceremonial order; the first, described in the prior section of this chapter, deals with the technical medical competence of server and client; the second, as described below, concerns their moral character.

Take, for example, the character proffered to mothers. As every Scottish doctor was (overtly) competent, so every Scottish mother was nominally treated as loving, honest, reliable and intelligent; not, of course, capable of passing judgement on medicine, but certainly fulfilling every maternal duty to her child. Consider the following extracts; the first from a routine consultation in a hospital clinic; the second from a local authority well-baby clinic, where the baby, at six months, is grossly fat (twice the expected weight) and from a family who have been notorious amongst health and social-service staff for three generations:

Doctor   Is there anybody in the house with you?
Mother   Well, my husband.

(Strong 1979: 46)

Doctor	And you feed him on Farex?
Mother	In the morning and evening.
Doctor	And porridge?
Mother	Aye.
Doctor	Does he get anything else for elevenses?
Mother	Just biscuits . . .
Doctor	How much does he get a lunchtime?
Mother	Oh just mince and tatties . . .
Doctor	And what does he get for his tea?
Mother	Oh a boiled egg or a scrambled egg.
Doctor	And this is as well as milk?
Mother	Aye . . .
Doctor	If I were you, I'd miss out the Farex and the porridge at breakfast and the biscuit as well. It's best to do this now because if children get fat now then they tend to be fatter later on in life. He's supposed to be twice his birthweight now and he's a good bit more than that, isn't he? This is very important. He's putting on a bit too much weight.

(Strong 1979: 46–7)

The first extract illustrates that all medical inquiry, however apparently trivial, routinely involves the production of potentially discrediting information; every consultation necessarily touches on the patient or parent's moral character. It also shows how, in the Scottish clinics at least, medical questioning was typically conducted with some delicacy; thereby preserving for every mother that pristine image of the ideal mother. This was most obvious where there was grave doubt about a mother's competence and character. In the second extract, the mother had ignored all previous medical advice about feeding her baby but the doctor's tone is still polite and friendly; she makes no mention of the mother's delinquency; her questions are posed in a neutral fashion; her advice is phrased simply as what she herself would do. Overtly the mother is treated as a good woman who simply needs to be informed of the best way to proceed.

In short, in the Scottish clinics, every doctor was an expert and every mother was good. Whatever their actual morality or expertise, consultation etiquette routinely cloaked them in these special and complementary identities. The sustained reality of their encounter was thus made possible not just by a special set of roles and events, but also by the rigorous exclusion of anything that might spoil such ideals. Rules of irrelevance enabled a prolonged mutual engrossment in the action almost regardless of circumstance – consultations were formal, polite and mostly free of emotion. Moreover, just as it sustained the internal action, so such ritual simultaneously celebrated key external, societal values; doctors were wise and mothers were motherly. But there are, none the less, three qualifications to be made to Goffman.

(1) *The unmentioned ideal*:   The rule of irrelevance could go rather further than Goffman implies. For it could rest on the routine omission of any mention of the very things that were being idealized. For example, in the Scottish clinics, medical expertise was never praised, it was just taken for granted. Likewise, mothers were never normally praised for their motherliness. A ritual is thus involved but one of some delicacy. This is (quite often) one of those religions where the name of God cannot be mentioned. Compare, however, the standard treatment of Scottish mothers with the following cases (also Scottish):

Doctor	You have children of your own?
Foster mother	Yes, one – and I've had nine foster children.
Doctor	Ah well, your opinion is worth its weight in gold.
	(Strong 1979: 179)
Doctor	What was the weight at birth then?
Father	Seven and a half pounds.
Doctor	Gosh, you've got a good memory! I expect mothers but not fathers to remember. It's seven and a half pounds, you think.
	(Strong 1979: 63)

Foster mothers (in very short supply) and fathers (who rarely came but were being encouraged to do so) could get lavish praise, but with mothers this was unnecessary. Mothers' competence was just not an issue, it was simply taken for granted. Moreover, overt praise might even be a sign that a character was seriously in doubt. (Note the way the doctor ends his response to the father with 'you think' – a qualification never made for mothers.)

(2) *Ceremonial orders*:   The second and third qualifications involve key aspects of Goffman's theory of etiquette which, though important, I have left for discussion until now. The first concerns the crucial issue of the *plurality* of ritual orders. Is the same set of events and roles, the same *activity system* (Goffman 1961c: 8) framed in just one standard fashion, all variations being simply variations on a theme, or must we speak of etiquettes instead of etiquette; of distinctive ceremonial orders, each with their own motif?

Goffman's own position is hard to judge. I have found no clear statement of his general views on the matter. However, his analysis of service encounters does imply that, here at least, there is only one basic, ritual order; that there is an 'ideal model' (Goffman 1961b: 326–9) which shapes the etiquette of every service encounter. There is thus a suspicion that, for all its sophistication, his own model of the ceremonial world still carries some of the unitary assumptions favoured in traditional role analysis – the implicit belief that each and every role relationship has just one socially specified form, thus allowing us to talk of the 'doctor's role', the 'patient's role' and so forth. But this is uncertain.

What he definitely says – at great length and in several different versions – is that within any one order, there can be many reasons for variation. Particular circumstances may not readily fit with the ideal roles (1961b); participants are often allowed a degree of 'distance' (1961c) from the roles they are given to portray; the original frame may serve as a base from which all kinds of transformations or keyings (jokes, rehearsals, etc.) may occur during the encounter (1974); and, finally, though a slightly different point, any one 'strip of action' (1974) may contain a series of different activities, each of which has a different frame.

All this can readily be granted; my discussion of the paediatric research has already shown some of the many variations that can occur within a single order. However, what that research also revealed was that amongst these consultations there were at least three basic ritual orders. The 'ideal model' which Goffman sketched of the server–client relationship was certainly among these but it was not the only one. Indeed, his assumption of just one ideal form looks rather parochial: ethnocentric, ahistorical and middle class.

The most common type of ceremonial order in my particular data set has already been described at some length. What I eventually termed the *bureaucratic format* was standard in every Scottish NHS consultation, and was also used with most non-fee-paying American patients. But there was in addition, as we have also seen, a *private* mode in routine use for the fee-paying patients (this is the model that Goffman describes as the ideal). And, as well as these – and not so far discussed – there was what might be called a *charity* mode, used for the very poor by one American doctor. The charity format is of some interest both for itself and for the other modes. Consider the following extract:

Doctor	Are there any other problems?
Mother	Well he chews cigarette ends . . . (she laughs) . . . It's very difficult to stop him.
Doctor	Why are you laughing? Do you think it's funny?
Mother	No, I don't think it's funny.
Doctor	Well, why did you laugh then? Do you always laugh at this?[8]

(Strong 1979: 44)

The private mode was like the bureaucratic mode in that mothers' character was idealized. But in the charity format the principle was reversed; the initial rule here being that every mother was now stupid, lazy, incompetent and unloving, unless she could prove otherwise. Thus, this particular ritual order contained, as one of its central ingredients, the overt and detailed investigation of the moral character of a key participant. Such investigation (which I term *character work*) is a very different kind of moral work to the cosmetic face work of the two ritual orders discussed so far. In these others, doctors glossed over the vast array of potentially discrediting material that medical inquiry necessarily revealed. In the charity format, by contrast, the doctor publicly seized on every shred of such evidence.

   This discovery of radically different expressive orders, co-existing within the same type of encounter, is not, from a common sense point of view, particularly surprising. Indeed, within the medical arena, it merely confirms the long-held view that doctors and patients behave in very different ways according to their relative status and the commercial basis of the transaction.[9] However, it seems to be an important break from Goffman's own discussion of the ritual order. For once we admit the possibility that the same activity may be ritually framed in very different ways, then we also give space for a mechanism through which systematic variations in the balance of power between participants may, in turn, have systematic effects upon the ritual order of their encounters.

(3) *The micro and the macro worlds*: At various odd points in Goffman's work, but particularly in 'Fun and games' (1961c) and in 'The interaction order' (1983b), a quick sketch is attempted of the relations between the micro and the macro. Here is a typical comment:

> An encounter provides a world for its participants but the character and stability of this world is intimately related to its selective relationship to the wider one. The naturalistic study of encounters, then, is more closely tied to studies of social structure on one hand, and more separate from them, than one might at first imagine.
>
> (Goffman 1961c: 80)

Goffman makes several other points too on micro–macro relations: that external effects are a mixed bag (and in some encounters as much weight may be given to noise as to social class); that some powerful external features are excluded from the ritual order while others take a rather different shape; that we can therefore speak of a *membrane* (1961c: 65–6) which surrounds the little world of the encounter, and of *transformation rules* which determine whether, and in what manner, the outside world may officially intrude; and, finally, that his own work had little relevance to the macro world (or to its students):[10]

> I make no claim to be talking about the core matters of sociology – social organization and social structure. These matters have been and can continue to be quite nicely studied without reference to frame at all . . . I personally hold society to be first in every way and any individuals current involvements to be second . . .
>
> (Goffman 1974: 13)

This last quotation displays several important things about Goffman's views on the macro-social world: that he held it to be more important; that he wasn't himself that interested in it (his insistence on talking solely about the micro was not confined solely to *Frame Analysis*); and, finally, that he didn't think core sociology needed to bother itself with the interaction order. On the basis of my paediatric research, I want to agree with the first, discuss the second and challenge the third of these propositions.

Let's begin with the second: the notion that, to put it most strongly, Goffman respected the power of macro phenomena but was (sociologically) bored by them. 'Fun in games', the first paper in *Encounters* (1961c) analyses the links between the micro and the macro worlds, emphasizing both the power of the ties and the importance of the separation. But, in practice, almost all his examples are of ways in which the encounter is systematically detached from the outer world and, though he introduces the notion of transformation rules, he gives no serious instances of such rules. Twenty years later, in 'The interaction order' (1983b), the story is much the same. Though he emphasizes, once again, the priority of the macro, what he wants primarily to focus on is the separation, not the tie. Interactional practices, so he stresses, are only *loosely coupled* to the wider social structure, at least in our society. There is never a one-to-one relationship.

Why did he touch on but then ignore the crucial macro dimension? The answer, I think, lies in Goffman's particular interest in ceremony. What he loved to look at, above all else, was not the ceremony itself but the complex relationship between the individual and the ritual,[11] an interest which my paper has scarcely touched upon. Thus, while the macro is recognized, it doesn't particularly concern him. One can certainly produce, as Rogers (1980) has most valuably done, a reconstruction of what Goffman's theories imply about power, hierarchy and status, but these are not topics which he himself systematically explored. Nonetheless, the fact that he did not, does not mean we cannot. Indeed, it only makes sense to stress loose-coupling, if we also recognize the phenomenon of *tight-coupling* too; that particular power is liable to breed particular ceremony.

Like all social-science generalizations, this is only a rule of thumb, not a universal law. There will always be exceptions. Not every encounter will be tightly coupled to the external world. Likewise, even where there are tight links, not every detail of the ritual order will be so linked, and there will certainly never be a one-to-one specification such that members of a particular status will invariably be addressed in a distinctive fashion; the modern world is not like that (Goffman 1983b: 11–12). Moreover, the average encounter will also have a penumbra of ritual practices which are rarely, never or only loosely coupled to the wider social structure. However, what does need stressing is that such a penumbra will often surround a solid core, a central ceremony which stems from and is tightly linked to the outer world.

What's the evidence for this? I can only offer the findings from my own research which dealt solely with server–client relations – and indeed with one limited form of that. Nonetheless, an intriguing relationship (table 8.1) did emerge between the different ceremonial orders and particular balances of power; a relationship which *a priori* seems true not just of paediatric clinics but of many other kinds of customer service, and one which can also be illustrated from a wide variety of other research.[12]

TABLE 8.1 Four types of consultation etiquette

Ritual style	Distribution of power	Type of moral work	Medical authority
Aristocratic[a]	V. high patient V. low doctor	Face work + character work by patient on Dr	Individual
Private	Medium patient Medium doctor	Face work	Individual
Bureaucratic	Low patient High doctor	Face work	*Ex officio*
Charity	V. low patient V. high doctor	Face work + character work by Dr on patient	*Ex officio*

[a] The aristocratic mode is not to be found in any of the consultations in my study. However, something like it may well have been true in the past. See, for example, Jewson's (1974) account of the problems faced by some 18th-century doctors when their patient was an aristocratic amateur scholar who dabbled in medical theory.

Such a model needs a good deal of further empirical testing and, besides, even if correct, it is only one of the many, many links which bind the micro to the macro worlds, all of which need detailed exploration.[13] However, if such a programme of research were ever to be undertaken, it might no longer be possible to claim that the core matters of sociology could be nicely studied without any reference to the interaction order. But of course, so far at least, we are a very long way off that.

NOTES

I would like to thank Robert Dingwall, Anne Murcott and the editors for their extensive comments on earlier drafts of this paper.

1 There are two major exceptions to this rule. Some prefaces contain brief but important statements on general theoretical and methodological issues. See, for example, *Relations in Public* (1971), *Interaction Ritual* (1967)

and *Frame Analysis* (1974). In the last year or so of his life he also produced two valuable general essays in which he reflected at length on his own work, 'A reply to Denzin and Keller' (1981a) and 'The inter-action order' (1983b). All these seem worthy of detailed exegesis.

2 Gonos (1977) contains an excellent analysis of Goffman's views on structure which brings out this point well. Its only flaw is that it makes Goffman nothing but a structuralist. As I show later, this is only half the picture. See also Strong (1983a) and Goffman's crushing response (1981a) to Denzin and Keller (1981).

3 Goffman is thus a moralist (of a cynical and stoical kind) as well as a sociologist. On his account, public morality is necessarily and unreformably ambiguous and flawed.

4 These were made together with a co-worker, Alan Davis, who was con-ducting another study of paediatric clinics (Davis 1982). Handwritten notes are less accurate than machine recording but, for a given volume of resources, enable a larger body of data to be analysed.

5 Most of the non-fee-paying American patients were treated in similar ways to the British NHS patients. The exceptions occurred with one of the doctors in a charity clinic for the poor.

6 Every NHS patient has the right to a second opinion; in practice this rarely happens – they are never normally informed of such rights. Those who do make a fuss run some small (but felt) risk of being blackballed.

7 These details concern the components out of which frames are constructed (rights, duties, qualities, etc.). It seems likely these are limited in number. Strong (1979: 188–9) hazards preliminary guesses.

8 The field notes on this particular doctor were not (unlike the rest) written verbatim at the time, but reconstructed immediately afterwards in the clinic's lavatory.

9 'To put it rather unofficially . . . to put it rather crudely, in an (NHS) out-patient session, the patient listens to the doctor, whereas in a private practice, the consultant listens to the patient' (Sir Thomas Holmes Sellors, a consultant giving evidence to the Pilkington Commission on doctors' pay in 1958, cited in Ferris 1967: 34).

10 Attempts such as Collins (1981) to enlist him in the cause of micro imperialism and assert the priority of the micro over the macro realm were firmly squashed (Goffman 1983b).

11 As with frame, Goffman's model of the individual is Janus-faced. On the one hand, people are either puppets, mere devices for creating and sustaining ceremony, or else victims, trapped helplessly within frames unable to escape. On the other hand, and more optimistically, they are also subtle manipulators of frame, endlessly either using the ritual order to achieve their own ends, or else, cunningly slipping away, creating margins of freedom for their own interests and identity.

12 Three of these relationships are based principally on my own research. However, Silverman (1981, 1984, in press) has subsequently found

further evidence to support the analysis of the private and bureaucratic formats, while Dingwall, Eekelaar and Murray (1983) have shown that the latter relationship exists in client relationships with social workers as well as with doctors. There is also supporting evidence for the bureaucratic and charity frames from other contemporary research which, though not using this vocabulary, may still be interpreted in these terms (see Strong 1979: 198–201). Historical versions of the charity mode may be discerned in Ferris (1967: 200), Turner (1958: 102–3) and (an intriguing variant) in Bulgakov (1975) – see Strong 1983b.

13 A very tentative description of another such link is described in Strong and Dingwall (1983) and Dingwall and Strong (1985).

Goffman as a Systematic Social Theorist

ANTHONY GIDDENS

No one would question the claim that Erving Goffman was one of the leading sociological writers of the post-war period. His writings have been more or less universally acclaimed for their luminosity, their charm and their insight. Probably no sociologist over this period has been as widely read both by those in neighbouring social-science disciplines and by the lay public. Goffman's writings have an intrinsically accessible style that has convinced not a few sceptics that sociology is a rather more interesting subject than they may have thought it to be. But all this having been said, Goffman would not ordinarily be ranked among the major social theorists. His work seems quite different in scope and intent from that of authors such as Parsons or Merton in American sociology, let alone such figures as Foucault, Habermas or Bourdieu elsewhere. For one thing, unlike these authors, Goffman writes for the most part in plain language. His texts do not abound with the strange-sounding neologisms favoured by those who are more self-consciously 'theorists'. Moreover, his method seems cavalier. In his writings, observations drawn from social research jostle with illustrations derived from fictional literature, and with casual assertions made with very little apparent empirical backing at all.

And yet I want to propose that Goffman should indeed be ranked as a major social theorist, as a writer who developed a systematic approach to the study of human social life and one whose contributions are in fact as important in this regard as those of any of the other individuals mentioned above. There is a system of social theory to be derived from Goffman's writings, although some effort has to be made to unearth it and we cannot necessarily accept Goffman's own interpretations of his works in elucidating its nature.

There are several reasons why Goffman's ideas are not usually approached from this perspective. One is his own perception of what he sought to achieve. He quite deliberately avoided any sort of engagement with issues concerning the large scale or the long term – although I shall argue later that his ideas are much more relevant to such phenomena than he tended to suppose. Another reason is that Goffman's writings lack a certain cumulative quality. Virtually all of his books are assemblages of essays, rather than integrated works. There is a sense in which it does not matter where one starts to read them: the reader can dip in almost anywhere and pick up the flow of the author's reasoning. Moreover, although Goffman developed and modified certain of his key views over time, his books tend to stand in a similar relation to one another as do the chapters within them. That is, again one can start almost anywhere. Goffman's writings, as it were, mirror that episodic continuity characteristic of the day-to-day forms of social life he seeks to describe and analyse. But by this very token his works can appear light-weight, brimming over with acute and delicate insights, yet lacking the overall intellectual power that derives from the endeavour of an author to grapple with general problems of society and history. Goffman might seem to have a brilliant but butterfly mind, like Simmel who was indeed in some degree a source of his inspiration. Simmel wrote over a considerably greater spectrum of issues in history and sociology than Goffman. Nonetheless, as compared to the work of, say, Max Weber, Simmel's writings lack that raw intellectual power generated by the work of his contemporary and friend.

Goffman's writings, in my view, have been persistently misunderstood. To some degree these misunderstandings are the result of views of his work that Goffman himself tended to foster. But in some part they derive from a disinclination on the part of more 'orthodox' sociologists to grasp the significance of Goffman's writings for their own concerns. Goffman produced his major writings at a time at which sociology tended to be dominated by naturalistic and functionalist models of social activity. His work resisted incorporation within such perspectives. For many of those who thought that the major proccupations of sociology lay with the then dominant outlook, Goffman's writings tended to be seen as no more than light relief from the serious business of institutional analysis. Goffman himself undeniably helped to connive in this. He saw himself as working within a particular field of study that had few direct implications for the central areas of sociological interest. Thus in *Frame Analysis*, arguably his most openly systematic work, he comments

that his study is not about 'the organisation of society . . . I make no
claim whatsoever to be talking about the core matters of sociology
– social organisation and social structure. Those matters have been
and can continue to be quite nicely studied without reference to
frame at all' (Goffman 1974: 13). It is as if the forces that somehow
create the structural characteristics of social systems are quite distant
from the activities of individuals in their day-to-day lives. Actors
seemingly move in a pre-structured social world, of which they must
take account in their actions, but which they play no part in bringing
into being or perpetuating. It is no doubt for this reason that
Goffman's writings fit quite happily into that division between
macro and micro studies so characteristic of a good deal of modern
sociology. Goffman often labelled his work 'micro-sociological',
apparently feeling entirely happy with such a designation. But he
was usually careful to avoid the connotation that the micro level is
somehow more fundamental than the macro. If he was in some sense
a methodological individualist, it was not something he chose openly
to defend.

There are four respects, I want to argue, in which Goffman's
writings have been persistently misunderstood. First, it is commonly
asserted that Goffman's work is no more than a series of
idiosyncratic observations about trivial features of social life.
Brilliant, ironic and mordant such observations may be, they have
no overall intellectual unity. Goffman is thought to be someone
overtaken by the tumble of his own ideas, which scatter in all directions and resist any kind of overall consolidation. Commonly held
though such a view may be, it is surely quite mistaken. From his
earliest writings, Goffman has quite clearly been preoccupied with a
number of concerns that persistently reappear in all his writings. In
his words, he has been absorbed by the study of social interaction,
which 'can be identified narrowly as that which uniquely transpires
in social situations, that is, environments in which two or more
individuals are physically in one another's response presence . . .
My concern over the years has been to promote acceptance of this
face-to-face domain as an analytically viable one – a domain which
might be titled, for want of any happy name, the *interaction order* – a
domain whose preferred method of study is micro analysis'
(Goffman 1983b: 2).

Second, it is sometimes suggested that Goffman is primarily
nothing more than a cynical observer of white American middle-
class mores. However acute Goffman's insights might be, they only
apply over a very restricted milieu, to the self-seeking activities of

individuals living in a competitive, individualistic cultural environment. Goffman himself seems a little uncertain in this respect. Thus in one of his most well-known works, he remarks: 'my own experience has been mainly with middle-class conduct in a few regions of America, and it is to this that most of my comments apply' (Goffman 1963: 5). However while this may be an appropriate reserve in respect of some of the generalizations he seeks to make, nothing is more plain than that Goffman's writing is neither perceived by him, nor could be plausibly argued to be, merely a record of certain particular features of American culture. To the contrary, Goffman often makes it clear that he believes the forms of activity and the social mechanisms he describes are of very wide generality indeed. Far from only applying within a particular society, many may actually have relevance to social interaction at all times and places. Whether this be so or not, it is not difficult to see that Goffman's works contain a whole series of generalizing terms. These are not concepts that are incidental to the observations that he generates, but in very large part the means of generating them at all.

Closely related to this point is a misunderstanding concerning the nature of the actors portrayed in Goffman's writings. These are sometimes thought of as mere 'performers', concerned to pander to their own vanities by presenting themselves to others in a false or manipulative fashion. Construed in this way, Goffman's works might very well be thought to be a portrayal – and no doubt a slanted portrayal at that – of a culture in which appearance is all and self-seeking individuals predominate. But such a view is surely false. Goffman is neither a disillusioned observer of the modes of activity he analyses, nor are those whose behaviour is examined specifically self-seeking (Giddens 1984: ch. 2). Gouldner is surely wrong when he says that Goffman's work is expressive of, not merely particular sectors of American society, but that society at a particular phase of its development – following the decline of the moral discipline provided by the Protestant ethic. Goffman's writing, according to him, 'reflects the new world, in which a stratum of the new middle class no longer believes that hard work is useful or that success depends upon diligent application. In this new world there is a keen sense of the irrationality of the relationship between individual achievement and the magnitude of reward, between actual contribution and social regulation. It is the world of the high price Hollywood star and of the market for stocks, whose prices bear little relation to their earnings' (Gouldner 1971: 381). Goffman is thus held to portray an amoral social universe, in which everyone is busy trying to manipulate everyone else. But this is far removed indeed from the main thrust of his writings, which not only describe a highly moralized world of social relationships, but which tend strongly to generalize its moral nature also. Trust and tact are manifestly more fundamental and binding features of social interaction than is the cynical manipulation of appearances. Thus people routinely shore up or 'repair' the moral fabric of interaction, by displaying tact in what they say and do, by engaging in 'remedial practices', and helping others to save face. If day-to-day social life is a game which may be on occasion turned to one's own advantage, it is a game into which we are all thrust and in which collaboration is essential.

Finally, Goffman's writings are often mistakenly presented as though they were an ethnography, an anthropology of culture. The reason why is easy enough to see, because Goffman employs none of the sophisticated modes of quantitive research or analysis favoured by many sociologists. If anthropological method be identified with the qualitative study of the small scale, based upon participants' observations, then Goffman's writings do have a definite 'anthropological bias'. Nonetheless, it would be an error to make too much of this. As it is often understood, at any rate, ethnography involves the detailed study of specific communities, analysed over a lengthy period of time. Goffman's work has one of its main points of origin in just such a study, in the shape of the doctoral dissertation which he wrote describing a Shetland Isle community. But most of his subsequent studies do not fall into this category at all, or only marginally so. As has been mentioned, Goffman does not undertake any detailed cross-cultural comparisons in respect of the material he discusses and the examples he offers. The presumption is that others might test out the degree of generality of his ideas if they should be moved to do so. Goffman is interested in the alien and the exotic, but not in the sense of comparative ethnology. He seeks to disclose the unfamiliar in the familiar, to produce an intellectual estrangement from what is most common and habitual in our day-to-day activities. When offering an overall characterization of his writings, Goffman is more prone to invoke the example of ethology rather than ethnography. Social groups of animals interest him because animals lack that capacity so essential to human social organization – and hence outside the scope of Goffman's studies of interaction – communication with others absent in space and time. In animal groups, almost by definition, all that goes on is the result of the influences of physical co-presence. As Goffman puts this:

Ethologists are forced to end up being students of face-to-face inter-action. So they are a source. More important, they have developed a field discipline that leads them to study animal conduct in very close detail and with a measure of control on preconception. In consequence, they have developed the ability to cut into the flow of apparently haphazard activity at its articulation and to isolate natural patterns. Once these behavioural sequences are pointed out to the observer, his seeing is changed. So ethologists provide an inspiration.[6]

(Goffman 1971: 54)

When, as he quite often does, Goffman refers to his studies as 'naturalistic', this has very little to do with the 'naturalism' involved in the views of those influenced by logical positivism. It denotes both an attitude of the observer and a trait of the interaction that is observed.

Clearing up these misconceptions will allow us quite readily to disclose the systematic content of Goffman's writings. But there is more than one level upon which this can be done. We can first of all attempt to outline the systematic social theory that Goffman himself seeks to advance in his work. Given the rather seamless nature of his writings, this is not quite as easy to achieve as it might be. There is no overall study in which Goffman brings together his main ideas in a fully developed manner. But it is not enough only to set out Goffman's own understanding of his work. A critical analysis of Goffman's own interpretation of his ideas might help us see how far they might be incorporated into a version of social theory that escapes the brackets he put around his own writings.

ENCOUNTERS, FRAMING AND CO-PRESENCE

Goffman is above all the theorist of co-presence, not of small groups. His work therefore cross-cuts the distinction between primary and secondary group and other similar distinctions well entrenched in the sociological literature. For one thing, many small groups (for example, the family or kinship groups) endure over time. Goffman is not really interested in the mechanisms of such endurance. More-over, co-present gatherings can be quite large, as in the case of theatre audiences or crowds. Interaction in circumstances of co-presence tends to oscillate between unfocused and focused exchanges. Unfocused interaction, in Goffman's definition, exists in so far as individuals who are co-present in a particular setting have some kind of mutual awareness. Focused interaction, Goffman's main concern throughout his writings, involves individuals directly attending to what each other are saying and doing for a particular segment of time. While the prototype is conversation, many other activities may claim the attention of parties to a given situation of co-presence. Focused interaction, Goffman points out, does share certain properties with those of small groups (Goffman 1961a: 8). But the differences are at least as important as the similarities. All groups or collectivities, whether large scale or small, have some general traits of organization. These include a division between roles, provision for socialization, capability for collective action, and sustained modes of connection with the surrounding social environment. Groups exist when their members are not together. Encounters, on the other hand, by definition only exist when the parties to them are physically in each other's presence. From such togetherness a range of characteristics flow. 'Examples of such properties include embarrassment, maintenance of poise, capacity for non-distractive verbal communication, adherence to a code regarding giving up and taking over the speaker role, and allocation of spatial position' (Goffman 1961a: 11). In focused interaction, the participants must maintain continuous involvement in the mutual focus of activity. This cannot be a property of social groups in general, precisely because of their persistence across different contexts of co-presence. Encounters may be a particular aspect or phase of the existence of collectivites, but to assimilate the two is to miss the very distinctive features of encounters upon which Goffman wishes to concentrate attention.

Groups may come together in a regular manner, and their members may even all be frequently present together in particular settings. We might tend to think that these gatherings are 'meetings of the group' and that to study them is to study the group in an immediate fashion. In fact, Goffman says, we should regard such encounters as meetings of the individuals who are the members of a group, and seek to understand what goes on in terms of their participation within a particular form of encounter, not in terms of their membership of the group. Goffman insists on this very strongly, because it is a key part of his attempt to mark out a distinctive subject matter concerning the 'interaction order'. The processes which sustain group relations across time and space are not necessarily the same as those underlying such an interaction order. Thus, for example, Goffman proposes that the modes of tension management in each are different. Tensions develop in encounters when the 'official' focus of attention is disturbed or threatened. Modes of managing such tensions may actually act to inhibit bases of group identity or affiliation. Thus a particular attention focus may be altered or redefined by participants to an encounter in order to cope with perceived threats to the original focus of attention. But this may have the effect of dissolving, at least in the particular context, the group relations in which some co-present individuals are involved.

Goffman's concern is therefore with 'situated activity systems'. He is not interested in, nor does he seek to analyse, for example, the role of a doctor in relation to the wider medical community. He studies the doctor only in terms of his or her activities within the settings of a single social establishment. But even here Goffman choses to ignore the detailed round of activity which the individual follows. Only some of this round of activities involves the person in situated activity systems – encounters forming focused interaction with others.

> The performance of a surgical operation is an example. Illustrations from other walks of life would be: the playing through of a game; the execution of one run of a small group experiment; the giving and getting of a haircut. Such systems of activity are to be distinguished from a task performed wholly by a single person, whether alone or in the presence of others, and from a joint endeavour that is 'multi-situated', in that it is executed by subgroups of persons operating from different rooms.
>
> (Goffman 1961a: 96)

Of course, Goffman does on occasion make an attempt to approach the overall study of social organization directly – most specifically, in his account of 'total institutions'. But even here his prime concern tends to be with how the overall features of the organization influence modes of interaction within specific settings.

A concentration upon co-presence draws attention to the body, its disposition and display – a theme that runs throughout the whole of Goffman's writings. Information conveyed in contexts of co-presence is necessarily embodied and Goffman specifically contrasts this to communications of a disembodied type, such as those involved in a telephone conversation, or an exchange of letters. The body is not simply used as an 'adjunct' to communication in situations of co-presence; it is the anchor of the communicative skills which can be transferred to disembodied types of messages. There are some circumstances in which embodied messages may be essentially one way, as for example when one person spies on another through a hole in the wall, or when a psychologist observes subjects in an experiment through a one-way vision screen. Such circumstances however, are unusual.

Normally any individual who is in a position to receive embodied messages from others also makes himself or herself available for embodied information that is accessible to them (Goffman 1963: 15). In focused interaction, according to Goffman, this is of basic importance. For it presumes and calls forth a monitoring by each individual of the other or others' responses in relation to their own. Each individual, in other words, not only has an audience in relation to whom he or she must 'perform', but knows that others see his or her activities in the same light. 'Ordinarily, then, to use our naked senses is to use them nakedly and to be made naked by their use. We are clearly seen as the agents of our acts, there being very little chance of disavowing having committed them; neither having given nor received messages cannot be easily denied, at least among those immediately involved' (Goffman 1963: 16). The norms or rules that regulate behaviour in circumstances of co-presence thus have a special form, and a variety of nuances, not possessed by other types. In the matter of sustaining face-to-face communication, everyone is in the affair together and can be seen to be so. Certain desired outcomes may be facilitated by this, but there always are attendant risks. In the presence of one another, individuals become open to forms of psychic and physical molestation that cannot be operated at a distance. Given the inherent reciprocity of such interaction, others of course become equally vulnerable. Every case of interaction thus has an inherently confrontational character, but it is one typically balanced and managed by the resources individuals mutually apply to ensure respect and consideration for one another.

Every individual brings to an encounter a personal biography and a range of personality characteristics. Roles specify generalized expectations to which an individual has more or less closely to conform when in a particular situated context. However all roles can be performed in a manner giving them a particular personal stamp, and allowing the individual to utilize particular means of self-expression. In the theatre, the role 'is' the person – even though we may be fully aware that there is an actor playing the part. But in real contexts of social life, neither a single role nor a cluster of roles that an individual plays correspond to the person. The question that is frequently asked of Goffman's work – is there a self which stands behind the diversity of roles any given individual plays? – surely has to be answered in the affirmative. Goffman's definition of the acting self, to be sure, is usually fairly vague. But he makes it clear enough that the 'perduring moral character . . . animal nature, and so forth' (Goffman 1974: 573) has to be distinguished from the multiplicity of roles that are enacted. The person is not some sort of mini-agent, standing behind and directing various role performances. Such performances are integral to what agency is and to the demonstration of agency to others. The self consists in an awareness of identity which simultaneously transcends specific roles and provides an integrating means of relating them to personal biography; and a set of dispositions for managing the transactions between motives and the expectations 'scripted' by particular roles.

All roles involve situated performances. But these are neither exhaustive of the role nor are they necessarily the same as the 'situated roles' that emerge in encounters. Situated roles may consolidate the expectations involved in a more encompassing role, or they may inhibit them. To illustrate this, Goffman gives the example of riders on a merry-go-round (Goffman 1961a: 97). A merry-go-round seems to provide both an objectively prescribed distribution of positions and an 'activity circuit' that is mechanically given. But when individuals are arranged in this fashion, a type of social interaction typically emerges which meshes together the individuals taking the ride. As in other circumstances of co-presence, there is much opportunity for reciprocal communication and the generation of feeling. While the ride goes on, there may be brought into being a sort of collective excitement linking all individuals involved. For children, the modes of expression thus involved may not be particularly discrepant from what is expected of their behaviour in other circumstances in which they are enjoying themselves. But for adults, succumbing to the mood of collective intensity created by the participants can cause problems because this might be seen to diverge from the usual expectations of an adult or parental role; a certain measure of embarrassment might therefore creep in once the ride is over. Those who run the roundabout maintain their distance from such activity systems by casual displays of mastery of the moving vehicle, nonchalantly carrying out manoeuvres which the uninitiated would not dare even to attempt.

Roles may be played at as well as played. Hence the possibilities for children, and stage actors, to mimic what in other circumstances is done with serious intent and with real consequences. The distinction is more blurred than may appear at first sight, however, because all roles demand some sort of authentication which the individual provides of his or her capability to play them. Hence the significance of the dramaturgical metaphor in Goffman's writings, a metaphor the limitations of which, contrary to what his critics often assert, he is acutely aware. Individuals who act out roles are not and cannot be just like individuals who act at roles. This is exactly why Goffman's analysis of role distance is so interesting and penetrating. Role distance is not available to those who play at roles – unless this is a child mimicking the specifics of a situated role performance of an adult. Role distance depends upon a separation between self and role, but may be the means whereby an identity with the seriousness of that role is maintained. Role distance can be a way of demonstrating supreme confidence in the performance of tasks involved in a particular role. By demonstrating to others that he or she does not fully 'embrace', in Goffman's term, the expectations involved in a role, the individual might actually validate rather than cast doubt upon its authenticity. Thus a surgeon who finds time for small talk, and even banter, during the course of performing an operation might be able thereby to reassure colleagues about his or her competence, and might do so more effectively than another who adopts a more sober and inflexible demeanour.

In *The Presentation of Self in Everyday Life* (1959), Goffman tends to concentrate upon situations in which performances are manipulated in such a way as to conceal the true motives of those who carry them out, and where such performances are deliberately staged – no doubt the view that Goffman portrays a cynical world of self-concerned agents, in which appearance counts above all else, derived from this. But it is a perspective that is corrected in Goffman's subsequent works. Performances do allow individuals to cut a dash; they may be used as a means of concealing feelings of indifference, or even of loathing, towards others with whom role expectations imply some kind of positive relationship. Performances are however just as frequently used to reassure others of genuine motives and commitments as they are to disguise insincerities.

Goffman's preoccupation with co-presence leads him to be constantly alert to the significance of time and space in relation to human activities. As Goffman defines it, social interaction is inherently circumscribed in time-space. The timing and spacing of contexts of encounters gives social life an episodic character. Episodes are 'strung out' in the day-to-day experience of the individual, but also are the occasion of daily collaboration in social settings. The architecture of locales is fundamental to encounters, because it focuses specific types of available co-presence and influences the spacing of contacts undertaken. All encounters tend to have 'markers' that establish their beginning and end. But all encounters are also limited by the character of the physical setting. Boundary markers, as Goffman puts it, 'occur before and after the activity in time and may be circumscriptive in space; in brief, there are temporal and spatial brackets . . . one may speak, then, of opening and closing temporal brackets and bounding spatial brackets' (1974: 251-2). The settings of interaction, for Goffman, are not just milieux within which activities happen to occur. Rather, they are routinely monitored, in common with the activities of co-present individuals, in the sustaining of encounters. The time-space zoning of encounters is often fundamental to the performances that are carried on. The existence of back regions, for example, helps to explain a good deal of what goes on in 'public' settings of activity.

The spacing of individuals within encounters is of vital importance to their form. Goffman's interest lies particularly in settings of interaction which are relatively fluid. In such settings, focused interaction occurs against the background of fluctuating relations of an unfocused kind. This is true, for example, of conversations at parties, of a couple who exchange the time of day against the background of a hurrying street crowd, or individuals who talk to one another in a hospital ward. Of course there are more highly organized and ritual settings of co-presence, in which the timing and spacing of appropriate responses is much more formalized. Goffman in general has much less to say about these than about more informal meetings and gatherings. The logic of this is apparent in the light of his professed concentration upon the interaction order. For there is in his view much more likely to be a direct relation between generalized roles and behaviour in the setting of co-presence in these latter circumstances than in the former. The very formalization of the setting, and of the nature of turn-taking in communication expresses this in, for example, a court of law.

The more formalized settings of interaction are those likely to be most closely linked with defined back regions, because in these regions control can to some degree be relaxed. Not just back regions, but a variety of barriers to perception can be used as 'involvement shields', behind which activities that would otherwise be disapproved of can be carried on. All organizations in which formalized role relations are called for have areas, or sometimes only nooks and crannies, which allow such shelter. As Goffman points out, actors may maintain a certain level of presentability in relation to likely responses of others even when alone. For if an individual is inadvertently discovered 'out of play', both that person and the intruder are likely to suffer embarrassment.

In circumstances of co-presence, it is not enough for an individual to be an agent, that is, routinely to monitor reflexively and organize what he or she does; that person must also be seen to 'demonstrate agency' to others. Goffman approaches the analysis of 'action' from three rather different angles. Action means first of all the capability of agents to understand what they do and to use that understanding as part of the doing of it. Action is this sense occurs within primary frameworks, which are the grounding of our experience of ourselves as agents. Goffman's preferred term for this is 'guided doings'. In guided doings we monitor both what we do in relation to the natural and to the social worlds. We employ primary frameworks both to direct the course of our own activities and to understand those of others as being different from events of nature. 'When the sun comes up, a natural event; when the blind is pulled down in order to avoid what has come up, a guided doing' (Goffman 1974: 24). Unlike most of those who have written about agency, however, Goffman suggests that the individuals must chronically display agency to others. Routinely actors have to display competence in terms of control of bodily manoeuvring and positioning and the interpretation of communications from others. That this is so, Goffman points out, can be demonstrated by what happens in situations where the individual experiences a lapse of control – either in what is done or in what is said. One category of 'response cries' is bound up with such lapses. A response cry is not a statement, even a highly elliptical one; nor is it apparently directed at another. However, a response cry uttered when one drops something, or otherwise makes a hash of something one can ordinarily accomplish without too much difficulty, has the consequence of demonstrating to others awareness of the lapse, and that it is only a lapse, not a sign of generalized incompetence of bodily management (Goffman 1981b: 101–3).

There is a third sense of action to which Goffman gives a good deal of attention. This is action in the sense of 'where the action is'. This might seem a rather inconsequential sense of the term, compared to the two others. But its importance in Goffman's eyes is considerable. For discovering 'where the action is' is an exploration and accentuation of those very qualities which define the particular character of experiences and encounters, setting them off from the wider world. 'Where the action is' is where the individual feels a sense of worth and engrossment, 'a plane of being, an engine of

meaning, a world in itself, different from all other worlds . . .'
(Goffman 1961a: 26).

Focused interaction always involves 'face engagements'. Where
two or more individuals are co-present, and not involved in a
focused way with one another, they may, in many circumstances at
least, gaze quite openly at others. It is equally possible for a person
to treat others present on the scene as though they were not there, as
not worthy of a glance – although this is something that has to be
controlled and is very rarely the same as genuinely not noticing
something in the environment.

But this kind of behaviour contrasts with what is normal, which
Goffman labels 'civil inattention'. The actor shows that he or she is
aware that the others are there, while not making those others the
object of any special curiosity. Thus the eyes of one person may
quickly look over the eyes of another, but no 'recognition' is
typically permitted. Glances of this sort are not sustained as the two
individuals actually pass one another, when there is normally a
mutual avoidance of gaze. There is, as Goffman expresses it, a kind
of 'dimming of lights'. Civil inattention, like all other aspects of the
monitoring of the body and its gestures demands chronic attention to
detail. Its significance is that each individual implies to others that
he or she has no reason to fear them, and *vice versa*. The management
of civil inattention demands that the gaze be neither too direct, nor
too averted or 'defensively dramatic'; in both cases this might
indicate to others the possibility that there is 'something going on'
(Goffman 1963: 84–5).

The complexities of civil inattention are many. We may ordinarily
inspect others in a more prolonged way if we are distant from them
and as long as eye contact does not occur. The closer an individual is
to another, the more exposed each will be to the other and the
greater the obligation they will tend to feel to maintain a clearly
demonstrated civil inattention. Mild embarrassment is likely to
result if one individual turns suddenly and catches the gaze of
another, thereby seeing that person looking too intently at him or
her. The person thus caught out might then in a prudent way act as
though this was just a coincidental crossing of glances during the
course of permissible observations, or perhaps indicate that he or she
is in fact trying to catch the attention of someone standing just
behind the individual involved. Staring in turn is frequently used as
the first mode of sanction when the proprieties of civil inattention are
not observed. As Goffman points out, it is very often the first and
last warning that it is necessary to provide to individuals who

transgress in such a manner. Those who bear visible stigmata may feel themselves especially vulnerable to transgressions of the rules of civil inattention; while others might find it particularly difficult both to maintain those rules in a judicious fashion in respect of them and to 'give off' the expression to the individual that he or she is being treated just the same as anyone else.

Focused interaction, requiring continuous face engagement, always involves the provision of 'openings' demonstrating the abandonment of civil inattention. Where individuals are strangers, the moment of discarding civil inattention is potentially perilous, since a range of misunderstandings can ensue about the nature of the encounter which is being established. Although there are many circumstances in which the nature of the setting allows for a clear-cut definition of the forms of encounter established therein, there are equally many settings in modern societies where such is not the case. Hence even the joining of eye contact may first of all be ambiguous and tentative. An actor who wishes to control the encounters to which he or she is likely to be subject in a particular setting will deliberately avoid certain eye contacts. Thus a customer might unavailingly try to catch the eye of a busy waiter, the latter taking some care to avoid such contact being made. Once a face engagement has been opened, via the maintenance of mutual gaze and by their spatial positioning individuals tend to maintain a 'huddle', providing the opportunity to monitor each other's contributions and reactions in an intensive fashion and by the same means to keep others who may be co-present more or less excluded. In situations where, for one reason or another, individuals find themselves in enforced physical proximity, such as in a lift, ordinary conversation may be suspended, or carried on in a limp fashion, being resumed when more normal spacing is possible. Even the most evanescent of encounters tends to establish something of a bond of moral solidarity between participants. The more protracted an encounter is, the more developed such a bond tends to be, and the mutual obligations associated with it to deepen. Once initiated, an encounter brings into being a 'relationship wedge' (Goffman 1963: 105). As soon as one has extended the consideration to another of attending to what that person says for a moment, some sort of moral commitment is established, which each may use as a basis of further claims put upon the other. 'In noting the implicit contract that makes persons present delicately accessible and inaccessible to each other, we can go on to note a basic margin of appetite and distaste to be found in social situations. The reason why individuals are obliged to restrain themselves from making encounter overtures provide many of the reasons why they might want to do so. And the obligation to be properly accessible often covers a desire to be selectively quite unavailable' (ibid.: 106). Naturally, what applies at the beginning of encounters also occurs when they are broken off, or the individual disengages from focused interaction. Signals or markers are ordinarily provided of the intention to close the encounter; in most circumstances these must be accompanied by the use of tactful devices whereby the moral bond that has been established between the individual and the other or others is not placed in question by the termination of the encounter.

Goffman gives a good deal of attention to the timing and spacing of encounters. When an individual is permitted to move in to a particular region, he or she is usually expected to display some sensitivity to the boundaries that surround it. Sometimes these boundaries are so complete that they insulate the situation of inter-action entirely. In the vast majority of circumstances, however, some kind of communication across the boundary is possible. Physical divisions, such as the walls between rooms, tend to be treated as though communication were cut off from the outside regardless of how far in fact this is the case. Walls are socially respected communication barriers as much as they are purely material divisions between the enactment of various forms of encounters. Eavesdropping is a breach of the tact which is expected to be displayed in respect of encounters of which one is not a part, and hence embarrassment is the likely consequence if someone stumbles across the eavesdropper. 'Accessible' face-engagements – those that are carried on in circumstances where there are others present – involve special forms of timing and spacing. In addition to the spacing of the body, this is accomplished also by the sound level of the voice, and by what is spoken about at particular phases of the encounter. 'Sensitive' topics will not be discussed when others co-present to whom they might be relevant are in the immediate vicinity. This very often has to be carefully managed, even if it is for the most part done quite routinely, or otherwise a given conver-sational huddle might look like a furtive knot of conspirators. However since all those co-present tend to co-operate in the maintenance of encounters, those not party to a particular face engagement will tacitly collaborate in maintaining 'conventional engagement closure'. Where participants in focused interaction cast their voices too low, this in fact is likely to be thought impolite, since it tends to discredit the disposition of others to display civil inattention.

Talk is the basic medium of focused encounters and the conversation is the prototype of the exchange of utterances involved in talk. Using the word 'talk' rather than 'language' is of the first importance to the analyses which Goffman seeks to provide. 'Language' suggests a formal system of signs and rules. 'Talk' carries more the flavour of the situated nature of utterances and gestures embedded within the routine enactment of encounters. In speaking of verbal 'conversations', rather than of 'speech', Goffman stresses that the meaning of what is said must be interpreted in terms of a temporal sequence of utterances. Talk is not something which is just 'used' in circumstances of interaction. The meanings which are deployed through talk are organized and specified by the whole range of subtleties of management of face, voice, or gesture and disposition of the body brought into play in circumstances of co-presence generally. In his early work, Goffman both anticipated and helped shape the development of what has subsequently come to be called 'conversational analysis'; in his later writings he has drawn upon it in developing his own discussions of talk and interaction. Only one person can talk at a time in a conversation, so all conversations are organized in terms of turn-taking procedures and mechanisms. The utterances of contributors to a conversation occur at different stages of 'sequence time'. What each individual says is oriented not just to what has been said before, but usually anticipates further contributions to the conversation. 'Sequence time' is most often organized dialogically, even in a conversation where there are several participants. Thus most conversations can be studied as composites of dialogical units, having interjections from other conversational participants. Turn-taking in conversations tends to cut across, and dismember, the units of speech grammarians are prone to call sentences. Sentences are often not completed, or have an 'incorrect' grammatical form, and indeed talk tends to have in general a much more fractured and dislocated surface form than most branches of orthodox linguistics tend to recognize (Goffman 1981b: 22ff.). Neither sentences nor even utterances correspond to the units of talk in a conversation, 'turns at talk'.

However, given that the nature of conversation is fundamentally dialogical, two or more turns can function as an interactional unit. To analyse this phenomenon, Goffman speaks of the 'moves' that are made over stretches of talk between conversational participants. A move in a conversation is like a strategy in a game, normally having a ritualized character. Moves include silences as well as actual utterances. Thus a suspension of talk during the turn of a contributor to a conversation may be very different in its implications from a silence maintained while another talks. While moves may consist of several sentences, they may also be composed solely of short interjections – as when, by uttering 'hmmm', 'gosh', 'gee', etc., listeners indicate sympathetic interest in what a speaker is saying. Speaking without having the floor, or even trying to get it, can be a move in the conversational game. On this basis, Goffman is able to show some of the limitations involved in thinking of talk in terms of statements calling forth replies. Many moves do seem to invoke rejoinders, but there are a variety of ways in which individuals can express intentions, provide approval or disapproval, or otherwise make their views known, without directly committing themselves to turn-taking within the conversation. A key aspect of all talk in situations of interaction is that both speakers and listeners depend upon a saturated physical and social context for making sense of what is said. For most purposes it is therefore not relevant that utterances do not generally consist of the 'well-formed' sentences often given primacy of place in linguistics. 'Well-formed' sentences can in a certain sense stand by themselves: they can for example be interpreted via media other than those of the spoken word. But it is a considerable mistake to assess the nature of talk in terms of models of 'perfect' language. Only in very special circumstances – for example, in the talk of radio or television announcers – is there any requirement that faultless speech should be maintained.

In analysing talk Goffman thus places a heavy stress upon communicative competence, in the manner in which the concept is developed by Hymes (1972b). Many branches of traditional linguistics have approached the study of language as though day-to-day talk were like radio- or television-announcing. But such an activity depends upon special forms of competence which isolate from the ordinary context of conversation certain capabilities of enunciation. Communicative competence depends upon a mastery of the whole range of proprieties observed in different forms and styles of encounter. Failure at the competent execution of an act or communicative move does not in itself compromise the perceived competence of the agent, and is likely to call forth remedial action. 'Remedial interchanges' are both a category of interaction and an aspect of certain forms of interaction. Consider an ephemeral incident on the street. An individual trips over another, says 'sorry', while as the other passes he answers 'okay' (1971: 139ff.). Here, as in lapses in other areas, the offender can be potentially seen as someone not competent to control the movements of his body. He or she might also be potentially perceived as an aggressor. The ritual interchange reassures the victim of the competence and the lack of malevolence of the offender; while the response reassures the first individual that this interpretation is to be accepted. To show that the interchange is a 'remedial account', rather than merely an 'apology', we can consider the fact that other glosses could have been offered to redeem competence. Thus the offender could pass on through calling out 'have to catch the train' or might replace the apology with a request: 'May I get through?' As Goffman says:

> The individual does not go about merely going about his business. He goes about constrained to sustain a viable image of himself in the eyes of others. Since local circumstances always will reflect upon him, and since these circumstances will vary unexpectedly and constantly, footwork, or rather self-work, will be continuously necessary. Each lurching of whatever the individual is standing on will have to be offset, often by his leading into the fall with a self that has been projected as unserious, the real person thereby made free to tacitly take up a counter-balancing position . . . However skittish he might be about behaving properly, he nonetheless takes care to have some behavioural reply ready in any situation where circumstances have suddenly called him into question. He need not honour a rule of conduct that applies to him. He need not even provide virtual accounts, apologies, and excuses for his deviations. But at least he must be at pains to portray an advocable relationship to the negative judgement of him which results.
>
> (Goffman 1971: 185–6)

The highly complicated and more or less constant dutifulness that individuals must display in sustaining their overall competence is perhaps most plainly revealed by situations where it is not observed or comes under pressure. Three main circumstances of such a sort are discussed in Goffman's writings – where individuals have to manage some kind of stigmata which inhibit the maintenance of ordinary proprieties; where the usual conditions of co-presence are systematically constrained, as in total institutions; and where individuals for one reason or another do not display normal competencies, that is, the behaviour of the 'mentally ill'. In modern societies the latter two are obviously often closely combined, because of the incarceration of mental patients. It is no doubt significant that the only type of regularized organization which Goffman discusses in an extensive way is the total institution. Other organizations seem to supply for him only the territories within which interaction is found and encounters occur. But the pressures of total institutions are such that proprieties observed elsewhere come under extraordinary strain (Goffman 1961b).

The maintenance of the competencies and proprieties that the majority of actors display and observe depends upon the time-space separation of some activities from others. Even within small oral cultures, there are a variety of spatial and conventional divisions separating 'inside' from 'outside' in contexts of interaction. Total institutions are physically circumscribed by barriers directed 'at the outside'. It is not just that they enclose individuals, often forcibly, within a restricted and communal milieu; it is that this specifically contrasts with the relative freedom of mobility that exists externally to the institution in the rest of society. By erecting impermeable barriers against the rest of the world, total institutions dissolve the divisions usually separating different spheres of life. All aspects of day-to-day life are subject to a single authority (ibid.: 17). Much of what is usually carried on in private has to be done in public, and much that is usually within the control of individuals is determined by the administrative authorities. In total institutions, incoming individuals are divested of most of the accoutrements of personal identity in the outside world. They may also be subject to specific forms of material and symbolic degradation. The staff of the organization may often ignore the forms of tact, remedy and respect found in interaction in the outside world. Information that ordinarily can be kept to oneself is available to staff in the form of dossiers or files; just as the spatial preserves that can be maintained between self and role in the external environment tend to vanish. Thus total institutions threaten a whole gamut of practices whereby actors are able to demonstrate both to others and to themselves their competence as agents. This is surely why they are often associated with forms of response that Freud would classify as regressive. This sort of enforced infantilism is the fate of many of those incarcerated within total institutions, and may be actively employed by members of staff to facilitate their control.

However, in Goffman's portrayal of total institutions individuals do not appear for the most part as broken beings. On the contrary, they find a multiplicity of ways of recovering their integrity, of creating personal territories of their own, and of combining together to resist the impositions to which they are subject. There are all sorts of 'dark corners' in which through their wit or their cunning inmates establish counteractive modes of interaction which 'breed and start to infest the establishment' (ibid.: 268). Many of these might involve conduct which would be regarded as quite unseemly or improper on the outside, but which in essence recapture for the inmate what is provided for by the orthodox proprieties in other settings. Those whom we choose to designate as the 'mentally ill' are perhaps in large part defined as such in terms of their inability, or unwillingness, to observe the standard proprieties on the outside. In the carceral organization, these traits may be accentuated, and thereby seemingly confirmed, by the nature of the settings which such persons experience. What might seem highly bizarre or quite incomprehensible behaviour in the external context of social life might come to seem quite normal even among those who were previously regarded as perfectly sane. In the study of 'mental illness' Goffman is thereby able to provide a particularly acute demonstration of what might be called the 'hermeneutic principle' that guides all his investigations. As he says, referring to the field work that he carried out in a mental hospital, 'it was then and still is my belief that any group of persons – prisoners, primitives, pilots, or patients – develop a life of their own that becomes meaningful, reasonable, and normal once you get close to it, and that a good way to learn about any of these worlds is to submit oneself in the company of the members to the daily round of petty contingencies they are subject to' (ibid.: 7).

MICRO CONTEXTS AND MACRO-STRUCTURAL PROPERTIES

In the foregoing section I do not claim to have provided an exhaustive analysis of the themes in Goffman's writings. I hope to have indicated with some plausibility, nevertheless, that Goffman's work is of a very systematic character indeed. Throughout his career he resolutely refused to tread upon two terrains that would seem to stretch invitingly open to him. On the one hand, with the exception of his work on total institutions, which in any case is expressed mainly in terms of their effects upon individual activity, Goffman maintained a strict separation between his work and that of sociologists interested in the macro-structural properties of social systems. On the other hand, various comments and allusions throughout his writings notwithstanding, he refused to be drawn into any kind of elaborated account of the psychology of the self. It is quite clear why he chose to work within these self-imposed restrictions. As he saw it, the study of situations of co-presence was something of an untrammelled field for social analysis, a field whose contours could only be explored by bracketing out most of the issues with which both sociologists and psychologists traditionally have been concerned. Who could dispute the fruitfulness of Goffman's decision strictly to confine the realm of his investigations? In so doing he not only brought into view substantively new arenas of study, but he was able to explore questions invested with a new significance as a result of trends in social theory and philosophy over the past several decades. Goffman was by no stretch of the imagination a philosopher. Yet in concentrating on the mundane, the apparently trivial, in the context of day-to-day life, Goffman's writings resonate strongly with some of the emphases of hermeneutic phenomenology and with the philosophy of the later Wittgenstein. The routine and the mundane have a great deal to teach us about quite fundamental issues of human experience, action and consciousness (cf. Giddens 1979: ch 1).

These philosophical schools of thought are certainly not without their shortcomings. And in some part these converge with those that can be discovered in Goffman's work. Rewarding though it may be, I want to argue that Goffman's obdurate preoccupation with situations of co-presence leads him to underestimate the generalized importance of his theories for more 'standard' – that is, macro-structural – problems of sociology.

Goffman's own views on the nature of his enterprise were clearly articulated in an article written as his Presidential Address to the American Sociological Association, at the end of his life. (He could not help approaching the occasion reflexively. What was going on in *this* particular situation of co-presence?) In the paper he reaffirms his overriding concern with the interaction order as 'a substantive domain in its own right' (Goffman 1983b: 2). Most of our day-to-day life is passed in the presence of others. Face-to-face interaction is not only clearly bounded in time and space, hence forming a clearly defined subject matter, it is mainly determined by exigencies of the very situation of co-presence itself. There is not a 'latent phase'; the mutual involvement of participants is of critical importance and structures the very same circumstances it is structured by. Goffman here seems much more confident about the universal or near-universal features of interaction in circumstances of co-presence than he does elsewhere. It is plausible to say, he avers, that frequently found characteristics of interaction are 'rooted in certain universal conditions of social life (ibid.: 3). But he also goes on to reject an exaggerated 'situationalism'. Most settings of social behaviour extend interaction in time and space well beyond any particular context of co-presence. Moreover each individual within any given situation brings to it a pre-given biography and personality, focused through forms of knowledge shared in common with others. It might be argued, Goffman points out, that the properties of large-scale collectivities are no more than a composite of what goes on in a variety of circumstances of co-presence. One might think that Goffman might find such an argument congenial, since it would seem to add very considerable weight to the importance of the sort of work he carries out. However, he will have none of such a view. Such a position, in Goffman's eyes, confuses the situation within which actions occur with the institutional consequences of those actions. We cannot infer from the study of social encounters what the institutional shape might be that those encounters in a certain sense 'support'.

Goffman also seems by this point in his career to reject any suspicion of methodological individualism much more strongly than he hitherto had done. Thus he disavows the view that interaction between co-present individuals is any more or less real than relations between social collectivities. 'I claim merely that forms of face to face life are worn smooth by constant repetition on the part of participants who are heterogeneous in many ways and yet must quickly reach a working understanding; these forms thus seem more open to systematic analysis than are the internal or external workings of many macroscopic entities' (ibid.: 9). While continuing to repudiate the idea that there are many direct connections between the interaction order and broader properties of institutions, Goffman does draw Durkheim into service in respect of characterizing the qualities of that order. Again, such a characterization is very distant from the view which sees Goffman as concerned above all with the interchanges of self-interested actors. Relations in circumstances of co-presence tend very frequently to be ceremonial and ritual. These may have connections with broader ritual occasions of a macro-structural kind. But for the most part more pervasive aspects of such ritual are internal to the interaction order. The ritual of social life should not be regarded as an 'expression' of the properties of institutions; it is a form of activity established 'in regard' of those institutions. There is only a loose coupling to the qualities of the institutions themselves. Most direct ties that can be discovered are between the interaction order and 'social relationships'. We might tend to think of the frequency of interaction between two related individuals as largely constitutive of what that relationship is.

However, how far there is an 'established' relationship between two individuals who meet in an encounter strongly influences the nature of the interaction entered into, the enquiries made of the other, and the forms of talk conducted. But once more the relationship neither defines nor brings about the range of interactive devices that are called into play in actual situations of co-presence.

What are we to make of these claims? Certainly at no time earlier in his writings has Goffman sketched out his overall position with such clarity and forcefulness. He provides what seems to be an effective rationale for his work, as a subdivision of sociology having potentially universal implications, yet distinct both from other major fields of sociological study and from the psychological analysis of motivation. Yet it does not need close scrutiny to see that this stance is not really adequately defended. Goffman has never demonstrated much interest in looking directly at how far the processes he discusses are generalizable beyond certain restricted cultural contexts of American society. This seems mainly because he adopts the cavalier attitude of the explorer of uncharted areas, preoccupied with opening up the territory but content to leave its precise mapping to others. But this is not very satisfactory. In the first place, it is one of the main reasons why his writings have seemed to most commentators much less systematic in form and intent than they really are. But, more seriously, it acts as a latent support to the assertion that the interaction order is a clearly separable domain in its own right. For it is only if the mechanisms influencing conduct in conditions of co-presence *are* generalizable across a wide range of cultural contexts that Goffman's arguments hold much water. If some of the traits of behaviour he analyses are really only the expression of limited cultural settings within a particular society, they do not support the claim that there is a distinctive interaction order stretching 'laterally' across differing institutional realms. Goffman's rather haughty disregard for examining in a concrete way the level of likely generality of his observations compromises the alleged autonomy of the interaction order.

It is striking that most of Goffman's work on interaction has a very 'flat' or homogeneous feel to it, something which is again certainly related to his wish to claim a distinctive order of investigation for his studies. I mean by this that virtually all of the illustrations Goffman gives of the forms of activity he analyses are on a par with one another in terms of their significance. Goffman's mode of procedure tends to be rather circular here. Since the interaction order is presumed to be a domain in its own right, no distinction is made between contexts of interaction which are fateful for others outside them and those that are not. Moreover, Goffman for the most part chooses to analyse situations in which there is neither an obvious disparity of power between participants, nor where the context is one inhabited by the powerful. His discussion of total institutions is again the major exception to this. Thus, although Goffman often notes that there are formalized settings in which institutionally sanctioned power is exercised – such as the courtroom – he rarely analyses such circumstances in the detail accorded to other settings of interaction. Nor does he often analyse the inter-action of the powerful – at least, in circumstances in which that power is being exercised. Decisions and policies that may have con-sequences for very large numbers of people are as much formulated in circumstances of co-presence as are the more mundane forms of interaction upon which Goffman usually concentrates. No attempt is made to differentiate these types. What should be actively established, that the interaction order is more or less everywhere 'the same', is not only taken for granted but tends to be used in a circular way to justify lack of interest in looking at such issues.

Goffman is surely right to resist characterizing his work as having any intrinsic relation to methodological individualism as a philo-sophical standpoint. The behaviour of individuals in situations of co-presence is no more or less real than the existence of more over-arching social relationships and social forms. He is also justified in suggesting that the division he draws between his studies and those concerned with structural properties of social systems does not recapitulate the micro/macro distinction as ordinarily formulated. That is to say, it is a mistake to confuse situations of co-presence with small groups, contrasting these to larger groups or collectivities. Circumstances of co-presence may involve large numbers of individuals, as where several hundred thousand people are present at a mass rally; while small groups may endure across time and space in a way in which encounters by definition do not. However, in persistently identifying his work as 'micro sociology' Goffman tends to obscure the originality of his position and at the same time glosses over some of its shortcomings (cf. Giddens 1984: 139–44).

Goffman is quite brilliant at demonstrating that what appear to be trivial and uninteresting aspects of day-to-day behaviour turn out to be fraught with implications for the sustaining of interaction between co-present individuals. But many of these features have much more to do with the reproduction of institutions than Goffman acknowledges. He recognizes several types of circumstance in which there might be, as he puts it, 'situational effects upon social structures' (Goffman 1983b: 8). But this is not an appropriate way to express the matter, since the use of the term 'effects' already presumes that situated interaction and more embracing institutions are different orders of phenomena. But such is most assuredly not the case. That this is so can be shown if we grasp the recursive character of the structural qualities of social systems. One of the plainest examples is language itself. Goffman analyses mechanisms of talk whereby communication is carried on between co-present speakers and whereby their doings are 'brought off'. Now talk is not just a situated expression of language, it is the prime means whereby language as an overall form exists at all. The overall structural properties of language, that is, the rules and generalized procedures of language use, are not properties of any individual subject, but of language communities stretching across very long spans of time-space. Knowledge of these properties is the means whereby talk is generated, while the situational elements that are used to 'make talk happen' reproduce what language *is* as a structured form.

We might take as another example Goffman's discussion of the use of tact and other supportive mechanisms as a means of maintaining trust between co-present individuals. Individuals who are co-present are inherently vulnerable to one another. Thus even between strangers engaging in a casual and passing encounter, forms of ritual tend to be observed that sustain mutual confidence and respect. Surely, however, it is apparent that the attaining of trust in this sense serves to make possible, or at least facilitate, the existence of a multiplicity of contacts and relationships that stretch across contexts of co-presence? As Simmel shows in his essay on 'The stranger', confidence in meetings with unknown others is not something that is characteristically part of traditional small communities (Simmel 1950). Studying how such confidence is created and reproduced in modern contexts might thus show a great deal about how large-scale societies are institutionally ordered across time and space.

Social institutions are formed and reformed via the recursiveness of social activity. The techniques, strategies, and modes of behaviour followed by actors in circumstances of co-presence, even in the most seemingly trivial aspects of their day-to-day life, are fundamental to the continuity of institutions across time and space. In his studies of co-presence, Goffman demonstrates that the predictability of much of social life, even on a macro-structural plane, is organized via the practices involved in what he chooses to call the interaction order. But this order is never separate from either the ordering of behaviour across contexts of co-presence, or the ordering of such contexts themselves in relation to one another. Consider again the example of trust. Trust, it might be said, is a device for stabilizing interaction. To be able to trust another person is to be able to rely upon that person to produce a range of anticipated responses. Goffman shows that there is a very significant sense in which we tend to trust strangers or chance acquaintances in the settings of modern social life. But of course we also characteristically in a deeper fashion trust certain individuals with whom we are particularly close. Trust in such instances certainly influences and orders what we do in co-present interaction with those individuals, but equally importantly it by the very same token orders our relations with them across a diversity of contexts. One might notice that analysing the means of sustaining trust in settings of interaction in modern societies cannot be meaningfully kept separate from examining other modes of sustaining confidence across separated contexts. Money, for example, may be understood as a token of confidence, allowing transactions between individuals quite ignorant of one another, but who would otherwise be disinclined to have confidence in what the other or others might promise. The pervasiveness of money transactions in modern societies is both relevant to the structuring of contexts of co-presence – influencing, for example, their 'impersonal character' – and intrudes into the very nature of interaction that might be carried on within those contexts.

Money is a vehicle of establishing relations between individuals who may be very widely separated indeed from one another in time and in space. What is interesting and important here is not just the relation between co-presence and 'transcontextual' interaction, but the relation between presence and absence in the structuring of social life. 'Presence' by definition of course exhausts the limits of our direct experience. 'Co-presence' is not really some sort of sub-category of presence in general. It is rather a form of experience, which may be assumed to be characteristic of large parts of most people's day-to-day lives, in which others are directly 'available', and in which the individual *makes* him or herself 'available' – that is, demonstrates agency in Goffman's sense. Interaction in contexts of co-presence obviously has characteristics not found in 'mediated' interaction – via the telephone, recordings, the mail and so on. But it is a mistake to see these as two opposed forms of social connection. On the contrary, each interlaces with the other in a multiplicity of subtle ways. 'Presence' – what the individual brings to and employs in any situation of conduct, whether there are others in that situation or not – is always mediated by what is absent. Goffman acknowledges, of course, that individuals come to any given situation of co-presence 'carrying an already established biography of prior dealings with other participants – or at least with participants of their kind', and also 'with a vast array of cultural assumptions presumed to be shared' (Goffman 1983b: 4). But the implications of this are very considerable. For individuals experience different contexts of co-presence as episodes within the time-space paths they trace out in the course of their day-to-day activities. Mediation between contexts in this sense – that is, the 'moving presence' of actors across time-space paths – strongly influences the nature of encounters that are entered into. Once more we are likely to have a misleading, or very partial, account of what goes on in circumstances of co-presence if we do not integrate an analysis of those circumstances with what connects them together in the continuous lives of individuals – and indeed groups.

One might point out that the difference between situations of co-presence and what might be called 'presence availability' is more blurred than Goffman usually seems to assume. In large gatherings, although individuals might be present in the same overall space with one another, they are not continuously within the range of vision or earshot of each other. They are 'available', in the sense that the individual might quite readily seek them out. But there may be more effort involved in so doing than in the case of individuals who are in adjoining rooms within a building, or in rooms on the same floor in a building. The study of the mechanisms of ensuring presence availability has to be closely tied to analysing what goes on in situations of immediate co-presence. This means relating the sorts of discussion Goffman provides with more extended analyses of the nature of the locales, and the modes of regionalization, whereby contexts of co-presence are conjoined. For example it seems entirely misleading to separate, as a distinct 'interaction order', the tissue of encounters in contemporary societies from urbanism as a social form.

The burden of the above observations is that Goffman's writings contribute much more to an understanding of 'macro-structural' properties than Goffman supposed; and that this very insight means seeking to connect in a direct way Goffman's analyses of co-presence with mechanisms of social reproduction across extended spans of time and space. However, Goffman's attempt to distinguish the interaction order as a clearly delimited field also gains plausibility from his disinclination to confront questions of motivation. If Goffman's writings are 'flat', lacking that vertical dimension which an enriched treatment of institutions would provide, they are also in a certain sense 'empty' in respect of the motivation that leads actors to behave as they do in day-to-day life. Perhaps this is another reason why, as portrayed by Goffman, actors might seem often to be shallowly cynical in their manipulation of what goes on in their social environments. Goffman makes it clear enough that there is a unitary person behind the roles that are played in the diversity of social contexts, but his discussion of this self tends to be very rudimentary indeed. He does have an analysis of motivation of sorts, established mainly as a critique of interpretations of the interaction order which he rejects. People might be seen to do the things they do in interaction with one another because they are motivated to form implicit contracts – everyone profits from following certainly mutually agreed conventions in their transactions with others. A rather different intepretation is that such motivation derives from the internalization of some sort of overall normative consensus, which is then applied in the situations of face-to-face interaction. Goffman does not so much show either or both of these interpretations to be false, as to reject the irrelevance of both of them to his endeavours. The conventions of conduct in situations of co-presence do not imply a general belief in the desirability or prudence of observing an implicit contract, nor a commitment to the value of norms that sanction the expectations followed. There are, Goffman says, 'mixed motive games' in interaction, and individuals conform to the relevant conventions 'for a wide variety of reasons' (Goffman 1983b: 5).

We might very well accept that this is so. Since, as Goffman defines them, situations of co-presence cover so much of social life, it is unlikely that conformity to the conventions involved would be reducible to any fairly simple formula. On the other hand, Goffman frequently (although, as I have mentioned, inconsistently) stakes a claim for the very general nature of the practices he analyses. If such should indeed be the case, it would definitely tend to suggest that generic mechanisms of a psychological sort are at work. I think it is in fact possible to speculate what such mechanisms might be, and although I shall not attempt to identify them here, it can be shown that we thereby add substance to the type of account that Goffman offers of interaction.

In conclusion, let me raise the question of social change. Have Goffman's writings any possible relevance to processes of profound transformation which social institutions might undergo? What relation, for example, could the study circumstances of co-presence possibly have to more encompassing issues such as examining the development of modern capitalism? In approaching such matters it might seem as though we have to decamp from Goffman's world completely. But this again would be mistaken. Social changes that are of a deep-rooted kind, by their very nature, involve alterations in the character of day-to-day social practices. So long as we do not accept Goffman's formulation of the autonomy of the interaction order, but think rather in terms of the intersection of varying contexts of co-presence, knit together by the paths that individuals trace out through the locales in which they live their day-to-day lives, we can see that it is not far-fetched to see a resemblance between the work of Goffman and that of Braudel. Goffman seemingly concentrates on the highly transient, Braudel on the long-established patterns of life of overall civilizations. But both shed light on the nature of day-to-day social life, and more specifically the modes in which everyday social activity is implicated in very broad patterns of institutional reproduction. There are long-term processes of change that are built into and expressed through the very contingencies of such reproduction. But there are also, obviously, more violent and dramatic processes of change. If Goffman's work does not seem, and indeed is not, of a great relevance to these it is not because there is an interaction order which somehow continues on regardless of them. On the contrary, it is because he does not examine how shifting institutional alignments condition, and are conditioned by, transformations of the settings in which social life is lived. But there is no reason why a more embracing approach to social theory should not undertake those tasks while incorporating the key ideas that Goffman has developed.

NOTE

This chapter is based on a paper first given at a conference called *Erving Goffman: an interdisciplinary appreciation*, held at the University of York in July 1986. In its present form it has also been published in A. Giddens, *Social Theory and Modern Sociology* (Polity Press, 1987).

References

REFERENCES TO WORKS BY ERVING GOFFMAN

A valuable bibliographical account of Erving Goffman's writings up to 1979, which also references reviews, appreciation and criticism of his work up to then, is J. Ditton's 'A bibliographic exegesis of Goffman's sociology' (in J. Ditton ed., 1980).

Goffman, E. 1952: On cooling the mark out: some aspects of adaptation to failure. *Psychiatry*, 15, 451–63.

Goffman, E. 1955: On face-work: an analysis of ritual elements in social interaction. *Psychiatry: Journal of Interpersonal Relations*, **18**, 213–31.

Goffman, E. 1956: Embarrassment and social organization. *American Journal of Sociology*, **62**, 264–74.

Goffman, E. 1957: Alienation from interaction. *Human Relations*, **10**, 47–59.

Goffman, E. 1959: *The Presentation of Self in Everyday Life*. New York: Doubleday Anchor.

Goffman, E. 1961a: *Encounters: Two Studies in the Sociology of Interaction*. Indianapolis: Bobbs-Merrill.

Goffman, E. 1961b: *Asylums*. New York: Doubleday Anchor.

Goffman, E. 1961c: Fun in games. In Goffman 1961a.

Goffman, E. 1963: *Behavior in Public Places: Notes on the Social Organization of Gatherings*. New York: Free Press.

Goffman, E. 1964a: *Stigma: Notes on the Management of Spoiled Identity*. Englewood Cliffs, New Jersey: Prentice-Hall.

Goffman, E. 1964b: The neglected situation. *American Anthropologist*, **66** (Part II, Special Issue), 133–6.

Goffman, E. 1967: *Interaction Ritual: Essays on Face-to-Face Behavior*. New York: Doubleday Anchor.

Goffman, E. 1969: *Strategic Interaction*. Philadelphia: University of Pennsylvania Press.

Goffman, E. 1971: *Relations in Public: Microstudies of the Public Order.* New York: Harper and Row.

Goffman, E. 1974: *Frame Analysis: An Essay on the Organization of Experience.* New York: Harper and Row.

Goffman, E. 1976: Replies and responses. *Language in Society,* **5**, 257–313. (Reprinted in Goffman 1981b.)

Goffman, E. 1978: Response cries. *Language,* **54**, 787–815. (Reprinted in Goffman 1981b.)

Goffman, E. 1979: Footing. *Semiotica,* **25**, 1–29. (Reprinted in Goffman 1981b.)

Goffman, E. 1981a: A reply to Denzin and Keller. *Contemporary Sociology,* **10**, 60–8.

Goffman, E. 1981b: *Forms of Talk.* Oxford: Basil Blackwell.

Goffman, E. 1981c: Radio talk. In Goffman 1981b.

Goffman, E. 1983a: Felicity's condition. *American Journal of Sociology,* **89**, 1–53.

Goffman, E. 1983b: The interaction order. *American Sociological Review,* **48**, 1–17.

REFERENCES TO OTHER WORKS

Anderson, S. and Keenan, E. 1985: Deixis. In T. Shopen (ed.), *Language Typology and Syntactic Description,* Vol. 3. Cambridge: Cambridge University Press.

Andronov, M. 1969: *A Standard Grammar of Modern and Classical Tamil.* Madras: New Century Book House.

Asch, P. and Asch, T. In press: *Video and Documentation on Balinese Trance.* Cambridge: Cambridge University Press.

Asher, R. 1985: *Croom Helm Descriptive Grammars: Tamil.* London: Croom Helm.

Ashworth, P. 1985: Goffman's Sartrism. *Human Studies,* **8**, 97–167.

Atkinson, M. 1982: *Explanations in the Study of Child Language Development.* Cambridge: Cambridge University Press.

Atkinson, J. M. and Drew, P. 1979: *Order in Court.* London: Macmillan.

Atkinson, J. M. and Heritage, J. (eds) 1984: *Structures of Social Action: Studies in Conversation Analysis.* Cambridge: Cambridge University Press.

Austin, G. 1966: *Chironomia: or A Treatise on Rhetorical Delivery.* Carbondale: Southern Illinois University Press. (First published London: 1806.)

Baldamus, W. W. 1972: The role of discoveries in social science. In T. Shanin (ed.), *The Rules of the Game.* London: Tavistock.

Bales, R. F. 1950: *Interaction Process Analysis.* Cambridge, Mass.: Addison Wesley.

Banfield, A. 1973: Narrative style and the grammar of indirect speech. *Foundations of Language,* **10**, 1–39.

Barker, R. and Wright, H. 1955: *Midwest and Its Children*. New York: Henry Holt.

Bateson, G. 1956: The message 'This is play'. In B. Schaffner (ed.), *Group Processes: Transactions of the Second Conference*. New York: Josiah Macy Jr Foundation.

Bauman, R. and Sherzer, J. (eds) 1974: *Explorations in the Ethnography of Speaking*. Cambridge: Cambridge University Press.

Beattie, G. 1983: *Talk: An Analysis of Speech and Non-verbal Behaviour in Conversation*. Milton Keynes: Open University Press.

Bellugi, U. and Klima, E. 1982: From gesture to sign: deixis in a visual-gestural language. In R. Jarvella and W. Klein (eds), *Speech, Place and Action: Studies in Deixis and Related Topics*, pp. 297–314. New York: John Wiley.

Bergner, J. 1983: *The Origins of Formalism in Modern Social Thought*. Chicago: Chicago University Press.

Bershady, H. 1973: *Ideology and Social Knowledge*. Oxford: Basil Blackwell.

Birdwhistell, R. L. 1952: *Introduction to Kinesics*. Louisville, Kentucky: University of Louisville Press.

Birdwhistell, R. L. 1970: *Kinesics and Context*. Philadelphia: University of Pennsylvania Press.

Birrel, S. J. 1978: Sporting encounters. University of Massachussetts: unpublished PhD thesis.

Bloor, D. 1983: *Wittgenstein: A Social Theory of Knowledge*. New York: Columbia University Press.

Bloor, M. 1978: On the analysis of observational data: a discussion of the worth and uses of inductive techniques and respondent validation. *Sociology*, **12**, 545–52.

Boas, F. 1911: *Handbook of American Indian Languages*, Vols 1 and 2. Bulletin 40, Bureau of American Ethnology, Smithsonian Institute.

Bridgman, P. W. 1936: *The Nature of Physical Theory*. Princeton: Princeton University Press.

Brown, P. In preparation: Tzeltal courtroom proceedings. Cambridge University.

Brown, P. and Levinson, S. C. 1978: Universals in language usage: politeness phenomena. In E. Goody (ed.), *Questions and Politeness*. Cambridge: Cambridge University Press.

Brown, P. and Levinson, S. 1987: *Politeness: Universals in Language Usage*. Cambridge: Cambridge University Press.

Buhler, K. 1982 [1934]: The deictic field of language and deictic words. In R. Jarvella and W. Klein (eds), *Speech, Place and Action: Studies in Deixis and Related Topics*, pp. 9–30. New York: John Wiley.

Bulgakov, M. 1975: The steel windpipe. In M. Bulgakov (ed.), *A Country Doctor's Notebook*, trans. M. Glenny. London: Collins and Harvill.

Button, G. and Lee, J. (eds) 1987: *Talk and Social Organization*. Avon: Multilingual Matters.

Carr, A. P. 1983: *Criminal Procedure in Magistrates' Courts*. London: Butterworth.

Cartwright, D. and Zander, A. 1953: *Group Dynamics: Research and Theory.* Evanston, Illinois: Row, Peterson.

Chafe, W. 1970: *A Semantically Based Sketch of Onondaga.* Bloomington: Indiana University Press.

Chapple, E. D. 1939: Quantitative analysis of the interaction of individuals. *Proceedings of the National Academy of Science, USA*, **25**, 295–307.

Chapple, E. D. 1940: Measuring human relations. *Genetic Psychology Monographs*, **22**, 3–147.

Chapple, E. D. and Coon, C. S. 1942: *Principles of Anthropology.* New York: Henry Holt.

Ciolek, M. and Kendon, A. 1980: Environment and the spatial arrangement of conversational encounters. *Sociological Inquiry*, **50**, 237–71.

Clark, E. 1978: From gesture to word: on the natural history of deixis in language acquisition. In J. S. Bruner and A. Garton (eds), *Human Growth and Development: Wolfson College Lectures 1976.* Oxford: Oxford University Press.

Clark, H. and Carlson, T. 1982: Hearers and speech acts. *Language*, **58**, 332–73.

Collins, R. 1975: *Conflict Sociology.* New York: Academic Press.

Collins, R. 1981: On the microfoundations of macrosociology. *American Journal of Sociology*, **86**, 984–1014.

Collins, R. 1985: *Three Sociological Traditions.* New York: Oxford University Press.

Collins, R. 1987: *Theoretical Sociology.* San Diego: Harcourt, Brace, Jovanovich.

Comrie, B. 1976: Linguistic politeness axes: speaker–addressee, speaker–reference, speaker–bystander. *Pragmatics Microfiche*, **1.7**, A3–B1.

Cooke, J. R. 1968: Pronominal reference in Thai, Burmese and Vietnamese. *University of California Publications in Linguistics, Vol. 52.*

Cressey, D. 1971: *Other People's Money: A Study in the Social Psychology of Embezzlement.* Belmont, California: Wadsworth.

Darwin, C. 1979: *The Expression of Emotions in Men and Animals.* London: Julian Freidman. (First published 1872).

Davidson, J. A. 1984: Subsequent versions of invitations, offers, requests and proposals dealing with potential or actual rejection. In J. M. Atkinson and J. Heritage (eds), *Structures of Social Action: Studies in Conversation Analysis*, pp. 102–28. Cambridge: Cambridge University Press.

Davis, A. 1982: *Children in Clinics.* London: Tavistock.

Denzin, N. and Keller, C. 1981: *Frame Analysis* reconsidered. *Contemporary Sociology*, **10**, 52–60.

Dingwall, R., Eekelaar, J. M. and Murray, T. 1983: *The Protection of Children: State Intervention and Family Life.* Oxford: Basil Blackwell.

Dingwall, R. and Strong, P. 1985: The interactional study of organizations: a critique and reformulation. *Urban Life*, **14**, 205–31.

Ditton, J. (ed.) 1980: *The View from Goffman.* London: Macmillan.

Dixon, R. M. W. 1972: *The Dyirbal Language of North Queensland.* Cambridge: Cambridge University Press.

Dixon, R. M. W. 1977: *A Grammar of Yidiny*. Cambridge: Cambridge University Press.

Drew, P. 1984: Speakers' reportings in invitation sequences. In J. M. Atkinson and J. Heritage (eds), *Structures of Social Action: Studies in Conversation Analysis*, pp. 129–51. Cambridge: Cambridge University Press.

Drew, P. 1985: Analyzing the use of language in courtroom interaction. In T. Van Dijk (ed.), *Handbook of Discourse Analysis*, Vol. 3, pp. 133–48. New York: Academic Press.

Drew, P. 1987: Po-faced receipts of teases. *Linguistics*, **25**, 219–53.

Duncan, S. and Fiske, D. 1977: *Face-to-face Interaction: Research Methods and Theory*. Hillsdale, New Jersey: Erlbaum.

Durkheim, E. 1954: *The Elementary Forms of the Religious Life*. New York: Free Press. (First published 1912.)

Elias, N. 1978: *The Civilizing Process: The History of Manners*. Oxford: Basil Blackwell. (First published Basel: 1939.)

Emeneau, M. B. 1951: Studies in Vietnamese (Annamese) grammar. *University of California Publications in Linguistics, Vol. 8*.

Evans-Pritchard, E. 1937: *Witchcraft, Oracles and Magic among the Azande*. Oxford: Clarendon Press.

Feld, S. and Schieffelin, B. 1982: Hard words: a functional basis for Kaluli discourse. In D. Tannen (ed.), *Analyzing Discourse: Text and Talk*, pp. 350–70. Washington, DC: Georgetown University Press.

Ferris, P. 1967: *The Doctors*. Harmondsworth: Penguin.

Fillmore, C. J. 1975: *Santa Cruz Lectures on Deixis*. Indiana University Linguistics Club (mimeo).

Fillmore, C. J. 1982: Towards a descriptive framework for spatial deixis. In R. Jarvella and W. Klein (eds), *Speech, Place and Action: Studies in Deixis and Related Topics*, pp. 31–72. New York: John Wiley.

Fischer-Jørgensen, E. 1975: *Trends in Phonological Theory*. Copenhagen: Akademisk Forlag.

Fisher, L. E. 1976: Dropping remarks and the Barbadian audience. *American Ethnologist*, **3**, 227–42.

Forchheimer, P. 1953: *The Category of Person in Language*. Berlin: de Gruyter.

Foucault, M. 1974: *The Order of Things*. London: Tavistock.

Frankel, M. R. 1984: The laying on of hands: aspects of the organization of gaze, touch and talk in a medical encounter. In S. Fisher and A. D. Tood (eds), *The Social Organization of Doctor–Patient Communication*, pp. 19–55. Washington, DC: Center for Applied Linguistics.

Frisby, D. 1981: *Sociological Impressionism: A Reassessment of Georg Simmel's Social Theory*. London: Heinemann.

Frisby, D. 1984: *Georg Simmel*. London: Tavistock.

Furbee-Losee, L. 1976: *The Correct Language: Tojolabal*. New York: Garland.

Garfinkel, H. 1956: Some sociological concepts and methods for psychiatrists. *Psychiatric Research Reports*, **6**, 181–95.

Garvin, R. L. and Reisenberg, S. H. 1952: Respect behavior on Ponape: an ethnolinguistic study. *American Anthropologist*, **54**, 301–20.

Giddens, A. 1979: *Central Problems in Social Theory*. London: Macmillan.

Giddens, A. 1984: *The Constitution of Society*. Cambridge: Polity Press.

Glaser, B. 1964: The constant comparative method of qualitative analysis. *Social Problems*, **12**, 436–45.

Goldberg, J. A. 1978: Amplitude shift: a mechanism for the affiliation of utterances in conversational interaction. In J. Schenkein (ed.), *Studies in the Organization of Conversational Interaction*, pp. 199–218. New York: Academic Press.

Gonos, G. 1977: 'Situation' *versus* 'Frame': the 'Interactionist' and the 'Structuralist' analyses of everyday life. *American Sociological Review*, **42**, 854–67.

Goodenough, W. H. 1969: Rethinking status and role. In S. Tyler (ed.), *Cognitive Anthropology*, pp. 311–29. New York: Holt, Rinehart and Winston.

Goodwin, C. 1977: Some aspects of the interaction of speaker and hearer in the construction of a turn at talk in natural conversation. Unpublished PhD dissertation: University of Pennsylvania. (Revised version as Goodwin 1981.)

Goodwin, C. 1979: The interactive construction of a sentence in natural conversation. In G. Psathas (ed.), *Everyday Language: Studies in Ethnomethodology*, pp. 97–121. New York: Irvington.

Goodwin, C. 1981: *Conversational Organization: Interaction between Speakers and Hearers*. New York: Academic Press.

Goodwin, C. 1984: Notes on story structure and the organization of participation. In J. M. Atkinson and J. Heritage (eds), *Structures of Social Action: Studies in Conversation Analysis*, pp. 225–46. Cambridge: Cambridge University Press.

Gouldner, A. 1971: *The Coming Crisis of Western Sociology*. London: Heinemann.

Greenfield, P. 1979: Informativeness, presupposition and semantic choice in single-word utterances. In E. Ochs and B. Schieffelin (eds), *Developmental Pragmatics*, pp. 159–66. New York: Academic Press.

Gross, F. and Stone, G. P. 1964: Embarrassment and the analysis of role requirements. *American Journal of Sociology*, **70** (July), 1–15.

Haas, M. R. 1964 [1944]: Men's and women's speech in Koasati. In D. Hymes (ed.), *Language in Culture and Society*. New York: Harper and Row.

Habermas, J. 1984: *The Theory of Communicative Action*. Boston: Beacon Press.

Hare, R. F., Borgatta, E. F. and Bales, R. F. 1955: *Small Groups: Studies in Social Interaction*. New York: Knopf.

Haviland, J. B. 1979a: Guugu Yimidhirr. In R. M. W. Dixon and B. Blake (eds), *Handbook of Australian Languages*, pp. 27–180. Canberra: Australian National University Press.

Haviland, J. B. 1979b: Guugu Yimidhirr brother-in-law language. *Language in Society*, **8**, 365–94.

Haviland, J. B. 1986a: 'Con buenos chiles': talk, targets and teasing in Zinacantan. (To appear in a special edition of *Text* edited by Allesandro Duranti.)

Haviland, J. B. 1986b: Complex referential gestures. Paper presented to the Conference on Talk and Social Structure, Santa Barbara, March 1986.

Heath, C. 1982: The display of recipency: an instance of a sequential relationship in speech and body movement. *Semiotica*, **42**, 147–67.

Heath, C. 1984: Talk and recipiency: sequential organization in speech and body movement. In J. M. Atkinson and J. Heritage (eds), *Structures of Social Action: Studies in Conversation Analysis*, pp. 247–65. Cambridge: Cambridge University Press.

Heath, C. 1986: *Body Movement and Speech in Medical Interaction*. Cambridge: Cambridge University Press.

Heilman, S. C. 1979: Communication and interaction: a parallel in the theoretical outlooks of Erving Goffman and Ray Birdwhistell. *Communication*, **4**, 221–34.

Heims, S. P. 1977: Gregory Bateson and the mathematicians: from inter-disciplinary interaction to societal functions. *Journal of the History of the Behavioral Sciences*, **13**, 141–59.

Helm, D. 1982: Talk's forms: comments on Goffman's *Forms of Talk*. *Human Studies*, **5**, 147–57.

Heritage, J. 1985: Analyzing news interviews: aspects of the production of talk for an overhearing audience. In T. A. Van Dijk (ed.), *Handbook of Discourse Analysis*, pp. 95–117. New York: Academic Press.

Hochschild, A. R. 1975: The sociology of feeling and emotion: selected possibilities. In M. Millman and R. M. Karter (eds), *Another Voice*, pp. 280–307. New York: Anchor.

Hochschild, A. R. 1979: Emotion work, feeling rules and social structure. *American Journal of Sociology*, **85**, 551–75.

Hockett, C. 1960: The origin of speech. *Scientific American*, **203**, 89–96.

Hollis, M. 1985: Of masks and men. In M. Carrithers, S. Collins and S. Lukes (eds), *The Category of the Person*. Cambridge: Cambridge University Press.

Homans, G. 1950: *The Human Group*. London: Routledge, Kegan Paul.

Hymes, D. (ed.) 1964: *Language in Culture and Society*. New York: Harper and Row.

Hymes, D. 1972a: Models of the interaction of language and social life. In J. Gumperz and D. Hymes (eds), *Directions in Sociolinguistics*, pp. 35–71. New York: Holt, Rinehart and Winston.

Hymes, D. 1972b: On communicative competence. In J. B. Pride and J. Holmes (eds), *Sociolinguistics*. Harmondsworth: Penguin.

Hymes, D. 1974: *Foundations in Sociolinguistics: An Ethnographic Approach*. Philadelphia: University of Pennsylvania Press.

Hymes, D. 1984: On Erving Goffman. *Theory and Society*, **13**, 621–31.

Ingram, D. 1978: Typology and universals of personal pronouns. In J. H. Greenberg (ed.), *Universals of Human Language*, pp. 213–48. Stanford: Stanford University Press.

Irvine, J. 1974: Strategies of status manipulation in the Wolof greeting. In R. Bauman and J. Sherzer (eds), *Explorations in the Ethnography of Speaking*. Cambridge: Cambridge University Press.

Irvine, J. 1981: Wolof praise singing. Paper presented to the Working Group on Language and Culture, Australian National University.

Jakobson, R. 1971: *Collected Papers*, Vol. 1. The Hague: Mouton.

James, W. 1890: *Principles of Psychology*. New York: Henry Holt.

James, W. and Lange, C. B. 1922: *The Emotions*. Baltimore: Williams and Wilkins.

Jameson, F. 1974: On Erving Goffman's *Frame Analysis*. *Theory and Society*, 3, 119–33.

Jefferson, G. 1972: Side sequences. In D. N. Sudnow (ed.), *Studies in Social Interaction*. New York: Free Press.

Jefferson, G. 1974: Error correction as an interactional resource. *Language in Society*, 3, 181–99.

Jefferson, G. 1978: Sequential aspects of storytelling in conversation. In J. Schenkein (ed.), *Studies in the Organization of Conversational Interaction*. New York: Academic Press.

Jefferson, G. 1979: A technique for inviting laughter and its subsequent acceptance/declination. In G. Psathas (ed.), *Everyday Language: Studies in Ethnomethodology*. New York: Irvington.

Jefferson, G. 1984: Notes on a systematic deployment of the acknowledgement tokens 'yeah' and 'mm hm'. *Papers in Linguistics*, 17, 197–206.

Jefferson, G., Sacks, H. and Schegloff, E. A. 1987: Notes on laughter in pursuit of intimacy. In G. Button and J. Lee (eds), *Talk and Social Organization*, 152–205. Avon: Multilingual Matters.

Jefferson, G. and Schenkein, J. 1977: Some sequential negotiations in conversation: unexpanded and expanded versions of projected action sequences. *Sociology*, 11, 87–103. (Reprinted in Schenkein 1978.)

Jewson, N. D. 1974: Medical knowledge and the patronage system in 18th century England. *Sociology*, 8, 369–85.

Jones, J. 1962: *On Aristotle and Greek Tragedy*. New York: Oxford University Press.

Kendon, A. 1967: Some functions of gaze-direction in social interaction. *Acta Psychologica*, 26, 22–63.

Kendon, A. 1972: A review of *Kinesics and Context* by R. L. Birdwhistell. *American Journal of Psychology*, 85, 441–55.

Kendon, A. 1977: Spatial organization in social encounters: the F-formation system. *Studies in the Behaviour of Social Interaction*. Lisse: Peter De Ridder Press.

Kendon, A. 1979: Some methodological and theoretical aspects of the use of film in the study of social interaction. In G. P. Ginsburg (ed.), *Emerging Strategies in Social Psychological Research*. New York: John Wiley.

Kendon, A. 1982: The organization of behavior in face-to-face interaction: observations on the development of a methodology. In K. R. Scherer and P. Ekman (eds), *Handbook of Methods in Nonverbal Behavior Research*, pp. 440–505. Cambridge: Cambridge University Press.

Kendon, A. 1985: Behavioural foundations for the process of frame attunement in face-to-face interaction. In G. P. Ginsburg, M. Brenner and M. von Cranach (eds), *Discovery Strategies in the Psychology of Action*, pp. 229–53. London: Academic Press.

Kendon, A. 1989: *Sign Language of Aboriginal Australia: Cultural, Semiotic and Communicative Perspectives*. Cambridge: Cambridge University Press.

Kendon, A. and Ferber, A. 1973: A description of some human greetings. In R. P. Michael and J. H. Crook (eds), *Comparative Behaviour of Primates*. London: Academic Press.

King, R. D., Raynes, N. V. and Tizard, J. J. 1971: *Patterns of Residential Care: Sociological Studies in Institutions for Handicapped Children*. London: Routledge, Kegan Paul.

Labov, W. and Fanshel, D. 1977: *Therapeutic Discourse*. New York: Academic Press.

Lakoff, R. 1973: The logic of politeness: or, minding your p's and q's. *Proceedings from the 9th Regional Meeting of the Chicago Linguistics Society*, 292–305.

Leech, G. 1983: *Principles of Pragmatics*. London: Longman.

Leeds-Hurwitz, W. 1986: Erving Goffman and the concept of social order. Paper prepared for the conference Erving Goffman: An Interdisciplinary Appreciation, University of York, 8–11 July 1986.

Leeds-Hurwitz, W. 1987: The social history of *The Natural History of an Interview:* a multidisciplinary investigation of social communication. *Research on Language and Social Interaction*, 20, 1–51.

Levinson, S. C. 1979: Activity types and language. *Linguistics*, 17, 356–99.

Levinson, S. C. 1983: *Pragmatics*. Cambridge: Cambridge University Press.

Levinson, S. C. 1986: Minimization and conversational inference. In M. Papi and J. Verscheueren (eds), *Proceedings of the International Conference on Pragmatics, Viareqqio 1985*. Amsterdam: Benjamins.

Lewis, G. L. 1967: *Turkish Grammar*. Oxford: Clarendon Press.

Lofland, J. 1980: Early Goffman: style, structure, substance, soul. In J. Ditton (ed.), *The View from Goffman*, pp. 24–51. London: Macmillan.

Lofland, J. 1984: Goffman's sociological legacies. *Urban Life*, 13, 7–34.

Lyman, B. 1973: Civilization: contents, discontents, malcontents. *Contemporary Sociology*, 2, 360–6.

Lyman, B. and Scott, M. 1970: *The Sociology of the Absurd*. New York: Appleton-Century Cross.

Lyons, J. 1968: *Introduction to Theoretical Linguistics*. Cambridge: Cambridge University Press.

Lyons, J. 1975: Deixis as the source of reference. In E. L. Keenan (ed.), *Formal Semantics of Natural Language*, pp. 61–83. Cambridge: Cambridge University Press.

Lyons, J. 1977: *Semantics*, Vols 1 and 2. Cambridge: Cambridge University Press.

Lyons, J. 1982: Deixis and subjectivity: 'Loquor, ergo sum'? In R. Jarvella and W. Klein (eds), *Speech, Place and Action: Studies in Deixis and Related Topics*, pp. 101–24. New York: John Wiley.

McDermott, R. P. and Roth, D. R. 1978: The social organization of behavior: interactional approaches. *Annual Review of Anthropology*, 7, 321–45.

McDermott, R. P. and Wertz, M. 1976: Doing the social order: some ethnographic advances from communicational analyses and ethnomethodology. *Reviews in Anthropology*, 3, 160–74.

MacIntyre, A. 1984: *After Virtue*. Notre Dame, Indiana: University of Notre Dame Press.

McQuown, N. A. (ed.) 1971: *The Natural History of an Interview*. Microfilm Collection of Manuscripts on Cultural Anthropology, 15th Series, University of Chicago, Joseph Regenstein Library, Department of Photoduplication.

Manning, P. 1986a: Reading Goffman: form and formlessness. Unpublished manuscript.

Manning, P. 1986b: More views of the lovingly empirical: a reply to Miller. Unpublished manuscript.

Matisoff, J. A. 1973: The grammar of Lahu. *University of California Publications in Linguistics, Vol. 75*.

Matthews, G. H. 1965: *Hidatsa Syntax. Papers on Formal Linguistics, 3*. The Hague: Mouton.

Mead, G. H. 1934: *Mind, Self and Society*. Chicago: Chicago University Press.

Montague, R. 1974: *Formal Philosophy: Selected Papers*. New Haven: Yale University Press.

Park, R. E. and Burgess, E. W. (eds) 1924: *Introduction to the Science of Sociology*, 2nd edn. Chicago: Chicago University Press.

Parsons, T. 1951: *The Social System*. Glencoe, Illinois: Free Press.

Phillips, J. 1983: Goffman's linguistic turn. *Theory Culture and Society*, 2, 114–16.

Pomerantz, A. M. 1978: Compliment responses: notes on the co-operation of multiple constraints. In J. Schenkein (ed.), *Studies in the Organization of Conversational Interaction*, pp. 79–112. New York: Academic Press.

Pomerantz, A. M. 1984: Agreeing and disagreeing with assessments: some features of preferred/dispreferred turn shapes. In J. M. Atkinson and J. Heritage (eds), *Structures of Social Action: Studies in Conversation Analysis*, pp. 57–101. Cambridge: Cambridge University Press.

Rauh, G. (ed.), 1983: *Essays on Deixis*. Tubingen: Gunter Narr Verlag.

Ricks, C. 1974: *Keats and Embarrassment*. Oxford: Clarendon Press.

Robinson, W. 1951: The logical structure of analytic induction. *American Sociological Review*, 16, 812–18.

Rogers, M. 1980: Goffman on power, hierarchy and status. In J. Ditton (ed.), *The View from Goffman*, pp. 100–33. London: Macmillan.

Rorty, R. 1980: *Philosophy and the Mirror of Nature*. Oxford: Basil Blackwell.

Rorty, R. 1982: *Consequences of Pragmatism*. Brighton: Harvester Press.

Ruesch, J. 1972: *Semiotic Approaches to Human Relations*. The Hague: Mouton.

Ruesch, J. and Bateson, G. 1951: *Communication: The Social Matrix of Society*. New York: Norton.

Ryan, A. 1978: Maximising, minimising, moralising. In C. Hookway and P. Pettitt (eds), *Action and Interpretation*. Cambridge: Cambridge University Press.

Sacks, H. 1963: Sociological description. *Berkeley Journal of Sociology*, **8**, 1–11.

Sacks, H. 1965–72: *Unpublished Lectures on Conversation*. Irvine: School of Social Science, University of California.

Sacks, H. 1972: Notes on the assessment of moral character. In D. Sudnow (ed.), *Studies in Social Interaction*. New York: Free Press.

Sacks, H. 1974: An analysis of the course of a joke's telling in conversation. In R. Bauman and J. Sherzer (eds), *Explorations in the Ethnography of Speaking*. Cambridge: Cambridge University Press.

Sacks, H. 1984 [1971]: Lecture, University of California, Irvine. Incorporated in 'Notes on methodology'. In J. M. Atkinson and J. Heritage (eds), *Structures of Social Action: Studies in Conversation Analysis*, pp. 21–7. Cambridge: Cambridge University Press.

Sacks, H. 1987 [1973]: On the preferences for agreement and contiguity in the organization of sequences in conversation. In G. Button and J. Lee (eds), *Talk and Social Organization*. Avon: Multilingual Matters.

Sacks, H., Schegloff, E. A. and Jefferson, G. 1974: A simplest systematics for the organization of turn-taking for conversation. *Language*, **50**, 696–735.

Sadock, J. and Zwicky, A. 1985: Speech act distinctions in syntax. In T. Shopen (ed.) *Language Typology and Syntactic Description* Vol. 1, pp. 155–96. Cambridge: Cambridge University Press.

Sansom, G. B. 1928: *An Historical Grammar of Japanese*. Oxford: Oxford University Press.

Schachter, P. and Otanes, F. 1972: *Tagalog Reference Grammar*. Berkeley: University of California Press.

Schatzki, T. 1983: The prescription is description. In S. Mitchell and M. Rosen (eds), *The Need for Interpretation*. London: Athlone Press.

Scheff, T. J. 1973: Intersubjectivity and emotion. *American Behavioral Scientist*, **16**, 501–22.

Scheff, T. J. 1977: The distancing of emotion in ritual. *Current Anthropology*, **18**, 483–91.

Scheflen, A. E. 1963: Communication and regulation in psychotherapy. *Psychiatry: Journal of Interpersonal Relations*, **26**, 126–36.

Scheflen, A. E. 1964: The significance of posture in communication systems. *Psychiatry: Journal of Interpersonal Relations*, **27**, 316–31.

Scheflen, A. E. 1972: *Communicational Structure: Analysis of a Psychotherapy Transaction*. Bloomington: Indiana University Press.

Scheflen, A. E. 1974: *How Behavior Means*. New York: Jason Aronson.

Scheflen, A. E. and Ashcraft, N. 1976: *Human Territories: How We Behave in Space-Time*. Englewood Cliffs, New Jersey: Prentice-Hall.

Schegloff, E. A. 1968: Sequencing in conversational openings. *American Anthropologist*, **70**, 1075-95.

Schegloff, E. A. 1972: Notes on a conversational practice: formulating place. In D. N. Sudnow (ed.), *Studies in Social Interaction*. New York: Free Press.

Schegloff, E. A. 1979a: Repair after text turn. Paper presented at the Social Science Research Council/British Sociological Association Conference on Practical Reasoning and Discourse Processes, St Hugh's College, Oxford.

Schegloff, E. A. 1979b: Identification and recognition in telephone conversation openings. In G. Psathas (ed.), *Everyday Language: Studies in Ethnomethodology*, pp. 23-78. Boston: Irvington.

Schegloff, E. A. 1980: Preliminaries to preliminaries: 'can I ask you a question?'. *Sociological Inquiry*, **50**, 104-52.

Schegloff, E. A. 1982: Discourse as an interactional achievement: some uses of 'uh huh' and other things that come between sentences. In D. Tannen (ed.), *Georgetown University Roundtable on Languages and Linguistics*. Washington, DC: Georgetown University Press.

Schegloff, E. A. 1984: On some questions and ambiguities in conversation. In J. M. Atkinson and J. Heritage (eds), *Structures of Social Action: Studies in Conversation Analysis*, pp. 28-52. Cambridge: Cambridge University Press.

Schegloff, E. A. 1985: Pre-apologies: on the interplay of truth, form and action, or 'Did I wake you up?'. Paper delivered at the Meetings of the Speech Communication Association, Denver, November 1985.

Schegloff, E. A. 1987a: Some sources of misunderstanding in talk-in-interaction. *Linguistics*, **25**, 201-18.

Schegloff, E. A. In press (a): On the organization of sequences as a source of 'coherence' in talk-in-interaction. In B. Dorval (ed.), *Development of Coherence in Conversation*. New York: Ablex.

Schegloff, E. A. 1987b: Between macro and micro: contexts and other connections. In J. Alexander, B. Giessen, R. Munch and N. Smelser (eds), *The Micro-Macro Link*, 207-34. Berkeley: University of California Press.

Schlegoff, E. A., Jefferson and Sacks, H. 1977: The preference for self-correction in the organization of repair in conversation. *Language*, **53**, 361-82.

Schegloff, E. A. and Sacks, H. 1973: Opening up closings. *Semiotica*, **8**, 289-327.

Schelling, T. C. 1960: *The Strategy of Conflict*. Cambridge, Massachussetts: Harvard University Press.

Schenkein, J. (ed.) 1978: *Studies in the Organization of Conversational Interaction*. New York: Academic Press.

Schieffelin, B. 1979: Getting it together: an ethnographic approach to the study of communicative competence. In E. Ochs and B. Schieffelin (eds), *Developmental Pragmatics*. New York: Academic Press.

Schieffelin, B. In press: *Language Acquisition in Kaluli* (provisional title). Cambridge: Cambridge University Press.

Schiffer, S. R. 1972: *Meaning*. Oxford: Clarendon Press.

Searle, J. R. 1969: *Speech Acts*. Cambridge: Cambridge University Press.

Sebeok, T. A., Hayes, D. and Bateson, M. C. (eds) 1964: *Approaches to Semiotics*. The Hague: Mouton.

Shannon, C. and Weaver, W. 1949: *The Mathematical Theory of Communication*. Urbana: University of Illinois Press.

Sharrock, W. W. 1976: Review of *Frame Analysis*. *Sociology*, **10**, 332-4.

Shattuck, R. 1986: Catching up with the avant-garde. *New York Review of Books*, 18 December, 66-74.

Silverman, D. 1981: The child as a social object: Down's Syndrome children in a paediatric cardiology clinic. *Sociology of Health and Illness*, **3**, 253-74.

Silverman, D. 1984: Going private: ceremonial forms in a private oncology clinic. *Sociology*, **18**, 191-204.

Silverman, D. In press: *Communication in the Clinic: The Place of the Social in Medicine*. London: Sage.

Silverstein, M. 1976: Shifters, linguistic categories and cultural description. In K. Basso and H. Selby (eds), *Meaning in Anthropology*. Albuquerque: University of New Mexico Press.

Simmel, G. 1950: *Sociology*. Glencoe: Free Press.

Smith, G. W. H. In press: Simmel, Goffman and formal sociology. *Human Studies*.

Spykman, N. J. 1925: *The Social Theory of Georg Simmel*. Chicago: University of Chicago Press.

Stalnaker, R. 1978: Assertion. In P. Cole (ed.), *Syntax and Semantics. 9. Pragmatics*. New York: Academic Press.

Streek, J. n.d.: Symbolic modes and interactive modes: a Goffmanian view of old ladies' verbal art. Paper presented to the conference on Goffman: An Interdisciplinary Appreciation, York, July 1986.

Strong, P. 1979: *The Ceremonial Order of the Clinic*. London: Routledge and Kegan Paul.

Strong, P. 1983a: The importance of being Erving: Erving Goffman 1922-1982. *Sociology of Health and Illness*, **5**, 345-55.

Strong, P. 1983b: The rivals: an essay on the sociological trades. In R. Dingwall and P. Lewis (eds), *The Sociology of the Professions*, pp. 59-77. London, Macmillan.

Strong, P. 1986: Erving Goffman and the sociology of health, disease and medicine. Paper presented to the conference on Erving Goffman: An Interdisciplinary Appreciation, York, July 1986.

Strong, P. and Dingwall, R. 1983: The limits of negotiation in formal organizations. In G. Gilbert and P. Abell (eds), *Accounts and Action*, pp. 98-116. Farnborough: Gower.

Terasaki, A. 1976: *Pre-announcement Sequences in Conversation. Social Science*

Working Paper 99. Irvine: School of Social Science, University of California.

Thomson, D. F. 1935: The joking relation and organized obscenity in North Queensland. *American Anthropologist*, **37**, 460–90.

Tsuchihashi, M. 1983: The speech act continuum: an investigation of Japanese sentence final particles. *Journal of Pragmatics*, **7**, 361–87.

Turner, E. S. 1958: *Call the Doctor: A Social History of Medical Men.* London: Michael Joseph.

Van Dijk, T. A. (ed.) 1985: *Handbook of Discourse Analysis.* New York: Academic Press.

Wada, J. A. 1961: Modification of cortically induced responses in brain stem of shift of attention in monkeys. *Science*, **133**, 40–42.

Warner, W. L. 1937: *A Black Civilization: A Social Study of an Australian Tribe.* New York: Harper and Row.

Watzlawick, P., Beavin, J. and Jackson, D. D. 1967: *Pragmatics of Human Communication: A Study of Interactional Patterns, Pathologies and Paradoxes.* New York: Norton.

Williams, R. 1980: Goffman's sociology of talk. In J. Ditton (ed.), *The View from Goffman*, pp. 210–32. London: Macmillan.

Wittgenstein, L. 1972: *Philosophical Investigations.* Oxford: Basil Blackwell.

Yeats, W. B. 1926: *Estrangement: Being Some Fifty Thoughts from a Diary Kept by William Butler Yeats in the Year Nineteen Hundred and Nine.* Dublin: Cuala Press.

Yngve, V. 1970: On getting a word in edgewise. In M. A. Campbell et al. (eds), *Papers from the 6th Regional Meeting of the Chicago Linguistic Society*, pp. 567–78. Chicago: Department of Linguistics, University of Chicago.

Zabor, M. 1978: Essaying metacommunication: a survey and context-ualization of communicative research. Unpublished doctoral dissertation, Indiana University.

Index